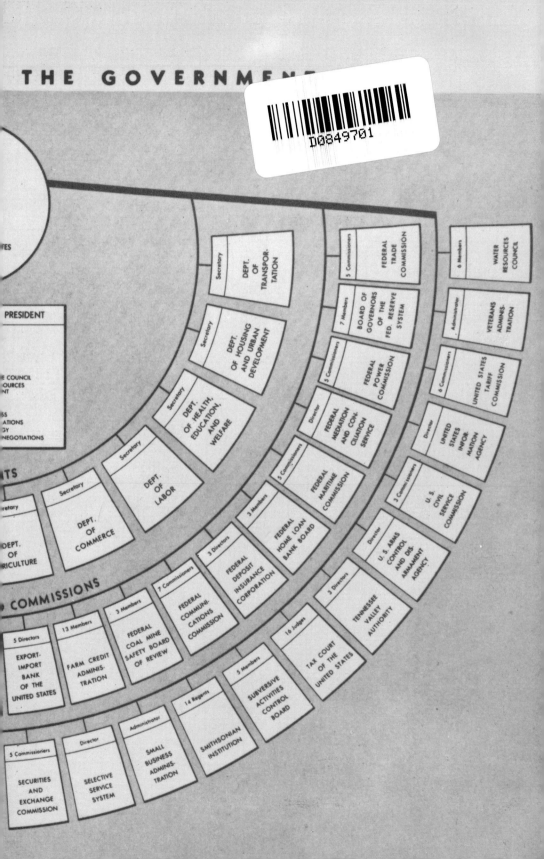

Research

in the

Administration of

Public Policy

NATIONAL ARCHIVES CONFERENCES

VOLUME 7

PAPERS AND PROCEEDINGS

OF THE

CONFERENCE ON RESEARCH IN THE ADMINISTRATION OF PUBLIC POLICY

NOVEMBER 19–20, 1970

THE NATIONAL ARCHIVES BUILDING

WASHINGTON, D.C.

RESEARCH

IN THE

ADMINISTRATION

OF

PUBLIC POLICY

EDITED BY

FRANK B. EVANS

AND

HAROLD T. PINKETT

HOWARD UNIVERSITY PRESS

WASHINGTON, D.C.

1975

This Special Edition
published by HOWARD UNIVERSITY PRESS for the
National Archives Trust Fund Board
National Archives and Records Service
General Services Administration
Washington, D.C.

NATIONAL ARCHIVES TRUST FUND BOARD

James B. Rhoads
Archivist of the United States

Gale W. McGee
*Chairman, Senate Post Office and
Civil Service Committee*

Thaddeus J. Dulski
*Chairman, House Post Office and
Civil Service Committee*

PRINTED IN THE UNITED STATES OF AMERICA

Library of Congress Cataloging in Publication Data

Conference on Research in the Administration of Public Policy, Washington, D. C., 1970.
  Research in the administration of public policy.

  (National Archives conferences, v. 7)
  1. United States—Executive departments—Congresses. 2. Political science research—United States—Congresses. 3. Archives—United States—Congresses. I. Evans, Frank Bernard, 1927-ed. II. Pinkett, Harold T., ed. III. Title. IV. Series: United States. National Archives. Conference v. 7.
JK411.C65 1970   353   74-7381
ISBN 0-88258-040-X

Foreword

The National Archives and Records Service has inaugurated a series of conferences for the exchange of ideas and information between archivists and researchers. These conferences are designed both to inform scholars about the wealth of useful research materials available in the National Archives and Records Service and to provide an opportunity for researchers to suggest ways in which their use of these records could be facilitated.

The National Archives and Records Service, a part of the General Services Administration, administers the permanently valuable, noncurrent records of the federal government. These archival holdings date from the days of the Continental Congresses to the present.

Among the approximately one million cubic feet of records now constituting the National Archives of the United States are such hallowed documents as the Declaration of Independence, the Constitution, and the Bill of Rights. However, most of the archives, whether in the National Archives Building, the regional archives branches, or the presidential libraries, are less dramatic. They are preserved because of their continuing practical utility for the ordinary processes of government, for the establishment and protection of individual rights, and for their value in documenting our nation's history.

One goal of the National Archives staff is to explore and make more widely known these historical records. It is hoped that these conferences will be a positive act in that direction. The papers of each conference will be published in the belief that this exchange of ideas and information should be preserved and made available in printed form.

ARTHUR F. SAMPSON
Administrator of General Services

Preface

The National Archives Conference on Research in the Administration of Public Policy held on November 19 and 20, 1970, was the seventh in a series of semiannual conferences sponsored by the National Archives and Records Service in the interest of increasing communication between archivists and the scholarly community. These conferences have been designated to provide archivists with guidance and counsel in how to serve better the needs of researchers and at the same time to provide directly to researchers information concerning the research potential of the federal government's archives.

The specific purpose of this conference was to stimulate interest in the relatively neglected study of the history and performance of federal government agencies by bringing together researchers concerned with this subject, by noting how archival resources relating to the subject have been profitably used in the past, and by suggesting ways in which they can be used more extensively in the future. The conference was proposed by Dr. Frank B. Evans, deputy assistant for the National Archives (now assistant to the archivist), in December 1969, and Dr. Evans invited Dr. Harold T. Pinkett, Records Appraisal Division (now chief, Natural Resources Branch, Civil Archives Division), to serve as codirector.

It was recognized that the conference dealt with a very broad subject that might well merit more detailed treatment in future conferences. It seemed desirable in 1970, however, to make an initial effort at proclaiming the value of archival sources for studies of federal administration. This volume serves as a measure of the success of this initial effort.

JAMES B. RHOADS
Archivist of the United States

Contents

Introduction

For over four decades there have been incorporated into the National Archives of the United States the most important extant records concerning the origin, organization, functions, decisions, procedures, and essential transactions of the United States government from the time of its establishment to the recent past. A principal reason for the preservation of these records has been the conviction that they are valuable for research concerning the administration of public policy. This conviction has been supported significantly by the use of archival sources in writings of federal government historians and occasionally in studies of specialists in federal administration and particular federal programs. The general use of such sources, however, has been surprisingly limited and has prompted some archivists and researchers to conclude that there exists a substantial unfamiliarity with the nature and potentialities of federal archives as sources for research in the administration of public policy.

Accordingly, the National Archives conference of November 19-20, 1970, dealing with this subject, sought to bring together historians, political scientists, specialists in public administration, and archivists for discussion and demonstration of particular research possibilities. The conference called attention to the wide range of documentation that delineates major characteristics of federal government agencies, especially their origins, involving functions and activities, organizational patterns, and public relations. It featured a discussion of some important techniques, problems, and results in using federal records for writing the history of federal agencies. It provided an opportunity for explanation of representative research concerning dilemmas in administering public policy and efforts for federal administrative reform. Furthermore, the conference was a forum for the presentation of some innovative proposals for research in the administration of public policy.

A few persons gave helpful suggestions to the directors in their planning of the conference. The codirectors are particularly indebted to Professors Louis Morton, Dartmouth College, James Harvey Young, Emory University, Thomas G. Manning, Texas Tech University, Francis P. Prucha, Marquette University, Norman A.

Graebner, University of Virginia, and Van L. Perkins, University of California; Mr. Charles E. Lee, director, South Carolina State Archives Department; Dr. Oscar Kraines, New York Judicial Conference; and Dr. Oscar E. Anderson, National Aeronautics and Space Administration. Professors Morton, Young, Manning, and Prucha and Dr. Anderson also made valuable contributions as participants in the conference. The services rendered by the following persons as speakers or chairmen were also greatly appreciated: Dr. Richard G. Hewlett, United States Atomic Energy Commission; Dr. John J. Corson, Fry Consultants; Mr. Dwight A. Ink, United States Office of Management and Budget (now deputy administrator, General Services Administration); and Professor Lowell H. Hattery, American University; James P. Johnson, Brooklyn College of the City University of New York; Richard Polenberg, Cornell University; Keith M. Henderson, State University College at Buffalo; and Sidney Baldwin, California State University, Fullerton.

The conference proceedings had the generous support and participation of Mr. Robert L. Kunzig, administrator of General Services (now judge, United States Court of Claims); Dr. James B. Rhoads, archivist of the United States; and Mr. Herbert E. Angel, deputy archivist of the United States (now retired). Papers were presented by the following National Archives staff members: Dr. Harold T. Pinkett, Mr. Jerome Finster, and Mr. R. Michael McReynolds. Dr. Frank B. Evans, who chaired the final session, made available to conference invitees "The National Archives and Records Service and Its Research Resources—a Select Bibliography," an updated version of which is appended to the volume.

Statements in the conference papers generally reflect conditions as viewed by the speakers in 1970. The directors are especially indebted to Kathleen A. Mach for her resourceful and diligent assistance in the editing of the papers and to the members of the Conference Papers staff for seeing the volume through press.

FRANK B. EVANS
HAROLD T. PINKETT
Conference Codirectors

Research

in the

Administration of

Public Policy

SESSION

I

Writing the History of a Federal Agency and Its Programs

CHAIRMAN

OSCAR E. ANDERSON

Director, International Program Policy, National Aeronautics and Space Administration Office of International Affairs ... A.B., Oberlin College, Ph.D., Harvard University . . . history faculty, University of Cincinnati, 1948–58; Assistant Historian, United States Atomic Energy Commission, 1958–62; National Aeronautics and Space Administration, 1962– . . . author, *Refrigeration in America: A History of a New Technology and Its Impact* and *The Health of a Nation: Harvey W. Wiley and the Fight for Pure Food;* coauthor with Richard G. Hewlett, *The New World,* 1939/1946.

Two weeks ago James McGregor Burns had an article in the *New York Times Book Review* entitled "The Historian's Right to See" [November 8, 1970, pp. 2, 42–44]. In that article Burns argued for the relaxation of the restrictions on access to federal records. Allowing for some gaps and oversimplification, I think he makes a good case for his point of view. Yet, this article, I believe, quite inadvertently distorts the problem and puts the focus on the wrong issue.

   As I see it—and, again, I look at it primarily as a historian—the principal difficulty is *not* that historians cannot use federal records, but that too few of them try. Historians often seem not to appreciate what is available, what can be done. Often they seem to think that the history of government agencies is not worth the trying, not worth the telling. There are a good many reasons for this feeling; at times I think it has something to do with the disenchantment with government that prevails in many academic circles, for whatever reasons. But I really do not think this is a cause for lasting concern. The work of the government is clearly central to understanding the problems of this century. Students of government and public administration need not be convinced of this proposition, and historians, I am sure, will not remain long on the sidelines. But why wait for these processes to proceed in their own way? I think it is important that we get on with the work. We are here today to see what *can* be done and to get some idea of how to do it.

Our first speaker is Dr. Richard G. Hewlett, chief historian of the United States Atomic Energy Commission. Dr. Hewlett conceived and brought forth the AEC history program. It is an impressive accomplishment, and it is no task for one faint of heart. I think Dr. Hewlett has succeeded so well because more than any historian I know he understands the bureaucracy. He knows how it works—if one works with it and not against it. He knows that the watchwords for dealing with the bureaucracy are reason and accommodation, not confrontation.

The AEC history program has resulted in two volumes: *The New World, 1939/1946,* published in 1962, and *Atomic Shield,* the volume that takes the story up to the fall of 1952. In 1969 *Atomic Shield* shared the David Lloyd Prize for history with Dean Acheson's *Present at the Creation.*

I speak with some hesitancy in talking about the AEC program because in its early stages I did have some part in it, but I think I have been away from it long enough to see it objectively. I certainly have no hesitation in stating my view that the volumes that have been produced in Dr. Hewlett's program have set a new standard for writing the history of public policy.

Dr. Hewlett's paper this morning will draw on his experience in conducting that program and in writing the history of the Atomic Energy Commission.

Our second speaker, Professor Thomas G. Manning, professor of history at Texas Tech University, is generally known to a generation of Americans for his widely used book of readings that, when I was teaching, was very popular in college introductory courses. To the scholarly community, however, Professor Manning is known primarily as the author of *Government in Science: The U.S. Geological Survey, 1867-1894.* This book is remarkable as a history of the politics of science in the United States and as a history of geology in the United States.

Dr. Manning brings a different perspective to the history of public policy. He will talk about an earlier era when many of the problems were different from today's, and he has approached those problems from the outside, as an independent scholar. But the technique, the approach, is similar to that of the atomic Energy Commission program because of the intensive use of the archives of a federal agency. The difficulties involved in writing the history of science agencies is the theme Dr. Manning will discuss.

And our last speaker for this session is Dr. Harold T. Pinkett, deputy director of the Records Appraisal Branch of the National Archives. I know of no one who has broader knowledge of how the records of the federal government are created nor a wiser view of their value for research.

Dr. Pinkett brings to his present position experience as both archivist and scholar. He is the editor of the *American Archivist;* he is an expert on the records of the United States Department of Agriculture; and for many years he was chief of the Agricultural Records Branch in the archives. He has not been content, however, to help other scholars use the records but he has made use of them himself. In addition to a great many articles, his work has found fruition in a study called *Gifford Pinchot, Public and Private Forester,* which was published this year and which the Agricultural History Society has selected as the book of the year.

THE FEDERAL EXECUTIVE.

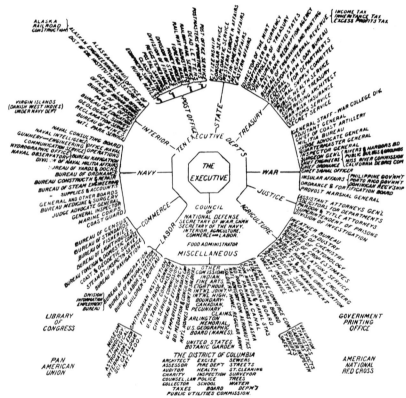

COMPILED BY W.I.SWANTON FOR THE COMMITTEE ON PUBLIC INFORMATION, 10 JACKSON PL., WASHINGTON, D.C.
JUNE, 1917.

This chart indicates the relations and
organization existing within the various
divisions of the Federal Executive.

National Service Handbook (Washington, D.C.:
Government Printing Office, 1917), p. 248.

Government History
Writing from the Inside

RICHARD G. HEWLETT

History for the Present

THE THEME OF THIS conference—research in the administration of public policy—assumes a proposition which may seem too obvious for comment. The proposition is that the study of recent public policy will help us to understand American society today and thereby enable us to attack some of the problems which threaten our nation. However widespread may be the acceptance of this premise, many scholars (and especially historians) do not seem to act as if they recognize it.

There are, to be sure, hundreds of books written each year on pressing issues of public policy, but very few of these are histories in any real sense. They are not written from a historical perspective. They do not, and really cannot, depend upon primary source materials. Even on a scholarly level, I find it discouraging to read journals in political science and public administration and to observe the scanty underpinning of historical fact upon which many of the published articles depend. And I am convinced that by and large the scholars who write for these journals are well aware of the inadequacies of their historical evidence. If better historical data were available, they would use them.

This is not a new problem in our generation, but it seems to have become more acute in recent years. The acceleration of change and the growing complexity of American life have not encouraged the historical approach. The rapid proliferation of new technologies with all their attendant economic and social problems seems constantly to distract our attention from a systematic study of the past to a harried preoccupation with the present. How can we worry about our past when our very existence in the present seems threatened? And, when many of the problems we face as a nation appear to have their origin in the events of last month or last year, what, after all, is the practicality of historical research? This is a question many Americans, especially young people, are asking today.

One answer, of course, is to give up. The "now" generation, full of exasperation, has discounted as "irrelevant" the historians and their tireless shuffling of the bones of the past. At the same time, many historians of the recent past take little professional interest in the issues of the day. In the long sweep of history the momentary preoccupations of the American people may be written off as fads like free silver and prohibition. We historians seem more than willing to write for each other, and if nonhistorians do not appreciate our work, so much the worse for them. Rather than face the challenge of the present, I suspect we find it easier to accept Lord Snow's thesis of the "two cultures" as sad but true, or to resign ourselves to the cliché that technological advances have outstripped the development of our social, political, and economic institutions. There is probably some truth in both of these laments, but we should not accept them as inevitable and irreversible.

There is a second, and I think much more promising, answer which the historian can offer in the present situation. It lies in the context of this conference—namely, that the historian's craft, applied in a new and perhaps unconventional way, offers some real hope for getting at some of the perplexing and even frightening problems which overshadow our national life. Although it would be much easier to accept the first alternative and to ignore the challenge of the present, I am becoming convinced that historians must begin to face up to that challenge.

The historian, I think, can play an important part in attacking the problems of the present, not because he has special knowledge of the past, but because he has mastered techniques that are particularly useful in understanding the present. The historian concentrates his attention on what has happened, not on what shall or should occur. He is committed to relating the truth within a chronological structure in which cause and effect are meticulously examined and explained. In an era of unprecedented social and technological change, the historian's ability to record what has and is happening is all the more important. Without a sound basis of historical fact, others in our society cannot hope to find workable solutions to the problems that beset us. I am convinced that contemporary historians must begin to consider themselves part of a team of experts whose combination of talents is chosen for the study of specific problems. My conviction stems from almost twenty years of experience in trying to write government history from the inside. Not, I hasten to add, from any success I may have achieved in writing history but rather from a sense of my own inadequacies and that of my profession in general.

When I speak of inadequacies, I am not thinking so much about such formal historical activities as criticism and synthesis as I am about the historian's understanding, as a historian, of his own age, and particularly of the possibilities for useful historical research into the recent past on the practical problems of the day. From the inquiries I receive from historians and graduate students, I would judge that there is little understanding within the profession of the possibilities for research in government records created within the last decade or of practical methods of going about such research.

The contents of our major historical journals give striking evidence of the historian's reluctance to hazard a study of the recent past. It is alarming to me to see how little attention is being devoted to the history of the administration of government policy in the half century since World War I. Presidential biographies, the crises of world conflict, international relations, and political movements in the conventional sense have attracted the interests of many capable historians, but beyond these obviously popular topics, the history of the United States government is virtually untouched. You can number almost on your fingers the professionally acceptable histories of the administration of public policy in the federal government at the agency or departmental level since World War II.

In contrast to this rather poor record of performance, the opportunities for historical research on recent public policy are almost staggering. In our research in the files of the Atomic Energy Commission and other executive agencies and departments my staff and I are frequently impressed by the exceptional opportunities for valuable historical studies. We recently reviewed the records of the Navy Department's General Board in the files of the Naval History Division. Only a few of these files are yet open for unofficial research after World War II, but under the twenty-five-year rule which applies to these records, some fascinating material will become available in the next few years. The files of the General Board, particularly for 1948, contain information which has a direct bearing on some of the crucial problems our defense establishment faces today. I am sure that many of you know of equally promising sources which have been unmined.

But I wish to go one step farther and to suggest that research in records of this type is not only attractive but is also in a literal sense desperately needed. Those of us who have been privileged to work behind the scenes in government, to observe living examples of the

administration of public policy, know how flimsy is public understanding of the nature of decision making in our government. In my
own area of special interest, the history of the Atomic Energy Commission, I cannot very well escape the fact that the government in a
new but terrifyingly real sense holds the power of life and death over
us all. When the stakes mount this high, it becomes impossible to deny
the right of citizens in a democracy to know how the government has
made decisions that affect their lives and liberties.

I hope you do not think I am simply issuing a call for public virtue,
such as our national leaders might proclaim in a political speech or in
congressional debate. I am convinced that the American electorate
would be much more effective if more of us understood, for example,
the complex of new relationships between American science and
government which has emerged in the last three decades. Don K.
Price, Jr., has suggested many of the themes in his book *The Scientific Estate,* but few historians have undertaken to examine the historical topics which Price suggests are significant.

There is another sense in which historical studies of the recent past
may prove even more starkly practical. It seems to me that the historical method can be applied with great potential to topics which
seem to typify critical issues of our day. I do not mean to suggest
that the historian should abandon his venerable craft and become an
analytic social scientist. Rather I would propose that historians be
urged to invest their talents in joint efforts with social scientists and
others to study contemporary problems.

For us in the Atomic Energy Commission, this idea of a practical
application of history emerged as we studied several topics for the
second volume of the AEC history. We knew, for example, that we
would have to handle the controversial subject of the hydrogen bomb.
But we also realized that this section could well serve as a case study
of the milieu and mechanism of decision making in the nuclear age.
We tried to describe the kinds of pressures public administrators faced
and the confusing array of technical factors they had to weigh. We
considered this subject of more than academic interest because it
seemed to represent the kind of situation that might often face federal
officials in the nuclear age. Indeed, congressional debates over the
antiballistic missile have borne striking similarity to the H-bomb debate in 1949. Looking back on that section of the book, I find that we
did not make this broader intention explicit and that the whole section tends to blend too smoothly into the larger pattern of narrative
history. Yet I think it is interesting that two graduate schools of public
administration are using this section as a case study in seminars this
fall. That fact demonstrates to me that others will use historical
studies if they have a reasonably direct application.

If this cautious first effort proved useful to someone outside the historical profession, it seems that a more deliberate and direct study of a crucial problem could be expected to have more social utility. We are not at all certain that we can write the kind of history that would even begin to meet the needs of social scientists and others, but I am convinced that historians must make a greater effort in this direction.

Writing from the Inside

If the need is so apparent and the opportunities so rich, why are only a few historians working on topics directly related to current problems of public policy? The answer is that it is extremely difficult for most historians to gain access to government records less than twenty-five or thirty years old, and such records are not very helpful for the kind of history that would seem most useful. In the last few years the government has made gestures in the direction of opening more recent, and even classified files for historical research, but the results have not been very satisfying, as James MacGregor Burns has indicated in a recent article in the *New York Times Book Review* ("The Historian's Right to See," November 8, 1970, pp. 2, 42-44).

In time it may be possible for some historians like Professor Burns to gain access to certain categories of records, but limited access of this nature will not provide the kind of history I am proposing. We need more historians who are willing to commit themselves to a career or at least to a period of several years as government historians.

I have often heard the objections raised to that idea. How can one trust the faceless bureaucracy? How can a historian on a government payroll maintain his independence? A common way of speaking about government employment is "selling one's soul to the devil." Furthermore, it is easy to cite horrible examples of the arbitrary termination of government history projects and the failure of government historians to produce a publishable product.

Granting that there may be some grounds for all these objections, I think we can say that writing on the inside is fast becoming an acceptable task for the historian. The series of volumes entitled *The United States Army in World War II* demonstrates that government historians can and do write good history. If I were to summarize my own experience as a government historian, I would say that we have never been seriously threatened by censorship, that we have enjoyed a remarkable degree of freedom in our research, and that we have received more than adequate support.

It would be misleading, however, to suggest that all these prerequisites for good history come automatically or instantly. The government historian must take certain precautions if he is to enjoy the freedom he needs.

First, the historian must make certain that he has firm support at the highest levels in his agency. There is sometimes a temptation to try to write history without attracting high-level attention, but to my knowledge such attempts have never been successful. Any history really worthy of the term will have too much significance for the head of the department or agency to be received with indifference. And even good history written without firm understanding at the top is not likely to be accepted for publication. If the top officials in the agency need to be educated about the value and purposes of history, the historian should begin the education process before he starts to write.

The best possible situation is that in which those who hold the authority already have an interest in history and seek out the historian. In all three projects which we have undertaken for the Atomic Energy Commission we have enjoyed this kind of interest, and I think this fact explains a large part of whatever success we have achieved.

The second precaution the historian should take stems from the first: he must be assured in a clear and formal way that he will have access to all records pertinent to his study. Unless he has support at the highest level, the historian is not likely to gain this privilege. But it is important to distinguish this right of access from the right to publish whatever one writes. Certainly if the government historian is to study really important policy issues in the recent past, he will inevitably stray into areas of classified information. And as a government employee, he must accept the responsibility to protect information that affects national security.

Access to all pertinent information may seem like a hollow right if the historian must in turn accept the obligation of censorship. But in practice, the obligation does not vitiate the right. One of the questions I am most frequently asked is how we handle the problem of classification. My answer, which many find hard to believe, is that the problem virtually takes care of itself. We are blessed in the commission with clear-cut regulations on classification, rules that leave the individual classification officer very little room for interpretation. Over a period of years we have come to know these rules almost as well as the classification officials. We do not, therefore, waste time writing about classified subjects and we manage in this way to avoid the frustration of seeing the red pencil desecrate our painfully constructed paragraphs.

In another sense, classification does impose some limitations and it always will. As we explained in the foreword to our second volume, there were important aspects of the commission's history in the early 1950s which we could not mention in the book. We could not, for example, describe all the intensely interesting and highly complex contributions to the hydrogen bomb by a number of Los Alamos scientists. We were not allowed even to mention the common name which the Los Alamos scientists gave to the successful design of the first thermonuclear weapon. We could not explain in any convincing way some of the key factors that went into major decisions on nuclear weapon policy during those years.

These limitations clearly marred the quality of our work, but we were confident that the essential truth would come through to the reader. Furthermore, because we had examined all the evidence, some of it bearing high security classifications, we were able to come to our conclusions on the basis of an examination of all the evidence. Within classification restrictions the historian may not be able to tell all the truth; but without full access to the records, he cannot be certain that he has told any of it.

This last point explains in part my contention that the kind of history I am advocating must depend to some extent on the historian on the inside. Getting all the evidence sometimes requires more than a formal clearance. An outsider coming into a government agency will not know what records exist, and without an intimate knowledge of the organization and its records, he will have to accept the judgment of others that he has seen all the pertinent files. It is even possible that the researcher may have to call the hand of some government officials who claim that certain records do not exist, but this option is not usually open to the outside historian.

A third precaution which the government historian must take is to keep his project on a high professional level. This seems obvious but it is not therefore easy to accomplish. Personnel officers often try to fob off on the historian employees with long service records who presumably know the agency's history rather than to permit the recruiting of people with formal training in history. There is also a tendency to discount the value of historical training and thus set positions at salary grades that will not attract good people. We have been lucky in the Atomic Energy Commission to avoid these pitfalls.

An important aspect of establishing a government history project on a professional level is to draw some sharp distinctions between the historians and the rest of the agency staff. The historian can attain this goal in part by keeping his group very high in the organization of the agency. In the Atomic Energy Commission the historical staff is directly responsible to the secretary of the commission and through him to the five commissioners. Thus the historians are completely independent of the operating staff of the agency, a freedom that is vital for two reasons. First, it protects the historians from a constant stream of current assignments, an abuse which has killed more than a few history projects in the government. Second, an independent position makes it virtually impossible for the operating staff of the agency to censor the historians' work in order to "protect" what the staff considers to be the "best interests" of the agency.

In the Atomic Energy Commission we have another device which perhaps more than any other has assured the independence of the historians. This is the Historical Advisory Committee. When I was asked to establish the commission's history program in 1957, I sought the advice of one of the best authorities on the subject, Dr. Kent Roberts Greenfield, who was at that time director of the army's historical program. Dr. Greenfield told me that a historical advisory committee would be essential, and I took him at his word. It was not easy to sell this idea to the commissioners, especially since I proposed that the committee, composed of independent historians and scientists, rather than the commissioners or the staff, would in effect determine whether a historian's manuscript was suitable for publication. But with the encouragement of several distinguished historians the commission did accept the proposal, and I am happy to say that the commission since that time has accepted the recommendations of the committee almost without exception.

In the last analysis the independence of the government historian depends upon the degree of responsibility he is willing to accept. The existence of a professional staff and an advisory committee of independent historians effectively cuts the historical staff off from the rest of the agency. With his new independence the government historian must stand alone. He and he alone is responsible for what he writes, and he must be willing to stand behind his work. All historians are at least resigned to accepting appraisals of their work by their professional colleagues. But the government historian is exposed to even greater hazards. He is ultimately vulnerable to attack by powerful political and economic forces on the national scene. The government historian does not enjoy the privilege of academic tenure, and indiscretion as well as harsh judgment from his peers may cost him his job.

Thus the government historian leads an exciting if precarious existence. He must maintain his independence and fight his own battles. He must be discreet in choosing topics for research, and he must evaluate the practicalities of publishing the results of his work. If he is reckless, he will probably not survive as a government historian; if he is too cautious he will fail to achieve his purpose.

In stressing the importance of independence, I do not wish to give the impression that the government historian must, like the captain of a ship, hold himself aloof from the operating staff of his agency. Indeed, he will never reach his full potential unless he establishes a relationship of confidence and even familiarity with his associates. He may best do this by assisting the operating staff on tasks which can make use of his special talents as a historian.

Over the years I have been fortunate in establishing a close working relationship with the commission staff. When we are occasionally called upon to prepare a study tracing the evolution of commission policy over several years, we pitch in with our best efforts. Projects of this nature have helped the operating staff to understand and appreciate the historian's special talents. And we historians in turn have found such assignments an exhilarating challenge to our abilities. In fact, studies of this nature have helped convince me that the historian can make significant contribution to the analysis of current public policy.

When we add up all the dangers and limitations which the government historian must face, I am not sure that they are more formidable than those the academic historian has learned to live with. I am not suggesting that the government historian has a hard life or that his task is impossible. Rather I would contend that writing history within the government can be a viable and respectable occupation.

If the government historian must tolerate certain limitations unfamiliar to the academic historian, he also enjoys some special advantages. He is free of the distractions which seem increasingly to beset the academic historian. He has the time and facilities to develop an expert knowledge of even the most complicated technologies, a capability often required of contemporary historians. Over a period of years of concentrated study, he can achieve an unusual depth of understanding and master the rather subtle relationships which may escape the general historian. Last and by no means least, as a government employee, the historian is free to draw upon the enormous resources of the federal government.

Some years ago Professor James Lea Cate of the University of Chicago, coeditor of *The Army Air Forces in World War II,* gave a delightful lecture on his experiences as a member of the Atomic Energy Commission's Historical Advisory Committee. In his paper, Professor Cate mentioned some of the dangers threatening the government historian. But he added one I have not yet mentioned today. Cate said that the greatest danger of all was that over the years the historian might develop too great a sense of loyalty to his agency and that his bias might damage the quality of his work. After thirteen years of a splendid association with the Atomic Energy Commission, I think I would say this is the greatest danger of all. An awareness of that danger as we continue to work toward the truth may keep us on our intended course.

Problems in Writing the History of
Government Science Agencies

THOMAS G. MANNING

Handling Archival Material

THE ASPECT OF RESEARCH in the National Archives that I most want to talk about is the problem posed by the massiveness of the records there. Managing their bulk can entail a disproportionate sacrifice of time and effort. A certain amount of waste motion is inevitable during every phase of original research. What seems unnecessary, however, is the cosmic helplessness or aimlessness which often must characterize the early behavior in the National Archives of research-minded persons faced with overwhelming numbers of documents. The genuine academic with a passion for knowledge traps himself by intending to master all the facts; or in his impatience to get at the primary sources and their promise of buried treasures of knowledge he rushes headlong into the documents. My statement will suggest ways of controlling enthusiasm by clarifying the purposes of research, thus avoiding confusion and delay at the archives. I include steps taken by the scholar before he comes to the National Archives and his attitude and behavior toward the documents after he has arrived there.

To fortify the researcher with ideas, questions, and information for an intelligent encounter with the mass of records, I recommend reading and studying in the libraries of government agencies and bureaus, which may have pamphlets, hearings, and even literature annotated by bureau members that cannot be found elsewhere. Beginning in the 1890s, the House Committee on Appropriations, probably at the behest of Congressman Cannon of Illinois, began to publish its hearings. For the fifty-year period before the upswing of government science in the 1940s, these hearings, printed for use on Capitol Hill and now to be found mostly in government libraries, are a major source of knowledge about government science agencies, because the money and sometimes even the organic laws of those agencies were managed as sundry civil appropriation legislation.

Anticipatory thinking about the final form of the book will give direction to this prearchival phase. If the researcher is planning on the narrative mode of organization, prior mas: y of outstanding events will enable him, once he is located at the National Archives, to pass rapidly through familiar documents and to concentrate quickly on those materials which elaborate or modify what he has learned elsewhere. An early selection of important persons, from information gained at the government libraries, will make archival note taking more relevant and focus it on the buildup of fresh knowledge. Even though the broad themes to uphold and energize the narrative may come at a relatively late stage in the research, whenever they appear they do wonders in sifting and grading the piles of facts for significance.

Tactical maneuvers save a person after he has made the plunge into the documents. Quantity of notes can prove as embarrassing as quantity of documents. To avoid simply shifting the locus of his problem by piling up notes, the researcher postpones note taking; he indexes materials where notes may be taken if further experience enhances the value of documents previously discounted. Many times he never returns to his own index. The sooner routine years are identified within the sources, the sooner the researcher can begin to skip large amounts of these sources. He may be reasonably certain that a particular year will not be fruitful if he knows from his preparatory study of no striking events during that year. Rapid sampling in the year suspected of barrenness enables the researcher to finalize the decision to bypass materials.

To urge thoughtfulness on those working in archives is not to imply that there are no limits to ratiocination. Sometime during his stay at the National Archives the scholar commits himself without reservation to the documents. His commitment is not blind, because he has done prior planning. Sooner or later, however, there is a submission to the materials in all their massiveness; the scholar finds the important documents by covering the ground. I have rarely found registers and indexes useful shortcuts; enormous amounts of time can be wasted consulting them. I have had more success coming upon valuable collections by surprise or by accident, within the framework, of course, of preparatory thinking. The reward for unrestrained embracement is more than the discovery of important sources. Names, places, and dates are imprinted on the mind of the researcher, because he keeps seeing them; his knowledge is made firm and authoritative through repetition. Perhaps, also, institutional forms and activity are better communicated through masses of documents; the regularized, repeated human behavior comes through more effectively.

To say that an archives is a place where the scholarly minded person thinks and learns is, I suppose, a truism. But this truism bears emphasizing in the face of the large amount of copying or reproducing of documents which is carried on in archives everywhere. If this copying precludes the acquisition of much more knowledge than one uses, if this copying does not provide for retracing one's steps in the documents, after further thought has inspired new demands on materials already examined, then I do not see how the serious researcher can accept such copying as his chief method. I am aware of the practical reasons for using this tool. Nevertheless, I affirm that the continual turning over of the documents and the selecting, winnowing, and thinking which note taking involves, are indispensable for serious works of historical scholarship.

I suppose that if I had known thirty years ago what I have said to you so far, my work since would have been better, or at least it would have proceeded more expeditiously. Could what I have said to you today been written thirty years ago? I am willing to answer this question in the affirmative. My research experience has not been so different or my statement of that experience so distinctive or profound as to lead me to believe that a similar statement could not have been written just before World War II. Would I have been willing thirty years ago to accept or learn from someone else's statement on research methods? I doubt it very much.

My subsequent remarks will not relate directly to the National Archives and its records; instead, I propose to survey nonarchival aspects of writing history of government science agencies. My justification is the opinion that the more archivists know about the frame of mind or intellectual concerns of the scholars who visit them, the better the collaboration will be between the two groups.

Writing the History of Government Science

I first wish to speak of scientific learning and the problem it creates for the historian desirous of introducing large amounts of such learning into their political, administrative, or institutional history. All too often this problem of scientific knowledge discourages important research in American history. But for the historian who is brave or rash enough to try his hand at mastering large parts of nineteenth- or twentieth-century science, the rewards are substantial. Research long overdue is accomplished, and from the marriage of science and history there emerges a new basis for judging past American politics and politicians.

To instruct himself in science the historian should undertake two tasks at once. Through textbooks that fit his intellectual grasp he should acquire the learning and vocabulary necessary to understand the past scientific knowledge that bears on his subject. Concurrently, he should consult expert opinion about this past science. In turn, this consultation of experts involves two approaches. Through book reviews and other commentary the historian discovers the initial response of the scientific world to the bureau and its work twenty-five, fifty, or one hundred years ago. And he also finds out what the best present-day scientists are saying about the work of their colleagues twenty-five, fifty, or one hundred years ago. He may indeed investigate opinion that intervened between the present and the scientific past which absorbs his interest, in order to have the history of criticism of the research he wishes to judge. Fortified with his own understanding and with professional opinion in depth, the historian is then in a position to grasp essential intellectual achievement and to weave the story of that achievement into his political narrative.

There is a skill to working the history of scientific knowledge into political history. Very early in the narrative, the author may wish to introduce long passages involving science to identify the bureau, before events rise to challenge it. A political attack on a bureau seems all the more extraordinary if beforehand the author has established the fact that extraordinary science has been done. Whenever a writer expounds on solid science, however, he runs the risk of suspending or sidetracking the narrative. Interspersion of the science can reduce such hiatuses in the narrative. For example, if politico-scientific issues are agitated at several points in the narrative, then each time the historian has the opportunity to develop important features of bureau science, thereby spreading his exposition of knowledge. Even if he still needs a whole chapter to relate the development of the relevant science, by opportune references to past or future persons and events he may convey to the reader the continuity of the narrative and its unification with the science.

Scientific versus Historical Training

Sometimes scientists propose a drastic solution for the problem of the historian in science: they would read the historian out of the business of writing the history of science. An intriguing moment for me came while I was reading a review of my history of the Geological Survey in the *Australian Journal of Science*. The reviewer, a field geologist in New South Wales and a senior lecturer at the University of Sydney, declared that the history of science "requires an author to be first a scientist, second a historian." The historian, he said, could have only a secondhand understanding of science. He closed his review with an earnest appeal to American and Australian scientists to take up writing the history of science, and not leave the field open to nonscientists. Scientists, I take it, would then do the writing of the histories of government agencies.

The problem is that no person can be an expert in both science and history, working, for example, simultaneously as a field geologist and as an archival historian. Yet a worker in the history of science needs to move with some sophistication in both fields, and the question is whether this worker should choose science or history as his primary, initial base of operation. No doubt if he starts with science, as the Australian geologist wishes, and takes his graduate training in that area, he will be less likely to make errors in technical matters when writing history than he would if he began with the discipline of history. Or the person trained from the beginning in history will be slower to learn the necessary technical knowledge than the person who began in science. Also, I have seen scientists do very well indeed writing history about some topic located on the frontier of emerging scientific knowledge if the exercise is in pure doctrine.

The disadvantage of moving from science into history comes in situations requiring the special techniques of the trained historian. The scientist may miss the importance of the primary sources which are a deep-seated and traditional interest of the historical discipline. It is not so much that he cannot find these sources, but rather that he neglects them, because he has not been impressed with the opportunities they present, or has never experienced the imperative to consult them. The nature of his current scientific involvement may mean that he will not develop fully the critical and open-minded attitude which historians set so much store by. If the scientist studies the past of a bureau that fosters his own discipline in the present, considerations of propriety may discourage his writing a full and frank history. His criticism might be regarded within the bureau or guild as rocking the boat. I have noticed a tendency among scientists to discount factionalism as a theme in the history of scientific bureaus. This factionalism, the scientists say, did not affect the caliber or productivity of the bureau. Whether that observation is valid or not, the historian would go ahead with the earthy theme, because his profession commits him to presenting the totality of the historical experience. Today's scientific worker may also assume that the government bureau has always pursued the science it is engaged in now. I was advised by one geologist to leave out a chapter on Yellowstone Park because the topic of the park had nothing to do with a geological survey. After the book was published another person called the chapter on Yellowstone "peripheral" to my subject, a judgment that certainly originated in a present-day conception of the United States Geological Survey.

Worst of all, the scientist may not be equipped to deal with the larger problems of historical organization. Needing broad themes to make his project a work of art and history, he may be tempted to borrow the commonplace periodizations of American history, and his work will appear mechanical. He will be typical of many scientists writing history if he uses only the good things about a bureau to order the facts. Or he may fall back on condensation and compression as means of control; no doubt this factual approach will render his narrative more scientific, but also heavy and slow. These organizational pitfalls a historian is in a better position to avoid, because he has learned, however painfully, to discover original, significant, and pervasive historical themes which elevate, excite, or give notable consistency to the narrative.

In effect what I have said is that both scientists and historians have something to contribute to the writing of the history of science. And the field is big enough to hold both groups. Comparisons should not extend to the origins of each of the groups; rather, these comparisons should focus on what each group contributes or fails to contribute to the profession of history.

Archival Sources for Studies of
Federal Administration

HAROLD T. PINKETT

IN A PROCLAMATION RELATING to the British invasion of Washington during the summer of 1814, President James Madison deplored the destruction of public buildings in the city. Those edifices were, in his words, "depositories of the public archives, not only precious to the nation as the memorials of its origin and its early transactions, but interesting to all nations as contributions to the general stock of historical instruction and political science."[1] In these words, a perceptive student of history and government voiced perhaps one of the earliest opinions concerning the value of federal archives for the study of history and governmental institutions. The growth and diversification of activities and interests of the federal government since Madison's time have made the resultant federal archives even more valuable through the years as sources for the study of the government in terms of administrative performance.

The archival sources useful for this purpose are vast, in spite of the considerable losses caused by the physical disasters and misguided disposal inflicted upon them for a century and a half before the establishment of the National Archives in 1934. Since that year, systematic efforts have been made to assemble these sources in the National Archives Building and in other special repositories. Meanwhile congress has enacted legislation that requires the creation and preservation of federal records that properly document "the organization, functions, policies, decisions, procedures, and essential transactions" of agencies and that are "designed to furnish the information necessary to protect the legal and financial rights of the Government" and the public.[2]

It is obvious that proper documentation of such facets of agency activities helps illuminate the origins, evolving functions and activities, organizational patterns, and public relations activities of federal agencies. These characteristics, in turn, can be used as a basis for describing major classes of records that are normally considered to possess value for studies of varied aspects of the administration of public policy.

Origins of Federal Agencies

The origins of federal agencies are often less conveniently documented than other characteristics because background material showing conditions leading to the creation of particular agencies is seldom accumulated comprehensively by the agencies in question. Records accumulated by other agencies, however, often provide such background information. Among these records are the material of agencies formerly charged with particular responsibilities, and records of investigative groups such as presidential commissions, interagency groups, and congressional committees may also exist. Moreover, public opinion communications of established agencies may deal significantly with problems considered to warrant creation of new agencies. In addition, new agencies usually very early reconstruct their own creation by assembling such authoritative documents as copies of statutes, executive orders, and legal opinions setting forth their power and responsibilities. Documentation of the origins of the General Services Administration, for example, illustrates these tendencies. The story of that agency's origins in functional terms is to be found in records of several agencies that were responsible for federal property, public works, and federal records functions for many years before 1949, the year GSA was established. The circumstances leading directly to its creation, moreover, are to be seen in records of the first Commission on Organization of the Executive Branch of the Government, popularly known as the first Hoover Commission, and in records of the Committee on Government Operations of the United States House of Representatives.

Functions and Activities

The evolving functions and activities of federal administrative organizations are captured in numerous types of records that are appraised as permanently valuable and that become major parts of archival sources. Indeed, the preservation of such records is the principal justification for the administration of federal archives at public expense. These records have long been highly valued for both administrative and research purposes. They include many tools that are useful in determining administrative responsibility or explaining of-

OCCUPATIONAL DISTRIBUTION

The diversity of Federal activities is reflected in the occupational distribution of the executives in the Inventory. There is a marked concentration of executives in 10 broad fields which account for 90 percent of the Inventory.

Ten Largest Occupations

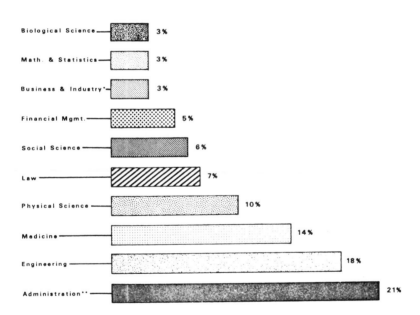

*Includes such specialties as contracting, procurement, marketing, real estate and finance.

**Includes management analysis, program management, computer systems management and general administration.

Characteristics of the Federal Executive (Washington, D.C.: Government Printing Office, 1969), p.5

ficial action. As such, they may be important instruments in the maintenance of accountability of the government to its citizens—an essential element in a democratic society. Moreover, the records are veritable fountains of administrative knowledge and experience from which may flow insight to solve present problems, or what is equally important, wisdom to avoid past mistakes. In this sense the records may perhaps help save policy makers, administrators, and citizens from the fate envisioned by George Santayana when he wrote: "Those who cannot remember the past are condemned to repeat it."

What are some of the classes of records that archivists seek to preserve in order that evolving functions and activities in federal administration may be documented? To begin with, they strive to retain all records that throw important light on all stages of the formulation and promulgation of policies to carry out basic functions. Policy formulation is frequently mirrored in minutes of top-level staff meetings, reports of advisory groups, office files of key staff assistants, and program correspondence. Policy promulgation is commonly evidenced in memorandums and other directives, speeches of upper-echelon officials, transcripts of press conferences, and formal statements of decisions. Documentation of basic procedures used in implementing policies also is a matter of concern for archivists. Here their efforts are directed toward preserving not only handbooks and manuals of program procedures and similar issuances but also representative records that show procedures in actual situations.

The implementation of policies designed to accomplish the purposes for which the federal agencies were established produces myriad documents, often called program records. Prominent among the records of archival value are annual or other periodic reports on agency goals and accomplishments. In recent years agencies have made these more uniform in contents and treatment than they once were to enhance their use as tools of administration. Consequently, they tend to lack much of the previous unexpected detail—detail unnecessary in the administrator's view—that has often been the delight of the researcher.

Among other reports valued by archivists are those that deal with comprehensive audits and investigations of programs or groups of programs and that contain evaluations of agency performance from the standpoint of congressional intent and operational efficiency. Such reports help to provide balance in weighing evidence from brief and uncritical periodic reports.

The program records continually preserved by archivists also comprise great bodies of correspondence that supply answers to the whys and wherefores of historic government actions. The "letters that flow in and out," Leonard D. White observed, portray the life of government departments and their subdivisions and thereby contribute to understanding of administration.[3] Samuel P. Hays, who examined general correspondence of several federal agencies during research on his provocative study entitled *Conservation and the Gospel of Efficiency,* called these records "gold mines." They provided, said this prominent historian, "invaluable insight into the attitudes and activities of federal resource agencies" and were especially useful in presenting "a view of policy-in-the-making and of the personal and group struggle over the formulation and execution of policy."[4]

In this connection it might be noted that the production of multiple copies made readily possible by the typewriter has tended to increase the researcher's chances of finding letters on particular subjects. During their research on the history of the Atomic Energy Commission, Drs. Richard G. Hewlett and Oscar E. Anderson were grateful that copies of pertinent letters had often been made in sextuplicate. Hence they pointed out that if an original was destroyed, the chances were better than even that one of the five carbons escaped the flames.[5] The possible blessings of multiple copies for researchers are also suggested in the following story told by Paul H. Appleby:

> Some years ago a man in the Department of Agriculture reported with a chuckle finding on his desk eight identical letters from a citizen who had addressed them to the President, the Secretary of Agriculture, the head of AAA, the head of the Southern Division of the AAA, two Senators, one Congressman, and the man on whose desk the letters accumulated.[6]

In many instances the great bulk of the program records of an agency consists of what are usually called "case files." These are units of records documenting dealings of the government with particular persons, places, or events. They differ importantly from so-called subject files in which the government's interest is centered on some phase of subject matter reflecting a wide variety of administrative events and interests.[7] Traditionally, case files have been bodies of records created in disputes between parties heard before courts of law. They have also been created for many years, however, in proceedings of the government's many quasi-judicial agencies and in operations of executive agencies that make administrative determinations not involving disputes between parties or regulatory action.[8] Because of their great volume and variety, these records create one of the greatest problem areas in archival administration. It has become increasingly impractical and probably unnecessary to preserve permanently all case files produced in the administration of public policy. Therefore, with considerable mental and physical anguish, archivists have striven to save these files on a selective basis. Criteria developed in this effort of selection have reflected the following basic considerations: (1) organizational levels of adjudications or administrative determinations, (2) uniqueness and value of data when compared with information in less voluminous records, (3) importance of persons, places, or things dealt with, and (4) illustration of the pattern or recurring nature of particular administrative actions. Mr. Jerome Finster of the archives staff will discuss case files in greater detail at the next session of this conference.

Still other classes of records yield significant information concerning evolving functions and actions of government agencies. Among these are legal and fiscal records. Archivists seek to preserve correspondence of chief legal officers and other records such as opinions and memorandums showing legal guidance in the formulation and administration of particular policies. Their appraisal of fiscal records centers importantly on budget statements and disbursement records documenting financial resources sought and used in the execution of substantive functions.

Organizational Patterns

Federal archival resources, furthermore, include varied documents delineating organizational patterns in federal administration. In one broad category there are records of investigative bodies created to study and make recommendations on reorganization of bureaus, departments, or the entire federal administrative establishment. R. Michael McReynolds of the Archives staff will describe some of these records in a session of the conference tomorrow morning. Suffice it to say here that these archival sources are vital for the study of a burgeoning bureaucracy that Charles A. Beard forty years ago saw as "a huge complex of wealth, political institutions, military engines, economic undertakings, and technological activities looming fatefully on the horizon of the ages."[9]

In the sphere of bureau and departmental administration several types of organizational documents are created and eventually retired to archival custody. There are statutes, executive orders, memorandums of department and bureau heads, and possibly supporting materials relating to creation, discontinuance, or consolidation of organizational units. Especially valuable are organizational and functional charts supplying information on the responsibilities assigned to major offices and depicting the interrelationships and specializations of component units. They yield significant data concerning the intricate administrative vicissitudes that characterize the life of many federal agencies. The information given in these charts is often supplemented importantly by that presented in official directories, organizational maps, and related records. Noteworthy also are correspondence and memorandums delegating or defining powers and responsibilities of administrative units and reports of staff or other advisors on organizational problems.

Public Relations Activities

Furthermore, another major class of archival material providing insights on administrative processes consists of records produced in public relations activities. This material includes press releases, brochures, charts, posters, bulletins, and other publications designed to interpret agency activities to the public. Archivists are especially desirous of preserving publicity issuances that contribute to an understanding of how agencies view their roles and accomplishments. Archivists are equally concerned, however, about the permanent retention of an ever-increasing quantity of communications the government receives from the public. This documentation, as Carl J. Friedrich states, contains "all sorts of communicable views, opinions, facts, and criticisms" and is becoming "a potent factor in the shaping of public-policy, particularly in areas where government is entering new or experimental ground."[10] This evaluation is supported by an account of the significance of letters the White House received during early, critical years of the New Deal. According to Rexford G. Tugwell, these letters "not only dealt with personal problems growing out of relief and unemployment difficulties but also provided much advice for governmental action in the nation's crisis and centered importantly on the desirability or undesirability of New Deal policy."[11]

Holdings of the National Archives and Records Service bulge with classes of records that have been described in this paper. It is not suggested, however, that this documentation furnishes answers to all questions that may arise in studies of federal administration. The simple fact is that many answers are not to be found in the records. This condition has provoked Arthur M. Schlesinger, Jr., to state:

> Nothing in my own recent experience has been more chastening than the attempt to penetrate into the process of decision . . . . The sad fact is that, in many cases, the basic evidence for the historian's reconstruction of the really hard cases does not exist— and the evidence that does exist is often incomplete, misleading, or erroneous.[12]

Several circumstances tend to contribute to this inadequacy of documentation in particular situations. Allan Nevins observes:

> Changes have come in communications which leave many transactions unrecorded. The telephone has annihilated much of the domain of the

written word; railways and airplanes have made face-to-face conversation easy; the radio has created intangible newspapers and magazines which, leaving no files, vanish into thin air.[13]

Other reasons for inadequate records were suggested several years ago by the Committee on Public Administration of the Social Science Research Council. These include the failure of administrators to appreciate the value of good documentation, lack of adequate staff for record-keeping work, necessity for secrecy in the public interest in certain cases, desire for secrecy in other cases where a written record is justified by public interest but not by personal welfare, and reluctance of some administrators to be committed in writing to decisions that may have to be changed later.[14]

These inadequacies, of course, should not deter the use of archival sources for studies of the history and performance of the federal government. There are large gaps in the records of all major enterprises—nongovernment as well as government. That research in administration can be profitably performed in archival sources is attested to by the work of a growing number of scholars. Leonard D. White's four volumes on federal administrative history from the founding Federalists to the ascendant Republicans at the close of the last century clearly suggest the great research potential of federal archives. What White, often handicapped by fragmentary sources, did for the nineteenth century, seems eminently feasible for the twentieth with its greater documentary abundance.

Attesting further to the research value of federal records are an increasing number of studies dealing importantly with the history of particular federal agencies and programs and administration of particular federal policies. As shown already and as will be demonstrated later, speakers at this conference have made notable studies of scientific agencies, regulatory programs, administrative reform, and policies relating to Indians and the rural poor. Noteworthy uses of records are also exemplified in the following studies: Arthur M. Schlesinger, Jr., and John Blum on New Deal policies; Arthur Johnson on government-business relations; Donald Swain and Elmo Richardson on conservation programs; Sidney Fine on labor policy; Gilbert Fite and James Shidler on agricultural programs; Wayne Fuller on the postal service; and Oscar Kraines on administrative reform.

Although these and other examples indicate a growing awareness of the value of federal records for analysis of federal policies and policy administration, such studies are signally outnumbered by publications on these subjects without the slightest adornment of citations of basic archival sources. This fact is shown in the most cursory examination of periodical and monographic writings in history, political science, and public administration. It is hoped that the situation will tend to be reversed by discussions at this conference and by subsequent research conferences of the National Archives and Records Service.

In helping to promote studies of federal administration, archivists are providing an unmatched abundance and authenticity of documentary sources. Because these materials are the products of the government of a large and populous nation, with wide geographical, economic, social, and cultural differences and with a frequent need to experiment, they can yield an understanding of some basic administrative features of this experimentation. These features are important elements in what many scholars have called the style and genius of American government.

DISCUSSION SUMMARY

Dr. Anderson first presented the following recapitulation of the papers: Dr. Hewlett has argued the need for histories of the recent past. He has asserted his belief that there is a need for inside jobs and has given some suggestions about how to keep inside histories honest.

Dr. Manning has given us a number of valuable suggestions on how to cope with the massive volume of records of federal agencies and has entered a strong plea for the role of the historian in carrying forward specialized studies.

Dr. Pinkett has shown us how a records appraisal officer thinks and works, has given us guides to the records of the federal agencies, and has strongly affirmed the research potential of those records.

After summarizing the papers, Dr. Anderson invited questions from the audience.

Paul J. Scheips of the Office of the Chief of Military History, Department of the Army, began the discussion by starting that he agreed with Dr. Hewlett on the importance of writing current history, but he spoke of the great difficulties caused by the classification and the disappearance of records. He also believed that because of the classification problem current history had to be written from the inside, yet he maintained that there was a limit to the amount of history that can be written in that way. The classification problem in Dr. Scheips's judgment had for some time been discouraging graduate students and others from getting into recent history.

Dr. Scheips was very much impressed with what James McGregor Burns, who at one point in his career did some work for Scheips's office, had to say. The classification issue involved not only historians but the public at large, because as a matter of public policy the public needs to know more than it often gets to know. He recommended that archivists and historians support the general position that Burns and others had taken.

Dr. Scheips also expressed his opinion that archivists had not really faced up to the problem that recent records are disappearing. They are disappearing not through any machinations on the part of anybody, but partly because records people do not have an archival and historical sense, partly because it is easier to destory records than it is to retire them, and partly—perhaps, most importantly—because the army's records retirement system, in Scheips's judgment, was oriented toward the destruction of records rather than toward their preservation, simply because it is cheaper to destory than to preserve.

Dr. Hewlett agreed with the remarks on classification. In his view much had yet to be done in the area, and impetus for reform would have to come from the historical profession and others outside the government. He felt that if enough pressure were put on the government, declassification would take place, and he indicated that he had seen engineers and the scientists in the government press for and obtain declassification of records.

On destruction of records, Dr. Hewlett agreed that some records officers were oriented entirely toward destruction, but he observed that he had some success in talking with records officers and trying to explain to them the value of records for historians.

James Harvey Young of Emory University discussed the problem of the outsider who approaches an agency to which he is a stranger. He observed that the agency often does not understand history, does not realize what the historian is about, and thinks that a few public relations releases are all the historian may want or need. As an example, Professor Young cited the case of one of his graduate students who was seeking to work on the background of pesticides. When a reporter got access to certain records at the Department of Agriculture and released material that made past policy look not as farsighted as the department might have wished, it became very difficult for the student to get access to essential records, even records that were not classified or otherwise restricted or protected by law.

Dr. Young suggested that researchers attempt to establish some kind of contact with someone in the agency who might understand scholarship at its most sophisticated level. He related that when he himself was trying to gain access to records relating to food and drugs he received help from various people. Probably ultimately the most crucial help he received was from the general counsel, who was himself a teacher of food and drug law and who understood what was involved in the broad scale of research scholarship. Professor Young recommended that researchers beginning work in new records, or who were sending their students to such records, study the people whom they were about to approach in order to find someone who had in his background some kind of college teaching and research experience.

Wayne D. Rasmussen of the Department of Agriculture observed that outside historians who are studying programs of the departments may well have an effect on government policy. He cited books by Dr. Oscar Anderson, Professor Gilbert Fite, and Professor Sidney Baldwin as having had considerable influence on government policy.

On the matter of access Dr. Rasmussen suggested that the scholar or student go to the agency historian, if the agency has a historian. Many of these historians in government agencies had developed indexes, files, or other aids that could help in shortcutting some material; most of them had been through masses of archival material and had some ideas where particular files or items were located and which were of particular value. He added that National Archives staff members, particularly those in charge of agriculture records, know the records thoroughly and would be of great assistance when the researcher came to the National Archives.

Dr. Rasmussen also observed that many government historians were concerned with creating a historical perspective on current programs and that in the Department of Agriculture the history group had affected agricultural policy through their staff studies.

Sidney Baldwin of California State University, Fullerton, recalled that when he wrote his book on the Farm Security Administration, he was a member of the Eastern Establishment who found it relatively easy to hop on a plane or train or into his car and to get to such Establishment places as the National Archives Building on Pennsylvania Avenue, the Franklin D. Roosevelt Library at Hyde Park, New York, the Library of Congress, and various other places along the eastern seaboard.

Now that he was a member of the Western Establishment, however, the world looked very different to him. From his western perspective, Dr. Baldwin wanted to know when the New Federalism would extend to the archival function so that members of the Western Establishment would not have to spend $292 to come to the East to do research on documents which, in their opinion, do not belong in Washington, D.C., but belong closer to the people in such places as the records centers in the Middle West, the Northwest, the South, and elsewhere. Placing all the archives in a building in Washington, D.C., in Dr.

Baldwin's judgment, did not effectively make them accessible to graduate students and particularly to junior faculty who lacked handsome stipends for airplane travel.

Dr. Pinkett replied that the National Archives and Records Service already had under way the establishment of regional archives in each of the federal records centers. In these regional archives would be concentrated records that are considered more useful for regional than for general or national studies. Two such branches had already been set up in California, and these units would also accumulate records of field agencies in the regions in which the records centers were located. If such records were appraised as being permanently valuable and most useful for studies by people in the locality of the creation, they would be preserved locally rather than brought to Washington.

Frank B. Evans of the National Archives added that the current issue of *Prologue* contained a listing of microfilm publications that are being distributed to the eleven regional archives branches. These were prints made from existing microfilm publications, and as the publication program continued and resources permitted, it was the intention of the archivist of the United States to make available in every regional archives branch copies of many National Archives microfilm publications. Dr. Evans also said that there is a problem in decentralizing field records if there is no opportunity to study those records in conjunction with related central office records, and he noted that the problem was further complicated by the government's decentralizing some of its central offices outside Washington.

Sherrod East, formerly of the staff of the National Archives, added that with regard to the problem of security review and classification there has been and will continue to be a problem, even for the insider, of getting the key documentation that is highly protected within an agency. He called attention to the policy General Eisenhower adopted two decades earlier that became the subject of an executive order enjoining agencies to implement procedures for the declassification of records in order to promote and permit greater access. Dr. East thought that results would come only from conscientious service on the part of the custodians of the records, and that, because of the volume of records and because the bureaucracy was what it was, no one was going to be able to wave a wand over the records and physically accomplish complete declassification in the foreseeable future. In his view the key was finding people who were willing to accept the responsibility of their positions as custodians of the documents or as officials who had played a part in the creation of the records. He pointed out how important it was for a researcher to come in at a high level, whether the researcher was on the inside or on the outside, because it is very hard in government to find the person who will exercise the declassification responsibility, even if that responsibility is written into the security regulation. But when a responsible official determined that a security classification should be removed, it could be removed.

"Freedom of information" procedures, Dr. East observed, had only tightened the procedures that already existed. If the researcher wants security classified access, he has to live with the problem of review within the existing system; security review could be handled if the researcher was willing to accept the responsibility of having a security check run on him and of submitting his manuscript.

SESSION

Dilemmas in Administering
Public Policy

CHAIRMAN

LOWELL H. HATTERY

Professor of Management and Public Administration and Coordinator of the Science, Technology, and Government Program, American University . . . A. B., Ohio University; Ph.D., American University . . . United States Department of Agriculture, 1939-41; National Research Council, 1946-48; faculty, American University, 1948- . . . developed and directed Center for Technology and Administration, American University . . . coeditor, *Information Retrieval Management; Executive Control and Data Processing; Scientific Research: Its Administration and Organization.*

It is a pleasure for me to be admitted to this program as a non-historian. I am happy to be able to serve as a switching center for this afternoon's session, which I think will be interesting and challenging. We are going to be moving from a very general perspective on research in administering public policy to some rather specific case studies representing the dilemma of administrators and their concern with major public policy.

The first presentation is by Professor James Harvey Young, who received his Ph.D. in American history from the University of Illinois and since finishing graduate school has taught at Emory University.

Dr. Young's writing has concerned the history of reform in America, especially in respect to public health. His publications include *The Toadstool Millionaires* and *The Medical Messiahs*. These books treat the history of health quackery in America and efforts to combat and control it. Professor Young is now working on a history of the Food and Drug Administration. He holds a grant from the National Institutes of Health and has developed oral history materials in his field. Today he is reporting on a case study in regulatory history.

Our second speaker this afternoon, Professor James Johnson, earned his Ph.D. in American history from Columbia University. He has been a Danforth Fellow and has won the Organization of American Historians' Louis Pelzer Award for an essay entitled "Drafting the NRA Code of Fair Competition for the Bituminous Coal Industry." He currently teaches history at Brooklyn College of the City University of New York, and his scholarly work has appeared in several historical journals, including the *Journal of American History*.

For this session's anchor presentation, we have Mr. Jerome Finster of the National Archives and Records Service, who was educated in American history at the College of the City of New York and at American University. A member of the National Archives staff for a number of years, Mr. Finster is now with its Records Appraisal Division and specializes in records of federal agencies operating in the socioeconomic field, particularly in labor and the regulation of transportation. He was director of the conference preceding this one on urban research, which met in June of this year.

Saccharin: A Bitter Regulatory

Controversy

JAMES HARVEY YOUNG

FEW FRANK EXPRESSIONS OF opinion uttered by a bureaucrat to a president have led to such extensive repercussions as those spoken one day in 1908 by Harvey Washington Wiley, chief of the Bureau of Chemistry in the Department of Agriculture, to Theodore Roosevelt. Four years later, during the final phases of the Bull Moose campaign, Wiley recalled the dramatic moment in a political address in which he was opposing Roosevelt and trying to get Woodrow Wilson elected.[1]

In 1908 Wiley had been seeking to provide rigorous enforcement of the Pure Food and Drugs Act of 1906 which his efforts had done so much to place upon the statute books. The law, in his mind, could be interpreted to mean the prohibition from processed foods of chemical preservatives like benzoate of soda. Industrial users of such preservatives were not convinced. They used their political connections to get a personal conference with the president, arguing that Wiley's policies would ruin many businesses owned by sound Republicans. Wiley, his colleagues in the bureau, and Secretary of Agriculture James Wilson, who were also present, all responded by terming the addition of benzoate of soda to foods injurious.[2]

"Then," as Wiley remembered the scene, "turning to the Republican representatives of business and striking the table a ringing blow with his fist, the President said, 'Gentlemen, if this drug is injurious you shall not put it in foods.'"[3]

At this point one of the canners, who happened also to be a congressman, interposed: "But Mr. President, how about the saccharin. My firm saved 4 Thousand dollars last year by using saccharin instead of sugar."

The research for this paper was done while the author held a fellowship from the John Simon Guggenheim Memorial Foundation and grants from the Emory University Research Committee.

"I unfortunately 'butted in,'" Wiley remembered, and said, "Yes, Mr. President, and everyone who eats these products is deceived, believing he is eating sugar, and moreover the health is threatened by this drug."

"Turning upon me in sudden anger and fierce visage," Wiley recalled, "the President said, 'Anybody who says saccharin is injurious is an idiot. Dr. Rixey gives it to me every day.'"

Many physicians were giving saccharin every day, and restricting sugar, to their patients who, like the president, tended toward corpulence. Saccharin was a coal tar derivative which had been discovered some forty years earlier by a chemist named Constantin Fahlberg working under the direction of the noted organic chemist, Ira Remsen, at the Johns Hopkins University. Remsen had suggested the line of research which Fahlberg had been pursuing, and the paper announcing saccharin's discovery bore both their names. Formerly a sugar chemist, Fahlberg recognized in saccharin's sweetness a possible bonanza. Without Remsen's knowledge, Fahlberg patented both the product and a process for its manufacture and assigned half his rights to a cousin, a German doctor, with whom he entered a partnership to produce the new chemical. Although much miffed by Fahlberg's deception, Remsen did not contest the patent, saying he would not sully his hands with industry.[4]

For a brief time saccharin blossomed as a panacea. "Like other new remedies," a scientist later wrote, saccharin "would cure all diseases. . . . The sick thought if they could get saccharin they would surely get well, and they got it to their heart's content." Then came the reaction. Sober second thoughts, based on clinical observation, discounted claimed cures and thus saccharin's therapeutic value. What was left was saccharin's sweetness, for use in the diets of diabetics, who dared not eat sugar, and in the diets of the overweight.[5]

The reaction went further still. Some scientists concluded that saccharin was not only not a beneficial medicine, but rather a positive poison. A French committee of scientists, set up by the government, decided that saccharin possessed no value as a food, interfered with digestion, and if widely used would expand the national dyspepsia. So the French government barred its importation. A number of other nations either banned saccharin or, as did Germany, put limits upon its production. Saccharin's friends saw in all this the powerful pressure of sugar lobbies.[6]

In the early twentieth century, one could find articles appearing in the medical literature which supported either a relaxed or a worried position on saccharin. Dr. Rixey could find support for his prescription for the president. Dr. Wiley could find support for his admonition to the president.[7] The evidence did not preponderate in either direction. At best, canons of clinical testing in these years, because not enough knowledge had yet accumulated, permitted certain errors that only a more sophisticated future could detect. At worst, deliberate distorted research circulated in the guise of honest science, because industrial stakes were high. In between, complicated biases, often unrecognized, influenced the formulation of hypotheses, the drafting of research designs, the interpretation of experiments, and the evaluation of research performed by others.

Dr. Wiley had such an honest bias, which caused him to distrust the putting into food of what he considered the artificial creations of the new chemistry. Wiley came from rural America. His whole career had been devoted to exposing adulterations of the processed foods, foods which an increasingly urbanized America more and more required. This tampering with nature's bounty, as Wiley saw it, cheated the consumer and harmed his health. Wiley's "poison squad" experiments persuaded him that chemical preservatives made the young men who ate them at his research table ill. While striving to secure a national law, Wiley stumped the country like an itinerant preacher, every rostrum a pulpit for the gospel of pure food. The makers of chemical additives and the processors who used them had been among the most stubborn lobbyists seeking to prevent, at least to weaken, a pure food law. When that law at last was enacted, and it fell to Wiley's lot to administer it, he naturally took an extreme position against chemical additives. These included saccharin.[8]

Even saccharin's coined name, Wiley held, was fraudulent, deceiving "the great majority" of Americans, who thought saccharin meant sugar. "For this reason alone, if there were no other," Wiley said, "it should be barred from the foods of the country." But there were other reasons, he believed, at least two of them specifically covered by the new law. Under the law a food was deemed adulterated "if it contain any added poisonous or other added deleterious ingredient which may render such article injurious to health." In Wiley's eyes saccharin fit this definition perfectly. Further, the law stated that a food was adulterated "if any substance has been mixed and packed with it so as to reduce or lower or injuriously affect its quality or strength." The substitution of saccharin for sugar in canned fruits and vegetables, Wiley held, fit this definition exactly, and he so advised all inquirers.[9]

So purist an interpretation of the pure food law panicked many food processors. Their pressure on Secretary Wilson and President Roosevelt quickly brought restraint on Wiley's sole authority to render decisions and propose legal cases. He was hedged in by a three-man

Board of Food and Drug Inspection created to hold hearings and make recommendations about policy and prosecutions. Wiley was chairman, but he could be outvoted by the department's solicitor, George Mc-Cabe, and a young chemist, Frederick Dunlap, imported from the University of Michigan.[10] The hedging effect became apparent almost immediately with respect to saccharin. Wiley's effort to restrict saccharin "solely to its medical use," to ban it from foods as part of a sweeping food inspection decision aimed at dyes, chemicals, and preservatives, met resistance from his fellow committeemen.[11]

Members of industry still did not feel secure and escalated their pressures on the president. Already uneasy about Wiley's scientific judgments, Roosevelt considered the chemist's attack on saccharin to his very face a sort of last straw. The president immediately yielded to a plan industrialists had been proposing to him, the creation of the Referee Board of Consulting Scientific Experts to render decisions bureaucrats must abide by with respect to chemicals in food. Wiley was outraged, not only because of loss of face, but also because he considered the board illegal, since the Congress, in its long study preceding passage of the law, had weighed just such a plan and had rejected it. Saccharin was one of the first problems presented to the board. By a certain irony, the board's chairman was Ira Remsen.[12]

In the acrimonious future, Wiley's partisans, even Wiley himself, would use Remsen's early connection with saccharin to cast suspicion on the board's integrity.[13] At the time of Remsen's appointment, despite his anger at the creation of the board, Wiley admired the Hopkins chemist, whose picture hung on his office wall. Wiley knew about "the fight Remsen had [had] with Fahlberg" and realized that if Remsen "had any prejudice at all in the matter," it would be against saccharin rather than in favor of it.[14] While the board weighed saccharin's fate, use of the chemical in food proceeded. This policy too Wiley opposed. "So far," he wrote in 1910, "the whole power of the government has been exerted to protect those who add certain deleterious substances to foods pending certain investigations instead of prohibiting the practice until the investigations are completed." The chemist added: "And such investigations!"[15]

This tone of scorn reflected Wiley's lack of agreement with nearly all the conclusions reached by the distinguished scientists who composed the Remsen Board.[16] The point at which they came the closest to concurring with the chief of the Chemistry Bureau's preconceptions, however, related to saccharin. The scientists had been posed two questions by the secretary of agriculture:

> 1. Does a food to which there has been added saccharin contain any added poisonous or other added deleterious ingredient which

may render the said food injurious to health? (*a*) in large quantities?
(*b*) in small quantities?
   2. If saccharin be mixed or packed with a food, is the quality or
strength of said food thereby reduced, lowered, or injuriously affected?
(*a*) in large quantities? (*b*) in small quantities?[17]

Using as their "poison squad" "young men in normal health," two
medical professors, Christian Herter of Columbia, a member of the
board, and Otto Folin of Harvard, conducted extensive clinical experiments with saccharin, which served as the basis for the board's report.
Small quantities of saccharin, defined as 0.3 grams or less each day,
the board concluded, did not injure "the health of normal adults." To
this judgment was added a protective clause: "so far as is ascertain-
able by available methods of study." Large quantities of saccharin,
the board went on, taken for long periods of time, were "liable to in-
duce disturbances of digestion." Mixing saccharin in food in quantities
either large or small, the board summed up, had "not been found to
alter the quality or strength of the food." Yet it was true that substi-
tuting saccharin for sugar reduced food value and hence quality.[18]

This report did not constitute the wholesale condemnation Wiley
might have hoped for, but it gave him ample regulatory leverage. The
use of saccharin was widespread; it was not hard to compile a list of
fifty-eight foods and drinks in which it had been found. So even diets
of healthy adults might easily move upwards past the 0.3-gram barrier.
What then of the young, the elderly, the sick? What of the poor,
whose diets already skirted the malnutrition line, whose purchases of
the cheapest foods brought the greatest risk of saccharin? What, moreover, about the thrust of Dr. Folin's discovery "that saccharin was
excreted from the kidneys [chemically] unchanged?" Consequences
for health Wiley deemed grim. "The continued pouring of a foreign
body of this kind," he wrote, "which must have active properties,
through the delicate cells of the kidneys can not fail in time to produce serious disturbances of function and even fatal disease." In addition to all this, in every food in which saccharin had been used some
other sweetening agent would suffice, so in no sense could it be
argued that saccharin was indispensable.[19]

Wiley's associates, in violent disagreement with him over other issues, agreed with him about the regulatory message inherent in the
Remsen Board's saccharin report. First McCabe and Dunlap of the
Board of Food and Drug Inspection, and then, in accordance with the
law, the three secretaries of the Agriculture, Commerce, and Treasury
Departments approved the text of Food Inspection Decision 135,
issued April 29, 1911. After the following July 1, foods containing
saccharin would be regarded as adulterated.[20]

If Wiley's victory seemed sweet, he had scant time to savor it. Immediately the saccharin manufacturers took up the gauntlet. The largest producer, Monsanto Chemical Works of Saint Louis, led the attack. Monsanto had begun to make saccharin less than a decade before and by now was selling some two million pounds a year, mainly to the food trades.[21] No manufacturer could have asked for a more imaginative or persistent attorney than Monsanto's Warwick M. Hough, ably assisted by Francis E. Hamilton, representing the smaller saccharin producers. On the grounds that the full text of the Remsen research was not yet available for study, they asked for and got a delay in the effective date of FID 135.[22] Upon seeing the research, Hough and Hamilton pleaded with the three secretaries for a reversal, saying Wiley had misled the cabinet members as to what the Remsen scientists had found, as to what the board itself had intended in its report. To permit FID 135 "to stand," Hough argued, "would be to commit as great a scientific error as that which condemned Bruno and Galileo as heretics because of their belief in the Copernican theory."[23]

Taft had taken Roosevelt's place in the White House, and the saccharin lawyers evidently did not manage to see the new president, although Hough wrote to him.[24] A vigorous debate involving textual criticism ensued, Hough and Hamilton eschewing Wiley's reading to stress instead the Remsen report's assertion that saccharin in small quantities posed no hazard to health. And the lawyers made gains. They won the privilege of presenting their views in new hearings before the three secretaries.[25] They jarred the secretary of the treasury loose from his allegiance to an antisaccharin policy.[26] They pushed the secretary of agriculture into asking the Remsen Board for a fuller elaboration of their conclusions, and when that document came it did indeed read—as Hamilton and Hough insisted—as if it were more favorable than the original report to the cause the lawyers were espousing.[27] The fact that large quantities of saccharin might impair digestion, the board said in its addendum, could not "consistently be accepted as an argument . . . that smaller quantities must constitute a menace to health." In fact, it was "improbable" that saccharin would ever be used in food "in quantities that might constitute a menace to health, since its extreme sweetness would naturally limit its consumption." While Hough and Hamilton prodded in private, they also proclaimed in public, insisting that the opposition to saccharin stemmed from the sugar trust.[28]

Despite their efforts, the attorneys for the saccharin interests did not win the victory they hoped for. When Food Inspection Decision 142 was issued in March 1912, the secretaries of agriculture and commerce, treasury dissenting, still forbade the use of saccharin in normal foods.[29] But the document confessed that evidence of saccharin's harmfulness was not strong, and the decision rested mainly on an argument against the displacement of a certain amount of sugar in food by saccharin because sugar possessed food value and saccharin did not.

Wiley must have much regretted the weakened tone in FID 142 as compared with the earlier 135. In any case, his labor in connection with the new version proved to be one of his last official duties. At odds with his superiors in much more serious ways, Wiley resigned.[30] Within a year, Taft, Secretary Wilson, McCabe, and Dunlap all followed Wiley into private life, as Woodrow Wilson, the candidate for whom Wiley took the stump, assumed the presidency.

Presidents and bureaucrats might go and come, but saccharin lingered on. Soon after the new administration entered office, lawyer Hough was back testing the regulatory temperature. The zealous attorney hoped that Wiley's successor as chief of the Bureau of Chemistry, Dr. Carl L. Alsberg, would give to him what Wiley so stubbornly refused. Hough desired the rules changed so that any saccharin-containing food could enter the marketplace, provided only that the saccharin's presence be plainly labeled.[31] Alsberg, however, was not persuaded, and he sought to convince the new secretary of agriculture, David Houston, that no changes should be made. While there might be legal technicalities favoring the course Hough wanted, Alsberg said, a loosening of labeling restrictions was "very undesirable," and would "open . . . the door to fraud." So Alsberg warded off Monsanto's initiative, while in due course planning a move of his own.[32]

Alsberg brought Monsanto into court charged with the crime of adulteration. In 1916 a food and drug inspector seized in Chicago a one-pound can of Monsanto saccharin, shipped from Saint Louis to a supply house selling items used in the manufacture of soft drinks. Included in statements on the label were the words: "The Perfect Sweetener," "Healthful," and "positively harmless," descriptions the government considered false and misleading.[33] Three years passed before the case came to trial. Initial delays broadened into the longer postponement of the war, as key witnesses donned uniform and went overseas. The war also shoved saccharin into public attention because of the critical shortage of sugar. Might not saccharin rush to the rescue? Monsanto certainly thought so, running full-page newspaper advertisements saying that, if saccharin replaced sugar in only those foods in which sugar's food value was not required, the nation's annual cost of living would be reduced by $11 million.[34] Letters from housewives deluged the Bureau of Chemistry. Alsberg made several public replies. Terming saccharin "a menace," he condemned the drug "from the standpoint of economy as well as health."[35]

When the trial finally got started in Saint Louis late in 1919, the judge limited the issue to whether or not saccharin was "positively harmless." The government did not seek, of course, to present saccharin as a violent or corrosive poison, like arsenic or lead, but rather as a harmful substance when used as a constituent in normal foods, all the more dangerous because its effect was slow, its actions obscure and not easily detected by the layman. To begin its case and to dramatize for the jury how impossible it was for the layman to know when he was getting saccharin, the government attorneys offered a feast of sweets. While jurymen and the defense attorney—the judge declined to participate—sipped sugar and saccharin versions of a grape beverage, a Bureau of Chemistry witness offered in evidence also lemon, cherry, and sarsaparilla flavors. Next came cakes of all sorts, pies, cream puffs, éclairs, ice cream, candy kisses, caramels, all made with saccharin. A short wrangle ensued over the question of whether or not it was legally proper to offer exhibits into evidence and then destroy them by eating them. The judge permitted this procedure, if the jury felt so disposed.[36]

The government presented many physician witnesses, some from Saint Louis, some from the most respected ranks of American medicine elsewhere, like Dr. Solomon Solis Cohen of Philadelphia and Dr. Haven Emerson of New York. They testified on the basis of their practice that the unlimited use of saccharin would be positively harmful.[37] The keystone of the government's case was the testimony of the University of Chicago's noted physiologist, Anton J. Carlson; this was one of many cases in which he served as expert witness supporting food and drug legislation during the course of his distinguished career. Dr. Carlson had experimented with saccharin, using dogs and goats and also human subjects, including himself and especially a man with a surgically created fistula into his stomach that had been made necessary because, as a youth, he had burned his throat shut when he swallowed lye. The experiments showed, Dr. Carlson testified, that the use of saccharin curtailed the appetite, markedly decreased the quantity and strength of the appetite gastric juice, and reduced peptic digestion. His dog experiments, he said, revealed that saccharin decreased the rate of absorption of water and food from the intestines. "In a normal individual of all ages," Carlson continued, "delayed absorption would be unfavorable and it would tend to increase the bacterial putrefaction in the gut." Saccharin spread throughout the body and affected the action of every cell, Dr. Carlson observed: he had found saccharin injected hypodermically into the veins in all body secretions, saliva, tears, bile, urine, milk. By using in vitro experiments, Dr. Carlson found that saccharin retarded the digestion of protein, and that it delayed the reabsorption of red pigment into red blood cells. Thus, he asserted, saccharin was not inert, not harmless.[38]

Dr. Carlson stressed that the human body had many built-in safety factors, which might disguise saccharin's harm in the normal healthy adult. "Now, if a substance is generally used," he added, "it will get to everybody, not only for three months or three weeks . . ., but from birth to old age, it will get to everybody, not only those who are physically sound and have large factors of safety but to those who are sick and do not know it, who are on the ragged edge and those who are below. . . . children, poor people, people in institutions, they will have to take what comes."

The defense brought to the witness chair a long parade of physicians who denied ever noting in their patients any deleterious effects from the use of saccharin.[39] Numerous laymen from Saint Louis also told their fellow citizens on the jury that they had taken saccharin for years without harm: one witness claimed that the chronic indigestion he had suffered before using saccharin had disappeared when he began to use the drug.[40] Efforts also were made to cast doubt on the thrust of Dr. Carlson's research. It would be unfair to place much reliance, a Chicago doctor said, in the results Carlson had secured by using his experimental man, who was "more or less of a scientific freak," so dependent on Carlson that he would want each experiment to turn out so as "to please his professor."[41] Also, this doctor said, Carlson's dog experiments were of questionable validity, because dogs do not eat candy. "I have seen lap dogs eat candy," the witness confessed, "but I have raised thirty or forty dogs and none of my dogs ever ate candy. I have tried to give it to them off and on, but they refused it." Despite the doctor's dog testimony, while the trial recessed for Christmas, the defense arranged a hasty effort to duplicate Carlson's dog experiments. The researcher arrived at conclusions contrary to Carlson's conclusions.[42]

Nor did the twelve members of the jury agree with Dr. Carlson and the other witnesses for the government. Seven of them did, but five did not, so a mistrial resulted.[43]

Nowhere in the ranks of government—in the Bureau of Chemistry, the Office of the Secretary of Agriculture, the Department of Justice— was any doubt displayed about proceeding as rapidly as possible to a second trial. Monsanto sent emissaries to inquire about compromising the case, one of them Dr. Wiley's former colleague and antagonist, George McCabe, who, like numerous regulators before and later, had shifted sides and now was espousing the cause of the regulated.[44] McCabe's efforts came to naught, and, during April and May of 1924, before the same judge, with "Ajax" Carlson again the star government witness, the issue of saccharin's explicit harmfulness again went before a jury.[45] Again the government lost. As in the first trial, seven jurymen favored convicting Monsanto, but five voted for the company's innocence.

Farce or tragedy, would there be a third act in the great saccharin courtroom drama? As far as the Bureau of Chemistry was concerned, the show must go on. And in the heart of the business-oriented Republican twenties, both Secretary of Agriculture Henry Wallace and Secretary of Agriculture Howard Gore backed the bureau to the hilt.[46] Nor was anyone in the Agriculture Department happy when Attorney General Harlan Stone overruled that department and determined that the case against Monsanto be stricken from the docket.[47] Stone's decision was pragmatic, resting solely on the district attorney's judgment that it would be impossible to win a jury trial in St. Louis.

A year later, in 1926, answering a letter of inquiry, a Bureau of Chemistry official termed food to which saccharin had been added adulterated in two respects: because it had been cheapened in quality and because it might have been rendered deleterious to health.[48] Almost a decade later, another inquirer about saccharin received in answer the same judgment, indeed in identical words.[49] But opinion is not legal decree. Had the government won the Monsanto case, it may be surmised, saccharin might not have appeared on the GRAS list—generally recognized as safe—at the end of the 1950s, in the aftermath of the enactment of the 1958 Food Additives Amendment, and its regulatory history from then to now might have been different.[50] But that is another story.

Almost all the data for the story of saccharin's early regulatory history come from records in the National Archives, in the Archives Branch at the Washington National Records Center, and in the Washington National Records Center itself. Some of the Wiley documents in these collections fit hand in glove with Dr. Wiley's private papers in the Manuscript Division of the Library of Congress, there being instances, indeed, of the appearance of an incoming letter in an archives collection while the reply shows up down Pennsylvania Avenue at the Library of Congress. There could be no better moment than now to say that the researcher's finding that indispensably relevant document inside that mysterious one of thousands of cubic feet of files on archival shelves requires the dedicated and imaginative aid of archivists. For such help rendered while he has studied the records of the secretary and the solicitor of the Department of Agriculture, the Bureau of Chemistry, and the Food and Drug Administration, this researcher now publicly expresses his heartfelt gratitude.

This researcher met in his studies one frightening revelation evoking the nightmare that there might have been no saccharin story, no early history of food and drug regulation in this country. The late John J. McCann, former records officer of the Food and Drug Administration, gave a speech in 1948 (filed in decimal file 047.3 for that year) reminiscing about earlier days.[51] In 1934, he said, special orders had been issued by the secretary of agriculture which would have permitted the complete destruction of all Food and Drugs Act records for the inclusive years 1907 through 1930. This did not happen; McCann saw that it did not happen. And shortly the National Archives Act was passed. Had FDA then had a records officer less conscientious than McCann, I might have been prevented from describing for you today the early regulatory history of saccharin.

The Attempt of the National Recovery

Administration to Raise Bituminous

Coal Prices

JAMES P. JOHNSON

ASIDE FROM MOBILIZATION FOR war this nation has never undertaken a vaster, more complicated governmental enterprise than that of the National Recovery Administration. When President Roosevelt signed the act, he remarked, "History probably will record the National Industrial Recovery Act as the most important and far-reaching legislation ever enacted by the American Congress."[1] Of all the tasks of the NRA, the attempt to restore profits to the chronically sick bituminous industry proved to be one of the most trying.[2]

Between October 1933 and February 1935, the NRA program for raising bituminous coal prices increased the average mine price for the major coal fields from approximately $1.25 to $1.87 per ton.[3] Success came primarily for two reasons. Significant wage agreements, one in October 1933, the other in March 1934, increased wages in two stages and for the first time created a nationwide wage scale. Because wages made up the largest ingredient in total costs, the agreements created a regularized cost base which forced operators to increase prices.[4] In addition, once operators began to fix prices by market areas and shifted from competition over prices to competition over quality of coals, they created price stability in hundreds of markets. New market stability, unknown for years in the industry, revived confidence, and price wars among individual operators abated briefly under NRA.[5]

Other forces aided in consumer acceptance of the increase in coal prices. The index of industrial production, seasonally adjusted, rose from seventy-seven in October 1933 to ninety in January 1935.[6] Marked increases in business activity of two of the largest coal con-

The author wishes to express his deep appreciation to all the members of the National Archives staff who have assisted him in his research at the archives, particularly to Mr. Joseph Howerton.

sumers, the railroads and the steel industry, generated increased coal production and helped sustain the new prices.[7] The enormous NRA propaganda campaign that encouraged acceptance of higher wages and prices as patriotic also contributed its part to the success of NRA attempt to raise bituminous coal prices. In an analysis of various attempts to stabilize prices under NRA, a presidential committee of review informed Roosevelt that coal had achieved better results than any other code.[8]

The administrative history of the effort, however, is one of harassed bureaucrats attempting to implement two vague mandates: one issued by Congress, the other written into the coal code that the operators developed during the late summer and early fall of 1933. During the short life of the code, from October 1933 to May 1935, operators marketed much coal at NRA minimums. Yet the operators and governmental officials in charge of the code wrestled with seemingly unanswerable problems of code machinery. The administrative debacles—the visible events of the code's history—are the main subject of this narrative.

The National Industrial Recovery Act mandated a sweeping challenge. The act directed the administration to stimulate the economy and "to promote the organization of industry for the purpose of cooperative action among trade groups." It asked the NRA to eliminate unfair competition, to reduce and relieve unemployment and otherwise "to rehabilitate industry and to conserve natural resources."[9] In the case of the depressed coal industry, this charge ordered the administration to generate cooperation among coal industrialists to raise both wages and prices. Because the United Mine Workers of America grew dramatically during the summer of 1933 and won a nationwide labor contract which raised wages, the NRA could concentrate on raising prices.[10]

Coal prices were then and still are determined by an exceedingly complex interplay of many forces. Geography determined quality and the ease with which the coal was mined.[11] Transportation facilities and the intricate structure of railroad rates affected price. Wage costs differed from mine to mine.[12] High overhead and taxes encouraged operators to sell coal at prices which covered only fixed costs or which put only a little toward variable costs.[13] Because coal could not be stored for long periods, once a mine had contracted sale of its larger sizes, it might dump its smaller, less expensive sizes on the market below cost.[14] Skilled buyers for the utilities and railroads, were able to force prices down by taking advantage of this system. Sometimes an experienced sales force could secure a better price for a particular kind of coal, but not often. Custom and habit affected buyers' decisions, and the age of a mine and the level of mechanization also altered costs and affected price.[15] Finally, although much coal was sold in competitive markets, some was not.[16]

Between 1915 and 1920, the industry had grossly overextended its capacity. During those four years, as war demand surged, prices skyrocketed from one dollar to nearly four dollars a ton.[17] Operators opened thousands of new mines.[18] The industry's annual capacity to produce coal jumped from 650 million tons to nearly a billion tons in 1920.[19] Actual production, however, never reached 600 million tons.[20] Monumental excess capacity of nearly 450 million tons spelled potential depression for the competitive industry.

In the 1920s demand for coal first leveled off and then declined after 1926. Many of the marginal mines closed down during the decade, but overexpansion continued to plague the industry. As price competition increased, prices declined from the momentary high of four dollars per ton in 1920 to two in 1925. Utilities doubled their efficiency in burning coal in the 1920s; railroads increased their traffic but used less coal. Fuel oil cut into midwestern coal markets.[21] Between 1926 and 1933 coal production dropped by nearly half. But supply still exceeded demand. Once the Great Depression slowed industrial activity, average coal prices sagged to $1.31 in 1932.[22] By then the coal industry found itself unable to end its own price wars, and a sick industry looked to the National Recovery Administration for assistance.

Although the National Industrial Recovery Act held out the promise of a thorough revamping of the nation's economy, it actually provided a contradictory mandate which generated confusion over objectives.[23] The law demanded both that the administration "remove obstructions" from commerce and at the same time promote organization of industry.[24] On two successive days General Hugh S. Johnson, the hard-talking former cavalry officer who headed the NRA, had declared himself to be both in favor and opposed to price fixing.[25] As historian Ellis Hawley has noted, "the very nature of the act made internal dissensions among its administrators virtually inevitable."[26]

Inconsistencies in the mandate, however, did not stop the NRA from forcing the operators to agree to a code of fair competition. As one of the big ten industries, soft coal received special attention from the irrepressible Johnson. After several months of negotiation, he finally won industry agreement to a code of fair competition on September 18, 1933. Johnson hailed the agreement—in his characteristic overstatement—as the NRA's "greatest achievement."[27] Like the law under which it was drafted, however, the code mandate reflected the industry's problems as much as it provided an answer for them.

Because they desired to retain as much freedom as possible under the code, the operators produced a deliberately vague section on price fixing. Operators who would control the twenty-five divisional code authorities won the right to fix prices in the code provision that outlawed the sale of coal for less than a "fair market price." But the code did not define "fair"; it said only that the "fair" price had to be high enough to "furnish employment for labor" and to pay the new nationwide minimum-wage scales that had been established in the Appalachian Agreement of 1933. At the same time, because of the accounting difficulties involved, the operators were not required to apply a strict cost system. The code also allowed operators to take "competition with other coals" and "the various conditions and circumstances" involved in particular coal sales into account when they were establishing prices. Phrases like these meant that operators could use almost any method to arrive at minimum price lists.[28]

To further protect local interests, the regional trade associations participating in the code drafting won the right to establish coal prices through twenty-five regional code authorities and marketing agencies. The National Recovery Administration had not even conceived the need for code authorities during the first months of NRA, and the act itself had not mentioned them.[29] Now in dealing with one of its most complicated problems, the central administrators had to oversee and coordinate twenty-five small industrial agencies, each with the responsibility to fix minimum prices for soft coal. These code authorities and marketing agencies in most cases grew out of regional trade associations, although some were ad hoc groups created to draft a local code. Thus the price-fixing agencies under the code were not always truly representative of the areas they administrated.[30] Nonetheless, Johnson approved all twenty-five sets of code authority bylaws soon after the code was signed.[31]

The code lacked any provision for joint or cooperative action among the regional agencies.[32] Although the code created a National Bituminous Coal Industrial Board as a capstone for the twenty-five code authorities, this board was the creature of the authorities, not their master. It met only twice in the life of the code. Moreover, Roosevelt's appointees to the code authorities, called presidential members, had neither a vote nor power to compel joint action among the authorities.[33] The presidential members could only approve or disapprove prices set by the industrialists. One presidential member felt that of all the important codes, coal had the weakest administrative structure.[34] Even Johnson lacked legal power to compel cooperation on prices among the industrial groups.[35]

Given these vague mandates, it is little wonder that NRA officials failed to offer leadership during the early months. The administration did not announce a general policy governing code authorities until nearly thirty days after the coal code was signed.[36] Then the executive branch delayed appointing the presidential members for another month.[37] When local code authorities sought assistance from NRA headquarters, they found the staff there unable to cope with the complex problem of establishing minimum prices for soft coal.[38] Left without a clear mandate in their code, without direction or assistance from Washington, operators in their code authorities and marketing agencies devised their own systems for establishing fair minimum prices.

Because most code authorities fixed prices by mining areas rather than by market areas, disputes among code authorities that competed in the same markets arose instantly. Indiana's subdivisional code authority set prices that both included freight differentials and established various market zones. Illinois had established mine prices only. Because Indiana's system allowed that state's mines to undersell coals from Illinois, Iowa, and western Kentucky, these subdivisions protested vigorously. Indiana retorted that its price system was temporary and blamed NRA for failing to give the industry proper leadership.

In fact, the code had allowed code authorities to establish prices "for the various grades and sizes in the various consuming markets." But in November 1933, Frank Haas, NRA technical advisor on coal, told Indiana operators that "zoning was out." In retaliation to Indiana's zones, Illinois retracted its minimums and left operators there to sell coal at any price. Amid this confusion, NRA division administrator Kenneth Simpson issued an order allowing Indiana her market zones—overruling Frank Haas. Then, as the midwestern subdivisions began to fix zone prices, the Appalachian Division announced that it might be forced to "enter the warfare" if the zone prices gave midwesterners an edge in competitive markets.[39]

Although this initial price disturbance sprang from the natural exploitation of vague code provisions by competitive businessmen, part of the blame lay with the NRA. General Johnson had failed to appoint a leader for the industry.[40] Instead, to run the Extractive Industries Division of the NRA, one of the four major industrial divisions, Johnson had appointed his old friend Kenneth Simpson, a mining engineer with a degree from the Columbia School of Mines. Simpson had helped to draft the code and later developed an extraction process for nickle which carries his name.[41] But he could not administrate.[42] In the crucial initial stages of the delicate effort to raise coal prices, the NRA had neither presidential members on the code authorities nor effective oversight from the NRA central offices. Simpson's support for price areas, however, would prove significant.

In part the confusions of the first months stemmed from the ambivalent attitudes that existed among the industrialists themselves. They sought leadership from NRA but wanted to keep control over prices in their own hands.[43] One informed observer felt that the operators were so desperate in 1933 that the NRA could have assumed dictatorial powers.[44] C. W. Reed of the mammoth Peabody Coal Company pleaded with the NRA to issue flat, direct statements of policy.[45] Another operator urged a meeting of coal men to "get behind your code authorities and protect their power; see that they are not shorn of that authority by some Washington bureau."[46]

Competition among subdivisions over the higher, NRA minimums replaced competition among individuals at the lower, pre-code figures. Although midwesterners worked out a price-filing system to resolve their differences temporarily, the operators from western Kentucky found themselves losing tonnage to the Midwest and disrupted the system. Different problems plagued the Appalachian Division. There operators underclassified their coals and competed on quality. Once the subdivisions finally agreed on some prices, the Appalachian code authorities appointed experts to the Technical Board of Value Correlation of Coals, which struggled to devise a "proper, uniform method of classification." Even when the board's findings were published, some of the subdivisions refused to follow them. By shifting from price competition to quality competition, however, the Appalachian Division raised its prices.[47]

Although subdivisional disputes occupied the first six months of the code experience, the majority of the operators were marketing coals at considerably higher prices than a year earlier. The midwestern dispute or that in Appalachia did not involve the bulk of the tonnage in either of those two regions, because each subdivision sold much of its coal within its own region or in markets where it had natural competitive advantages. James D. A. Morrow, chairman of the western Pennsylvania subdivisional code authority, claimed that his own company had lost much business during the first year of NRA. Yet his firm had regained the loss of customers through higher prices on the regional coals sold and through higher total sales. Despite his loss of customers, he feared the consequences of regional price disputes "just smashing this code."[48] *Coal Age* noted: "The essential point is that no sane operator wants to contemplate reverting to the chaotic and ruinous conditions which prevailed less than a year ago."[49] A code authority secretary wrote that the "constructive gains under [the]

Code of Fair Competition for [the] Bituminous Coal Industry have been wonderful."[50]

The price wars among subdivisions, however, made more news than the offsetting gains. General Johnson moved to end the conflicts. First, he appointed Wayne P. Ellis as deputy administrator under Simpson—so that there would be someone to work directly with the operators. Ellis, an Iowa lawyer who had worked in the Fuel Administration during World War I and who had acted as counsel for coal companies before the Interstate Commerce Commission during the 1920s, had been serving in the weak post of presidential member for the Appalachian Division. Although Ellis understood the industry better than Simpson, he faced and failed to overcome the same problems.[51] Then Johnson summoned the National Bituminous Coal Industrial Board into session for the first of its two meetings.

Although the general could not attend the mid-January 1934 meetings because of illness, NRA General Counsel Donald Richberg addressed the coal men in blunt language. Some operators had suggested that some kind of tonnage allocation system be devised to keep prices up. Treating the industrialists as schoolboys, Richberg chided that until they could pass "the first grade" of establishing effective minimums, how did they expect to graduate to tonnage allocation. "I think," he continued, "you are at a very serious crisis in the affairs of the bituminous coal industry, and you have your opportunity and if the opportunity is not taken advantage of, so that we simply have to degenerate back into a disorderly, lawless, anti-social industry, in which everybody tries to cut everybody else's throat," then further governmental action "can be expected." Most operators got the point. They faced the threat of special legislation if they could not cooperate.[52]

Yet the coal board, like the industry, remained torn between wanting governmental assistance and seeking to keep local control over prices. Some operators advocated making the presidential members arbiters of the subdivisional disputes. James D. Francis, president of Island Creek Coal Company, argued that this step would put the price-fixing powers into the government's hands. Various board members spoke to each other of calling intersubdivisional meetings, but they took no positive steps. The board appointed two committees, one on price regulation and one on interdivisional disputes, later heard reports, but failed to act. UMW president John L. Lewis threatened that his union would strike if price cutting did not stop. Even this warning could not jar the board into action during January 1934.[53]

During the spring and summer of 1934 bituminous price wars among **subdivisions intensified. The Appalachian Division system for price** filing did not work well. Many subdivisions continued to absorb freight rates. *Coal Age,* the industry's leading journal, reported that "price schedules were filed, and then suddenly withdrawn, moratoriums were set up against contracting, modified and withdrawn."[54] In June 1934 at Cincinnati, midwestern operators met to consider the competitive situation in their region, where the increased NRA levels were the focus of controversy. Appalachian operators traveled to New York City to seek an adequate way to review price changes, and even to consider centralized allocation of production. As the operators met, *Coal Age* sounded the alarm. All hopes for thorough price stabilization among regions under the code seemed to be evaporating. Perhaps, the editors feared, the code itself would disappear "under a wave of sectional jealousies."[55]

In late May 1934 General Johnson offered those who sought stable minimums new cause for optimism. He finally removed Simpson and appointed a new divisional administrator for extractive industries. In Charles E. Adams, a dapper Yale graduate, one-time stockbroker, and then board chairman of several chemical companies, Johnson found a man who might bring some direction to the coal industry. Adams had been NRA deputy administrator in charge of finance and insurance codes previously, and so he was not particularly knowledgeable on coal. He was, however, decisive.[56]

Adams got the coal men in the Appalachian Division to agree to a system of tonnage allocation. Quotas based upon the 1929-33 average production were set for each subdivision. If any subdivision exceeded its quota in one month, it had to raise its prices. It was hoped these prices would reduce the subdivision's tonnage gains and bring its production back into line with its quota. *Coal Age* cheered this "first definite step in the administration program to end the longstanding and multiplying disputes over the correlation of interdistrict prices under the bituminous code."[57] Yet even this system failed. Ohio claimed the base years were unfair, since they were years when only Ohio operators were paying union wages. Western Kentucky objected to its quotas. Western Pennsylvania withdrew. Begun in June, the Adams plan collapsed in December 1934.[58]

Despite the failure of the Adams plan, the subdivisions increased their prices measurably during 1934 simply by establishing price areas. Originally the code authorities had fixed prices by mining area. Once this system proved defective, the Appalachian Division established price areas in July 1934. Other divisions followed suit. Although correlation and value classification continued to upset various subdivisions, prices were maintained at higher levels. Once quality competition replaced price competition, prices held up.

Just as the coal price techniques were beginning to take hold, however, top officials in the NRA retreated from support both of price fixing and of production controls.[59] Within NRA, free-price advocates like Leon Henderson, whom Johnson had rashly appointed as head of research and planning, led a formidable attack on fixed prices. In a general reshuffle of May 1934, Johnson appointed Dr. Leverett S. Lyon, another advocate of free prices, as head of the trade practices section of the new NRA policy group. Within a month, Lyon's recommendations had resulted in a policy statement opposing fixed prices except in emergencies. Although Johnson quickly claimed that the memo did not apply to codes already drafted, in the summer of 1934, NRA stood on record against price fixing.[60]

Later that summer the Washington rumor mills were correctly predicting a complete change of personnel at the top level of NRA. Johnson and Richberg could not work together. Johnson's paranoia was disrupting the entire operation. Although Roosevelt delayed the inevitable for months, he finally accepted Johnson's resignation on September 24, 1934. The president replaced Johnson with the National Industrial Recovery Board, a five-member panel, on which sat Leon Henderson.[61] At a fireside chat the following week, Roosevelt told the nation that the government planned to delete the price-fixing provisions from the codes. Richberg echoed the sentiment at the National Press Club shortly afterward.[62]

Although governmental officials specifically explained that the new policy on price fixing did not extend to the bituminous industry with its particular problems, coal operators were stunned. Divisions I, II, and III passed a joint resolution which asked that the new recovery board issue a statement that all provisions of the coal code were "in full force and effect."[63] Operator fears intensified when coal buyers in Buffalo, Pittsburgh, and Charleston, West Virginia, stopped purchasing coal in anticipation of the end of minimum prices.[64] The secretary of one code authority described his anxiety. The jobbers, wholesalers, and coal buyers, he said, were a "bunch of buzzards" who would seize on anything to weaken the fragilely constructed minimum price structure. He stated that Richberg's speech produced "incalculable damage" to the industry.[65]

As anxiety among coal men increased following Richberg's speech, John L. Lewis pressed the NRA into calling a second meeting of the National Bituminous Coal Industrial Board.[66] At these January 1935 meetings, the operators and governmental officials created another new agency, the National Coal Board of Arbitration, to settle intersubdivisional disputes. The arbitration board proved somewhat effective but had little time to function before the Schechter brothers won their famous court decision and invalidated the NRA.[67]

Despite the lack of direction regarding price fixing in the National

Industrial Recovery Act, in the soft coal code, and among officials in
the NRA hierarchy, the bituminous industry succeeded in increasing
its prices under NRA. Much of the success came when the operators
in the code authorities shifted from a system of fixing prices at the
mine and adding freight charges to the system of fixing prices in consuming markets. By the summer of 1934, market areas had been
established in most regions. The use of price areas shifted the focus
from price competition to quality competition and presented consumers with uniform prices in most markets.[68]

In no small part, however, the increased cost structure resulting
from wage increases forced the shift to market areas. The Appalachian
Agreement of 1933 increased labor costs by 60 percent in many
regions; the second wage increase of April 1934 pushed labor costs
up an additional 20 percent. Since these wage increases became an
integral part of the code and were policed both by the NRA and an
invigorated UMW, they could not be violated at will.[69] The increased
wages gave operators little choice but to cooperate in maintaining
prices.

Although the only significant general economic improvement at-
tributable to NRA came in the spring and summer of 1933 when
businessmen stepped up production to beat codification of industry,
the mild increase in demand between October 1933 and January 1935
aided the maintenance of bituminous prices. Once coal exports rose
and demand from the steel and railroad industries increased, coal
production advanced. However slight, this economic revival gave
operators the sense that the bottom of the price spiral had been
reached.

Although operator attitudes are impossible to measure precisely,
the code caused many operators to change their outlook on government regulation. Despite past fears of governmental interference in the
industry, coal men in every section worked with government officials
to end the competition which had destroyed price levels. James D. A.
Morrow, one of the leading conservative operators, offered this evaluation of the code after the first year: "You can call it government control, state socialism, or whatever you like. I don't care. It's the practical answer for those who have money invested in the business and
for those who are employed in the industry."[70] The *Mining Congress
Journal* editorialized, "Even the most ardent exponents of 'rugged
individualism' admit that the code has been beneficial and that the
industry is emerging from at least some of its chaos."[71]

Thus, despite bureaucratic difficulties, the Code of Fair Competition for Bituminous Coal helped raise average per-ton prices from
$1.25 to $1.87. Cooperative effort, a slight increase in production, a

solid nationwide wage base, and the code authorities' development of price areas all contributed to a major NRA success. When coal men were polled after one year of NRA, they responded with enthusiastic support for the code. In summarizing the poll's findings, *Coal Age* praised the price stability and orderly marketing under NRA.[72] Although historians must take Hugh Johnson's remarks at some discount, the general, who often extolled the achievement of the bituminous code, asserted that the code was "the finest product of NRA."[73] At the very least, the code program halted what Sidney Hale, the editor of *Coal Age,* called the "plunge toward chaos."[74]

Records concerning Decisions in
Federal Regulatory Work

JEROME FINSTER

THIS PAPER IS CONCERNED with the records in the National Archives
that document decisions of the independent federal regulatory agencies. After some definition of terms I shall describe the principal
varieties of these records and the practices of these agencies in respect to their archival transfer and disposition. I shall try to include
some remarks on the distinctive features of agency records that depart
from the normal pattern. The paper will close with a discussion of
policy and practice regarding access to the records.

Let me begin with some simple (perhaps oversimplified) definitions
in order to set the context for my remarks. I am concerned with nine
federal agencies—the Civil Aeronautics Board, the Federal Communications Commission, the Federal Maritime Commission, the Federal
Power Commission, the Federal Reserve System, the Federal Trade
Commission, the Interstate Commerce Commission, the National Labor
Relations Board, and the Securities and Exchange Commission—that
make rules and administrative determinations in respect to certain
fields of economic activity and entrepreneurs in those fields. The
making of a rule or a determination constitutes a decision. The functions of the FTC, the NLRB, and the SEC, of course, cut across many
fields of economic activity, but, for the purposes of this discussion,
they can, I think, be considered together with the other regulatory
agencies.

These nine agencies are termed "independent" because they are
not components of other federal agencies. Another mark of their independence is that the members of these commissions (as the agencies
are usually called) are, insofar as the legalities go, relatively safe from
removal from office at the whim of the president. Moreover, there is
no provision in law, except in respect to a few matters, for clearance
of their decisions by superior authority in the executive branch of the
government.

Rule Making and Administrative Adjudication

Let us look a bit more closely at the two types of decisions, rule making and determinations in the course of administrative adjudication. The rule-making function may be viewed as having three aspects: the stipulation of conditions under which the regulatory process contemplated by the basic legislation takes effect; the institution of supplementary and interpretive rules that give specificity and fuller meaning to the legislation; and the prescription of standards of conduct and performance to be observed and achieved by the enterprises subject to regulation. On the side of administrative adjudication there are four general categories of decisions: the award, continuation, suspension, denial, and revocation of licenses; findings upon charges of violations of standards of conduct or performance; establishment of eligibility for privileges; and findings upon claims of injury as a result of administrative action.

Although I am not now discussing nonindependent regulatory components of the conventional federal departments, I will note, and this will be of interest to the students of economic regulation in general, that the activities of such agencies result in records that are subject to the same problems that affect—shall I say afflict?—those of the independent agencies. Some notion of the number of types of regulatory proceedings in the nonindependent agencies can be gained from a statistical report for the year 1961, during which, to cite a few examples, there were twenty-three such proceedings in the Agriculture Department, ten in the Interior Department, and nine in the Labor Department. As in the independent agencies, these proceedings were concerned mainly with the promulgation of rules, charges of violations, and licensing.

Before looking at the actual archival records that bear on decisions, I will generalize briefly about the stages in which decisions are made. Rule making involves the study of a problem, the holding of hearings and other consultation with interested parties, the formulation of a tentative rule, the receipt and consideration of reactions to the proposed rule, and the final promulgation of the rule. An administrative adjudication, on the other hand, may be triggered by a complaint or an application of a private party or by an action of the agency. There then follow the preliminary preparation of the case and the holding of hearings with the presentation of testimony, exhibits, briefs, and other papers by the parties immediately at interest and/or by intervenors. Next ensues a summary of the case by the examining officer and the officer's recommendation to the full commission as to what should be its action, finding, order, etc.—in short, its decision. This report of the examining officer is acted on by acceptance, modification, or rejection at a meeting of the commission, and the commission's decision is rendered. The agency, of course, may make provision for appellate proceedings within its own structure, and there are also procedures for appeals to the courts.

Obviously, the foregoing is a very generalized and skeletal characterization of the decision-making process, and, in the case of a given agency, there will be some departures from it. Nevertheless, the description contains elements common to regulatory work in many agencies and therefore refers to the operational contexts in which were created many records series that are mentioned below.

Agency Records

It is important to understand that the archival transfers of regulatory agencies are principally materials that document the formal steps in decision making. This means that what most of the documentation reveals are the actions at relatively high levels, that is to say, the levels of the commissioners and persons who report directly to them. These materials are case files and minutes of meetings at which the decisions are formally adopted. Decisions, of course, can be made at any level, regardless of the level at which they are formally rendered. A thorough analysis of the making of any decision should reveal who made it, who contributed to its being made, what alternatives were available or considered, and the reasons for it. Reasons for decisions may well be affected with a variety of legal, economic, and personal elements—and by bureaucratic considerations as well. Unfortunately, the case files and the minutes are only slightly reflective of these factors, and the records that might reflect them are largely not in the custody of the National Archives. Indeed, many personal factors are never documented, and the existence of the telephone, to say nothing of face-to-face discussion, accounts for a further lack of documentation. For these reasons there is lost to us, except to the extent that the future acquisition of correspondence and other noncase materials may provide, knowledge of the decision-making roles played by the actual competence of officials, their sense of responsibility, and their attitudes toward others whose skills and work affect decisions. What goes on in a person's mind is not always clear to that person himself, let alone to others; thus, such considerations as the anticipated effect of a decision on a person's career, what he conceives to be the expectations of his superiors, his fears for the reputation of his agency, and his estimate of the administrative resource that the agency can marshall to support a decision—all of these considerations are frequently not committed to paper.

But I had best depart from these negative remarks and turn to a consideration of what is in the National Archives. A few moments ago I said that the principal records series here that relate to decisions are case files and minutes. Of the nine agencies under review, we have case files for six (or their predecessors) and minutes for four (or their predecessors). One agency has sent the Archives neither type of record.

Case Files and Minutes

Case files consist mainly of documents that show the formal steps in the progress of cases from the actions that initiated them to their conclusions. These documents fall into what I shall call initial, intermediate, and final categories. Typical of the records in the initial category are applications, petitions, and complaints by private parties and charges of violations and resolutions embodying rules or ordering investigations, both generated by the agencies. The intermediate documents are answers, objections, rebuttals, briefs, depositions, and similar papers filed by the principal parties or intervenors, similar papers filed by the agencies, and transcripts of testimony and related exhibits presented at public hearings.

Sometimes the case files contain case summaries that were prepared by the hearing officers (or trial examiners) and the officers' recommendations as to what the decisions should be. The final documents are decisions, orders, and opinions (including dissenting opinions). If the cases are taken to the courts, the files also usually contain copies of the various substantive legal documents that result from the judicial proceedings, but these papers are also in the litigation files of the agencies and in the court records.

Many case files contain, in addition to the records already specified, considerable quantities of correspondence and various forms, but these relate in overwhelming number—except in some FCC case files—to procedural rather than substantive matters; they are transmittals, notifications, proofs of delivery of documents, and instruments that reflect the agencies' internal administration of the cases—for example, the assignment of hearing officers and the setting of dates for argument of motions.

There are case files for the following agencies and/or their predecessors: the Federal Communications Commission, the Federal Maritime Commission, the Federal Trade Commission, the Interstate Commerce Commission, the National Labor Relations Board, and the Securities and Exchange Commission. The kinds of case files will be specified later.

Minutes vary in their context from agency to agency, but all contain the substance, if not the texts, of decisions, orders, and opinions. Some agencies' minutes contain the texts of documents that were considered at commission meetings, documents that often were the bases of the actions taken. Also in some minutes are summaries of the discussions that revolved about the matters under consideration. In one set of minutes, for example, there are exhibits that consist partly of the official file copies of the documents presented at the meetings and partly of anterior documents to which the file copies themselves referred. These cases thus provide an occasional glimpse into levels of decision-making two steps below that of the full commissions.

The National Archives has received minutes of one sort or another from the following regulatory agencies and/or their predecessors: the Civil Aeronautics Board, the Federal Communications Commission, the Federal Maritime Commission, and the Federal Reserve System. More will be said later about the individual collections.

There has been no uniform pattern of transfer of case files and minutes to archival custody. Three agencies, the NLRB, the FTC, and the FCC, transfer case files regularly every few years; the ICC and the SEC have not done so for many years, and the remainder have never done so. Large quantities of case files have been transferred to the National Archives's Washington National Records Center in Suitland, Maryland, a nearby suburb of the capital; but these transfers do not change the legal custody of the records—it remains vested in the agencies concerned. As for minutes, the FRS, the CAB, and the FCC are very much up-to-date in their archival transfers, but the other agencies have done nothing in this regard, although the minutes of the predecessors of the FMC are in the Archives.

In principle, the National Archives would like to continue to accession case files, and I am sure that some agencies that maintain large accumulations at the Suitland center would not resist action to this end. But there is an obstacle: the extreme proliferation of bulky case files makes it necessary to assess carefully the archival values of the files as against the Archives's limited space for their storage and the costs of their reduction by microfilming or other techniques. The Archives is thinking increasingly of the use of sampling techniques to retire case files so that it may obtain both cases that are representative of the universe and those to which special importance is attached. As will be explained later, such a system is already in effect for some files.

Regulatory agencies publish in book form their decisions and with them summaries of the facts in each case and the opinions rendered. These bear such titles as *Federal Communications Commission Re-*

ports and *Opinions and Decisions of the Federal Power Commission.* If these decisions, summaries, and opinions were all one needed to understand any given decision, one would not need to trouble to visit Washington, D.C., to view the records. But transcripts of proceedings are seldom published, nor is there much publication of the many adjunct documents—the briefs, the exhibits, and the other presentations. This fact means that those researchers who wish to examine the ramifications of a case must use the archival material. The opinions, one may find, are selective in the facts mustered in their support or for the sake of downgrading alternative judgments. The records, on the other hand, contain the full evidence adduced for consideration. The public record, whatever its shortcomings, is therefore closer to being a full source than the published record.

Having made these generalizations about case files and minutes, I will now speak in some detail of the archival transfers of each of the nine agencies. I shall take them in alphabetical order, beginning with the Civil Aeronautics Board.

Civil Aeronautics Board

The only decision-related records of the CAB that have been sent to the National Archives are its minutes and those of its functional predecessor, together covering the period 1938-62. These minutes, which are transferred periodically, are summaries showing the actions taken at each meeting; i.e., the texts of the orders and the opinions of the board are given. Although the minutes do not show the course of the discussions at the meetings, they refer to the documents that were there considered and that are exhibits. These exhibits, which are bound with the minutes proper, are of several varieties: memorandums from CAB bureau and division chiefs and its hearing examiners and legal officers, letters from other sources, and copies of proposed orders and regulations. An important feature of these minutes is the incorporation in each volume of an extensive alphabetical index keyed not only to subjects but also to persons, air carriers, geographic locations, and types of CAB actions, case files, and documents. The facility of research such an index affords is obvious. The board itself also maintains a card index to its minutes.

Although the National Archives has not as yet accessioned case files from the board, it may be worthwhile to say something about the arrangements for their disposition. The Archives has proposed to the agency a plan for the selective retention of this very great mass of materials. Until a decision is made upon this proposal the present disposition arrangements govern. Under these, only those case files of relatively minor significance can be destroyed after periods varying from two to twenty years. These files relate to minor amendments to and dismissals of applications for certificates of convenience and necessity for air carriers, dismissed proceedings in connection with violations of laws or regulations, economic cases that have been consolidated with other cases, and appeals from denials of an airman's certificate or a medical certificate. A study by a National Archives staff member disclosed that over fifteen thousand docketed case files were closed by the CAB between 1938 and 1964. It is the intention of the Archives's proposed retention plan to extract from this collection those files worthy of preservation for historical purposes. Their retention in entirety is not warranted in view of the inherent lack of interest in some of them and adequate summary information available in other records.

FEDERAL COMMUNICATIONS COMMISSION

The Federal Communications Commission is one of the agencies for which the National Archives has both minutes and case files. These total about three thousand cubic feet. The minutes, which cover the period 1927-67, include those of the FCC's predecessor, the Federal Radio Commission. These records derive from the licensing, frequency allocation, and related functions of these agencies and their issuance of regulations. The minutes dated after 1945 include those of officials or agents to whom the commission delegated some of its functions.

The case files also cover the period 1927-67. They are concerned with petitions and complaints of private parties or actions initiated by the commission in respect to communications common carriers and broadcasters and their rates, facilities, allocation of frequencies, changes in ownership, service practices, and other aspects of their business. Besides the usual papers found in case files, there are techical drawings, rate schedules, contracts, and other evidence of transactions between the parties. One interesting feature of the correspondence in the FCC case files is the extent to which it consists of communications from the public. Applications for broadcasting licenses sometimes become controversial and thus generate pressures—sometimes clearly organized—that may influence the decisions. This type of correspondence is not normally found in publicly available case files. Incidentally, the case files include those for the communications carriers when the carriers were under the jurisdiction of the Interstate Commerce Commission.

There are several series of correspondence files in the FCC record group, although the files stop short of the beginning of the FCC period, that will be of interest to researchers in early federal regulation of radio broadcasting. Overall these records cover the period 1910-34 and are valuable supplements to the materials in the minutes and the case files.

Although the FCC is very regular and current in transferring its minutes and case files to archival custody, none of its other records that bear on decision making is here. Thus, the various correspondence and memorandums accumulated and generated by the commissioners and similar supportive papers of bureau chiefs are still under the control of the agency, including files that have been transferred to the physical custody of the Suitland center.

FEDERAL MARITIME COMMISSION

Next to be considered in the alphabetical run-down is the Federal Maritime Commission, an agency that was established in 1961 as the heir to the regulatory functions exercised by the former Federal Maritime Board, the still earlier United States Maritime Commission, and the relatively ancient United States Shipping Board. The Archives has no records of the FMC in its custody; it has only six cubic feet of the minutes of the FMB, which cover the period 1950-57. In separate record groups, however, it does have the minutes of the two earlier agencies for the period 1917-50. Typically, these minutes—which, including exhibits and some duplicates, measure about five hundred cubic feet—contain not only the formal action documents and the documents that were presented at the meetings but also, in separate sections, many exhibits submitted with the documents that were presented. The exhibit documents thus carry the researcher well beyond the minutes proper and reinforce his knowledge of how the decisions were reached. The volumes of minutes are elaborately internally indexed by subject, name of person or organization, vessel, and document type, and there is a separate card index through the USMC period, that is, to May 1950. Additionally, there are minutes of an advisory board to the Shipping Board in the period 1933-36.

Although the Federal Maritime Commission has not transferred any case files to the National Archives, those of the United States Maritime Commission and the Shipping Board for the period 1917-48 are in the Archives and are maintained as part of the record group for the USMC. In contrast to the case files of other agencies, those of United States Shipping Board and the Maritime Commission, as those of the FCC, sometimes contain substantive as well as procedural correspondence.

Federal Power Commission

The Federal Power Commission has neither minutes nor case files in the Archives, but it recently offered to transfer its minutes from its beginning in 1920 through 1967. These minutes record the formal actions of the agency but carry no discussion. An adjunct series of records, not yet offered to the archives, is the set of Secretary's Meeting Folders, which contain drafts of documents considered or discussed at meetings, actual or contemplated changes of the drafts, and copies of staff memorandums directed to the commission or the secretary.

Federal Reserve System

The only records of the Federal Reserve System in the Archives are minutes of the Federal Open Market Committee, 1936-65, and some of a related executive committee. Although these are summary minutes, they report in great detail not only formal actions but also the remarks of the participants in the meetings. So far as I was able to determine from a sampling, the minutes fully include the texts of formal statements made by those in attendance. The 1936-60 minutes have been reproduced as a National Archives microfilm publication, and the Board of Governors has also made copies of these minutes widely available at the Federal Reserve Banks and elsewhere. Except for these transfers of minutes, the Federal Reserve System has followed a policy of maintaining its records with no transfer to National Archives custody.

Federal Trade Commission

The Federal Trade Commission is one of the older federal regulatory agencies, having been established during the Wilson administration. The contents of its docketed case files through 1952, which are in the National Archives and which amount to about thirteen hundred cubic feet, are much like those in the comparable files of the other regulatory agencies. But there is one notable difference: the trial examiners' reports are lacking. These reports, which are not public documents, are in the so-called auxiliary case files that contain other substantive materials supportive of the records in the case files. Among these materials are excerpts from the commission's minutes, memorandums from examiners and staff attorneys, and correspondence with prospective witnesses. Another records series in Archives custody, the applications for issuance of complaints, documents the preliminary process of receiving complaints from private parties who wish action against alleged violators of statutes or regulations. Such papers as reports of interviews with informers, attorneys' recommendations, and correspondence between the parties at odds are useful for understanding the development of a case. There has been selective disposal of portions of the complaint files after 1925, and both the auxiliary case files and the applications for issuance of complaints are under restricted access.

INTERSTATE COMMERCE COMMISSION

The patriarch of the independent regulatory agencies is the Interstate Commerce Commission, which was established by an act of 1887. Despite its age the archival transfers of the ICC have been relatively limited. The National Archives has ICC case files relating only to rail carriers, although the agency's jurisdiction extends to motor carriers, pipelines, and other carriers. Moreover, most of these files pertain to actions initiated only about 1925 at the latest.

The rail carrier files fall into four categories: the so-called formal files, which document actions arising because of complaints against carriers either by private parties or the commission, because of proceedings initiated by the commission (for example, in investigation of practices of carriers), and because of applications by carriers for relief from provisions of the regulatory statutes; investigation and suspense case files, which arise from challenges to proposed rates; finance case files, deriving from (to take a few examples) carriers' proposals for the issuance of bonds, pooling arrangements, mergers, and abandonment of service on certain routes; and rail carrier valuation case files resulting from the commission's obligations under an act of 1913. By far the largest of these series—larger than the other three combined—is the collection of formal dockets. These series contain the usual types of documents found in case files.

The sheer volume of ICC dockets has led the National Archives to devise a tentative plan for their selective retention. As of 1965, there was a total of about thirty-four thousand five hundred cubic feet of dockets, of which about forty-four hundred were in the National Archives, fourteen thousand six hundred in what is now the Suitland center, and fifteen thousand five hundred at the agency. The Archives has not accessioned from the ICC any other records that disclose the process by which decisions in these cases were reached. Such records remain in agency custody, although some are actually at the records center.

National Labor Relations Board

The eighth of the agencies that I shall consider is the National Labor Relations Board, which dates from 1935, or 1933, if one includes its predecessors under the National Recovery Administration. The principal records bearing on NLRB decision making are the various case files, which, to facilitate treatment, can be said to document the so-called representation and complaint cases. In representation proceedings employees in a given plant or company have the opportunity to select or to reject a proposed collective bargaining agent; in complaint proceedings the board determines the validity of a complaint that an employer or a union is engaging in an unfair labor practice. Together with their related transcripts of public hearings the case files in National Archives custody amount to about five thousand cubic feet and extend to matters closed as late as 1959.

In a representation case file the principal papers are the petition for certification of a bargaining agent, the decision of the board to hold or not to hold an election, and the order indicating that an agent has or has not been chosen. These case files contain also what the agency terms "informal" papers and which are not necessarily regarded as public. The informal file contains, among other documents, memorandums from trial examiners that analyze cases and make recommendations and sometimes documentation of the views of NLRB regional officials. Comparison of these recommendations and views with the decisions rendered sometimes yield interesting conclusions about the processing of decisions.

In a typical complaint case file the expected substantive papers are found: the complaint, the board's charge, the respondent's reply, and the board's decision. The decision gives the board's asserted reasons for its conclusions and refers to the recommendations of the trial examiner, whose intermediate report is part of this file. In the informal complaint file one finds internal memorandums exchanged between NLRB attorneys and trial examiners; these documents contribute toward an understanding of the legal aspects of the case.

It was said earlier that the NLRB is one of the agencies that regularly transfers its case files to the National Archives. It may be instructive to speak of the arrangements for the disposition and transfer of these files. First, however, a few words about the records that antedate the Wagner Act. The NLRB had a predecessor known as the National Labor Board and another known also as the National Labor Relations Board. Their case files are in the Archives, and they are not subject to distinctions between formal and informal records. One finds in the variegated papers of these agencies comments by board members and correspondence that may contribute to an understanding of the decisions.

As for the files of the statutory NLRB, these are retained and transferred only on a selective basis. The proportion of files retained for cases that occurred before the enactment of the Taft-Hartley law in 1947 is somewhat different from later files. Nevertheless, in both cases the selection process gives preference to headquarters records over regional materials. A merger of regional and headquarters files takes place, and from 1 to 3 percent of the complaint and representation case files each year is now selected for retention. (Of the files created under the Wagner Act 10 to 12 percent of regional complaint cases and no regional representation cases were retained.) Transfers to the National Archives are made triennially and only after the cases are six to eight years old. But what may interest us more is the manner of selection.

NLRB headquarters, with the assistance of the regional offices, is required to make the selection in accordance with certain criteria defined in the relevant National Archives disposal jobs. Essentially, these criteria seek to define files of the cases that are important. A case may be important for one or more reasons: the issues involved or the principles, precedents, or standards of judgment that affected the board's decision in respect to such matters as the board's jurisdiction, the nature of an unfair labor practice, or the nature of an appropriate collective bargaining unit. Or, a case may be important because it contributed toward the development of NLRB's methodology, because of the extent of public interest in it, or because of its economic impact. The intent of the sampling process is, to quote the language of the disposition instruction, "that all significant cases in each category are considered for selection." In addition to the case files retained under the percentage formula, all complaint and representation cases that are originally processed at headquarters are retained. The disposition procedures also call for the elimination of routine procedural papers from the retained files. A file not selected for retention is destroyed six years after the case is closed.

Securities and Exchange Commission

The last of the agencies under review is the Securities and Exchange Commission. In the commission's record group the National Archives has only the registration statement dossiers that resulted from the Securities Act of 1933. These records occupy about eight-hundred forty cubic feet. Under the Securities Act parties wishing to offer securities to the public must file statements containing financial and other information about themselves and the securities. The files contain reports of the prices of the securities, related prospectuses, transcripts of hearings, periodic financial reports, correspondence, and the orders, findings, and opinions of the commission. Only the records for the period 1933-43 are in the National Archives; these include the FTC records covering FTC administration of the registration function before the SEC assumed that duty. The correspondence and the transcripts of private hearings are debarred from public access.

Correspondence and Other Records

Most of the foregoing remarks have been about case files and minutes. This is so because, as a matter of fact, these are the varieties of records that the National Archives has, in the main, accessioned from regulatory agencies. It is in the other records—the correspondence with regulated parties and other organs of government, the internal memorandums among hearing examiners, other specialists, attorneys, and the commissioners and their principal deputies, and papers detailing the backgrounds of key officials in the decision-making process—that reasons and motivations for decisions not evident in the formal records are sometimes disclosed. The National Archives has relatively few records of these types for the regulatory agencies. The most notable exception to this generalization is the United States Shipping Board record group where there are many, many records of various forms; yet, even here, the continuation of the regulatory aspects of that agency's work resulted very largely in the transfer of the records for that function to its successors, from which the Archives has made few accessions beyond case files and minutes. Another exception is the FTC, but, again, its correspondence accessioned by the Archives stops about a generation ago, and some other records are under restricted access.

Restrictions on Access to Agency Records

Reviewing the statements of regulatory agencies about the accessibility of their records, one perceives that there are certain types of materials commonly not regarded as public (that is to say, not considered to be amenable to the disclosure provisions of the Freedom of Information Act). Security-classified minutes, unapproved minutes, and minutes on matters still pending are in this category; so are investigatory files. And so are a host of papers—work papers, memorandums, and correspondence—that are asserted to reflect "the internal practices" of the agencies. In my opinion, the nine exemptions to public disclosure that are contained in the Freedom of Information Act are, if one considers them together, both concrete enough and vague enough to include in their scope all of these categories of records. I am sure that our knowledge of decision making suffers for the lack of access to these records. The attitude of regulatory agencies toward public access to the so-called internal papers is epitomized in a regulation of the Securities and Exchange Commission that regards as exempt for disclosure "records which reflect discussions between or consideration by members of the Commission or members of its staff, or both, of any action taken or proposed to be taken by the Commission or by any member of its staff."

Some agencies place special limitations on access even to records open to the public under the Freedom of Information Act. Thus, the FCC will search correspondence only in response to very specific requests. The Federal Reserve System will defer availability of records if this action is necessary to avoid interfering with the object of the action contemplated in the papers or to avoid giving speculators inside and advance information. The FTC will not disclose the votes of its members upon issuances of complaints or in connection with the initiation of proceedings by the agency. I am not arguing that these constraints are necessarily unreasonable, but rather that their existence does impose obstacles to research in decision making.

Finally, it should be noted that some agencies impose conditions on access to case files and minutes, although these conditions do not always have the effect of denying access. Typically, one must obtain permission from the secretary of the agency, but in most cases this is a pro forma matter.

In closing, I wish to reiterate that the prime records of agency decisions are in the National Archives and that they are far superior to the materials available in print, especially for large-scale studies of agency procedures or in-depth studies of notable episodes in regulatory administration. The National Archives will continue to accession the prime records—case files and minutes—and it will, through its records retention plans and its review of agency proposals for records disposition, seek the ancillary records relating to decision making. The National Archives and the agencies have to reconcile the needs of scholars and others for documentation, the public's right to know, the legitimate considerations of privacy, the long-term values of the records, and the social costs of their long-term or permanent preservation. In this effort at reconciliation it is essential that the Archives receives help from scholars, administrators, and the public at large. The Archives would like to be informed of the trends in research, the problems that attend the processing of records, the kinds of sensitive information that may affect access, and the rights, privileges, and interests that are served by access to these records. It therefore hopes to hear from scholars and others individually and from organizations that represent them—and the more often, the better.

DISCUSSION SUMMARY

Sherman L. Richards, Jr., of Central Michigan University began by inquiring about the possibility of the Archives's microfilming the population censuses from 1900 on.

Jerome Finster responded that there are legal obstacles to access to the population censuses. These schedules are closed to research for seventy-five years from the year of the census, and the only way a researcher can gain access to any of the closed population schedules at all is through the Census Bureau.

Meyer H. Fishbein of the National Archives and Records Service suggested that when researchers are requesting access to 1900 and post-1900 census data from the Census Bureau they should state whether they actually need unit information—information on individuals—or whether some system of cohorts would be satisfactory. Mr. Fishbein proposed that scholars explain to the Census Bureau what uses they intend to make of the records and that the Census Bureau then review each case on the basis of actual need and make a determination about access.

Albro Martin of American University introduced the topic of access to privileged communications or interoffice memorandums of members of commissions and of important subordinates of those members that document how decisions are reached. He asked whether there is any limit on how long those files will be closed to research.

Mr. Finster replied that, as far as he knew, even under the Freedom of Information Act of 1967 [U.S., *Statutes at Large,* vol. 81, p. 54] there have not been many changes in what agencies can or cannot make public because the act removed only a relatively small area of discretion from the agencies. The only way a person can challenge a denial of access by an agency is to go into litigation and to see what the courts rule.

Mr. Finster also observed that even though agencies have certain specific obligations to live up to under the Freedom of Information Act —notably, to publish their decisions and public hearings and so forth—

there is a provision in the act that exempts them from making public papers relating to their "internal personnel and other practices." He explained that there is a host of papers that can be subsumed under that exemption and remarked that until that particular exemption is narrowed there is not much hope that researchers can gain access to much more than they have been seeing.

Robert Gremner of Ohio State University next requested that Professor Johnson comment on the problem of undertaking research into large volumes of records.

Dr. Johnson replied that from his experiences with NRA records he agreed with Professor Manning that the researcher should first learn the history of the agency, at least in rough outline, and he then can make better use of the enormous resources of the agency's records.

Dr. Young, tending to agree with Dr. Manning, said that if, before he began his research, he had read his own paper about what every young researcher in the federal records should know, he would not necessarily have followed the suggestions himself. The advice might have been helpful, and yet one has to do a certain amount of blundering, of sampling, of getting the feel of things.

In the case of food and drug records, Dr. Young continued, after about 1918 there was a decimal file system set up for everything except case records. One of the difficulties was that not all of the decimal file guide books were available in the National Archives. Another problem Dr. Young encountered was trying to guess what decimal numbers might be important for a certain topic. The only recourse he had was to sample files under the numbers through certain periods of time to see if they, in fact, proved out for the kinds of things in which he was interested. Pragmatically, Dr. Young found that there was no rhyme or reason to the system: a particular decimal file for one year might contain a large amount of material that related to high policy, and then in a later year when this material on high policy came down to be filed, someone decided to use another decimal number for it.

Dr. Young also remarked that the in-house, multihistorian approach will cover the material more thoroughly than a single historian can, but there is no absolutely certain way to win. There is no scientific way for a single, outside historian to be perfect, and he has to realize that there will be some very good and important material that he may have missed. (And he added that oral history may occasionally help fill in gaps.)

Mr. Finster suggested that one place scholars might find the administrative history of an agency is in National Archives publications called preliminary inventories. Before the inventory entries describing the records there are usually introductions that give at least outlines of the administrative history of the agency dealt with in the inventory. Some of the better inventories include discussions of units as low as the divisional level, or even lower, in agency history. Using the information in these publications and the knowledge of National Archives specialists, one can often discover what unit performed what function in a given period. This step represents the beginning in tracing an elusive file.

Alten B. Davis of the Bureau of Reclamation next asked a general question about the implications for political science of the studies presented at the session.

Mr. Finster cited the fact that the internal structure of the Food and Drug Administration had been completely changed many times and suggested that the problem of the relationship of structure to function in a given agency is a question with which both historians and political scientists might be concerned.

Dr. Johnson stated in response to the question about political science that in his study he did focus on the question of interest groups and interest group cohesiveness. The fact that there was no national voice for the coal industry (even though there was the National Coal Association) and that the localities produced twenty-eight codes that had to be amalgamated into one was the central problem in drafting the code. Thus, his overall study of the industry was along the lines of David Truman's governmental process framework and of Ted Lowi's interest group analysis.

Wallace F. Janssen of the Food and Drug Administration noted that the process of decision making on the question of food additives had changed very substantially from the time of Theodore Roosevelt and that there are now statutes and procedures that delineate how the FDA must approach such a problem. Mr. Janssen also expressed the opinion that Professor Young's study was a good illustration of the manner in which a professional historian can shed light on a topic of current controversy, for saccharin had once again become a matter of considerable public interest because of the disclosures about a year ago regarding the safety of cyclamates (artificial sweetners). He added that although a scientific advisory committee nominated by the National Academy of Sciences-National Research Council had reviewed the question of the safety of saccharin and had recently rendered the judgment that based on present usage saccharin was safe, the committee also had recommended that more research be conducted. Research was therefore being done on questions such as the carcinogenic effect of saccharin.

William R. Petrowski of the University of Nebraska at Omaha next observed that sometimes there are multiple copies of records and that neither the National Archives nor the agency that created the records is able to retain the duplicates because of space limitations. He asked whether instead of destroying the duplicates the archives could discover if another institution wanted them and take steps to transfer them to that institution.

Mr. Finster replied that there are provisions in law for transferring federal records that have been authorized for disposition from the federal government to educational and other such institutions—the archives can dispose of records, but it does not necessarily have to destroy them. He thought that the problem was to improve the relations of the National Archives with the academic world in order to make arrangement of that sort.

Dr. Young commented that he thought perhaps the National Archives's reliance upon scholars when it comes to the tremendous decision of destruction it too casual and haphazard, and he suggested that scholars who are recognized as experts in their fields ought to give the Archives and the agencies an opinion about whether the use of records for social policy is or is not worth the cost of preserving the records. He reiterated that the advisory system should be worked out on a formal basis and should not be haphazard.

Mr. Finster also commented that the National Archives had no advisory panels on specific fields of research. Archivists, however, do try to engage scholars to get their opinions and judgments about the disposal of records in their areas of specialty. He added that there is also the National Archives Advisory Council, which consists of historians and other scholars who have their own specialties, and that there are advisory councils in several GSA regions that function similarly; perhaps, however, such a mechanism should be established for specific areas of study.

Deepening the Wellsprings of Public Policy

CHAIRMAN

ROBERT L. KUNZIG

Associate Judge, United States Court of Claims . . . B. A., L. L. B., University of Pennsylvania . . . Coprosecuting Attorney, United States Buchenwald concentration camp case, 1947; associate member, firm of Clark, Ladner, Fortenbaugh and Young, Philadelphia, 1948-69; Deputy Attorney General, Pennsylvania, 1948-53; Administrator, General Services Administration, 1969-72.

We are fortunate in having with us an experienced practitioner of public administration and a leading exponent of its study. After receiving a doctorate from the University of Virginia, he became an associate of the *Richmond News Leader* and later joined the faculty of the University of Richmond. His important work as a federal administrator began in 1936 when he became Assistant Executive Director of the Social Security Board. Later he served as Director of the Bureau of Old Age and Survivors Insurance and as Director of the United States Employment Service. He has also been Deputy Director General of the United Nations Relief and Rehabilitation Administration. Since World War II he has had experience in public affairs and has served as an executive of the *Washington Post,* a director of the international management consulting firm, McKinsey & Company, Inc., and Professor of Public Administration and International Affairs at Princeton University. He is a past President of the American Society of Public Administration and has written independently and extensively, including the books *Executives for Federal Service*, published in 1952, *Public Administration in Modern Society*, published in 1964, and *Men Near the Top*, published in 1966. Now Chairman of the Board of Fry Consultants, Inc., our speaker is Dr. John J. Corson.

Deepening the Wellsprings of Public Policy

JOHN J. CORSON

MY THESIS CAN BE stated simply. The political leaders who come to Washington every four or eight years, with the pageantry of inaugural day, and who steal out mouselike, one by one, over the next four or eight years, get in performance, in zeal, and in loyalty from the bureaucracy over which they rule just what they pay for—not in cash, but in terms of policy and administrative leadership.

I would not expect any of you to challenge this thesis. Many of the dozens of secretaries and assistant secretaries, administrators and board members that have come and gone over the decades during which I have observed the functioning of the executive branch, however, would not accept this thesis. A majority come (and mind you in the decades I have been around here Democrats as well as Republicans have come and gone) with a conviction that bureaucrats were time-serving, inefficient dullards of the opposite political conviction, and a minority left with the opinion they brought with them even more firmly fixed in their minds.

The periodic change of political leadership at the top is essential to the functioning of a democracy. But the effectiveness of "men near the top," the career civil servants who provide the program, technical know-how, and continuity that makes the federal departments and agencies run, is equally essential. And that effectiveness is contingent, in major part, upon the care, feeding, and leadership that the 7,000 occupants of supergrade positions are given by the political leadership that comes and goes.

It is time, hence, that the incoming political leaders give more thought to the pragmatic questions: How do we turn them on? How can we stimulate these career civil servants to produce? How, in short, can we motivate them?

The Federal Environment

As a consultant, I have plied my trade in a score of industries, in universities and hospitals, in nonprofit associations, in government— federal, state, and local—and even in an American League ball club. From this range of experience, I have concluded that there is much that is common in managerial practice—in planning, organizing, motivating people, coordinating, and evaluating results—but there is much, very much, that is unique in the environment of each industry, of universities, of hospitals, of nonprofit agencies, and even among governments. Whatever is common in managerial practice can be applied only by someone who truly understands the environment. And the relationship of a knowledge of environment to the substance of management is a much neglected area of research in public administration.

This fact explains why at least one out of four (and possibly three out of five) of the businessmen who come to Washington in political leadership jobs are not notably successful in the executive branch. They bring experience and a high order of capability, but lacking an understanding of the environment of government and lacking a willingness to learn what this environment is like, they are unable to put that capability to work effectively. What they really need to learn can be boiled down into a statement of five characteristics of the environment that obtains within the executive branch.

First, the upper levels of the executive branch—the corridors of power inhabited by the secretaries, assistant secretaries, and supergraders—is a rather heady environment. Those who tread these corridors, if they are not themselves responsible for decisions that affect many lives or many dollars, are close to those who do make such decisions. And decisions of the political leaders and the implementation of decisions by the supergraders are right out in public view.

Consider, for example, the thirty-eight-year-old fellow who now serves as director of the Federal Bureau of Prisons; he is closer to the crime and drug problems, seemingly problems of great national concern at the moment, than all save a very few people. A revolt among prisoners in one of his institutions, or the escape of an Angela Davis or a Timothy Leary, is news.

Or consider the fellow who heads the Air Traffic Control Service in the FAA; he knows that on the effectiveness with which he manages this service, and a very unruly group of controllers, depend the lives of many, many air travelers. A mid-air collision puts him squarely and promptly before the press or before a congressional committee.

The responsibility of either of these men—the director of the Bureau of Prisons and the head of the Air Traffic Control Service—is greater and more subject to public exposure any day than, let us say, the responsibility of the vice president for operations of the Esskay Meat Packing Company of Baltimore, Maryland—who incidentally is paid more than either of those two government employees.

Second, they work—both the political leaders and the career civil servants—in an environment marked by initiative-inhibiting irritations. (I might more precisely have said constraints, but that would have ruined the Agnew-esque quality of my phrase.)

Much of that inhibition flows from a quaint doctrine that has long been maintained in the federal executive branch and zealously nurtured by the Bureau of the Budget; that is, the doctrine of the "president's program." The idea that the president shall determine what legislation shall be presented to the Congress and what policies shall be followed in implementing all legislation is obviously sound. But this doctrine of the "president's program" as interpreted by the White House staff, the secretaries' staffs, the Bureau of the Budget, the Civil Service Commission, and sometimes the General Service Administration, and a few other agencies (for example, the Council of Economic Advisors, the Office of Science and Technology, and the Office of Emergency Planning) may mean whatever a staff member wants it to mean at the moment. Thus authority is transferred from the program manager who is accountable to a congressional committee or an interest group to a faceless official in one of these "control agencies."

The president is referred to as the "general manager," and it is implied that the executive branch is similar to a private corporation. On the basis of such superficial reasoning, these same control agencies set ceilings as to the number of people to be employed and as to the number of executives above a certain rank; they may dictate the structure of the organization, the relative importance of particular jobs and who shall be appointed to them, the times at which equipment may be bought, and, of course, the dollars to be expended.

Harold Geneen of ITT and Jim Ling, once of LTV, preside over wide-flung conglomerates marked by as great diversity as is found anywhere in private business, but neither tries to impose anything like the degree of centralized control that is imposed over the much larger, and more diverse executive branch. Tom Tierney who runs the Medicare program, for example, must conform with a variety of policies and practices that owe their existence to the size, public exposure, and the variety of other health activities of the federal executive branch, and that are *not* conceived solely to make Medicare a more efficient and economic operation. Tom operated with much more freedom when he ran the Colorado Blue Cross, even though that was a regulated private enterprise.

I am describing—not appraising—the integrated, unitary kind of organization that the federal executive branch tries to be. There are reasons unique to the public service for much of this overcentralized control, but whatever the reasons, it is part of the environment in which these men work.

Third, the environment in which these men and women operate is one of conflicting ties and allegiances. Formally, each is responsible to the secretary of his department and through him to the president. Realistically, each agency (if not each supergrader) bears some simultaneous responsibility to a congressional committee (or committees) and to one or more pressure groups (preferably two or more, if any). The supergrader serves the president and his secretary well only if he maintains harmonious relations with the pressure groups and the congressional committees.

Mind you, I am not referring to partisan political interference. The environment includes some of that but not a great deal (except immediately after each change of administration). But decision making in a democratic government involves the continual reconciliation of the views of various interest groups and the legislative branch.

Fourth, these men and women operate (as I noted earlier) in a highly specialized environment. Specialization is required by the character of most or many programs, and is enforced, in some measure, by the interest groups that look over the agency's shoulder. A graduate of the Harvard Business School, a well-equipped generalist, may move from one company to another in a succession of sales, accounting, or administrative jobs, although only a minority do. But a man with such relatively generalized capabilities will find few opportunities in the Office of Education, the Federal Aviation Agency, the Bureau of Indian Affairs, the National Bureau of Standards, NASA, or the Defense Intelligence Agency. Each such agency has its own family of specialists, and it is rare for a nonspecialist to break into one of these xenophobic families.

Finally, these men and women live out their careers in what has been described as a discontinuous hierarchy. They know that they can rise only so far—and realistically no further. The only real parallel in the industry is the family owned and operated business, in which top executive positions are reserved for family members. Others can and do rise to substantial, important, and prestigious jobs. But the most prestigious jobs are reserved for those who arrive through another door, and the supergrader must be one content to live in such a limited environment.

If they understand these aspects of the environment within which the work of the executive branch is carried on, the men and women who assume political leadership posts will be more effective themselves and will be better able to discharge a prime responsibility—that of motivating the top career people on whom they depend.

What Motivates the Supergraders?

The environment I have pictured does not conform with what textbook writers picture as ideal for the motivation of human effort. The environment within the federal service does not offer the compensation—in current income or capital, in freedom, or in unlimited opportunity—that many men in business enterprise have come to take for granted. Why then are capable individuals found in supergrade jobs? —for indeed, there are capable men and women in most of these jobs. What satisfactions attract them, hold them, and stimulate them to make the contribution to public policy that they do make?

Many are there because of the relative unattractiveness of alternative opportunities in the late depression years, the war years, and the postwar years. Some of these men and women entered the federal service, keep in mind, in the 1940s, a few in the late 1930s. At those and at other times since, the public service or particular programs, for example, the poverty programs, were relatively glamorous. Once in the federal service (and most started at beginning levels), they were trapped by the process of establishing a family. Since then, few have had opportunities to leave. The recital of those three facts sounds more negative than I intend, for there are in the federal service satisfactions that hold men and women and motivate them to do their utmost.[1]

These men and women exhibit an innate desire to achieve; they were born with a desire to get ahead. David McClelland, a Harvard psychologist and author of *The Achieving Society*,[2] has demonstrated, at least to my satisfaction, that some people want to achieve, to get ahead, more than others do. Those in supergrade jobs comprised, among all those who entered the federal service twenty to twenty-five years ago, a substantial proportion of those who wanted badly to excel. I am not suggesting that this motivation is unique to the federal service. Nevertheless, it is a positive motivational force that works if it is not destroyed by unfair treatment, narrow political partisanship, or just simple lack of leadership. In short, the political leaders can, if they will, cultivate this desire.

A substantial proportion of these men and women also place a relatively high value on security. The ease of mind provided by relative assurance of a steady job with some prospect of a stepladder-like raise over the years is a satisfaction that claims the diligent, earnest application of a goodly number. I do not count this factor as a positive energizing force, rather it is a passive force breeding satisfaction and contentment.

A more positive stimulus is the opportunity for professional accomplishment. Several federal agencies—the National Institutes of Health, the National Bureau of Standards, NASA, the Bureau of Labor Statistics, the Foreign Service, and the Beltsville Agricultural Research Center—offer the preeminent opportunity for individuals who place discovery or professional reputation high on their scale of values. This factor attracts especially qualified individuals to the service, holds them, and stimulates them.

These individuals are also motivated by program commitment—a deep belief in what they are doing. If you will forgive personal example, I can assure you that I have never worked as hard or wanted the enterprise I was associated with to succeed as earnestly as when I was a part of the Social Security Board more than a quarter of a century ago. I have been paid ten times as much by subsequent employers, but I never gave more of myself than I did then. My colleagues and I thought we were doing something very important, we were proud to be associated with the agency, and we tried to do the very best job possible. I have seen the same commitment in many other programs— in the TVA in the late 1930s; the WPA under Harry Hopkins; the Anti-Trust Division of the Justice Department under Thurman Arnold; the foreign aid program in Paul Hoffman's day; the Veterans' Administration when Omar Bradley breathed life into a moribund agency in the period when veterans were returning after World War II; the Atomic Energy Commission at its start; and the poverty program and the Peace Corps in the early Shriver days.

These illustrations suggest this is a transitory motivational force. For many agencies it is, but in still other agencies a deep concern for those who are served has long been a positive motivational force. The Children's Bureau was headed for decades by men, and more by women, who deeply cared about children; the Bureau of Indian Affairs by men who truly believe the Indian has been wronged. The Forest Service similarly is peopled by men who believe, as their progenitor Gifford Pinchot did, that this nation's forests are an invaluable resource that must be protected. The Rural Electrification Administration attracts people who believe that the farmers deserve electric power and that only the federal government will make it available to them. This concern for those who are served is a positive and substantial motivating force that I have seldom seen in private enterprise.

What I regard as a closely related motivational force is pride in organization. (Galbraith speaks of this as "identification.") I have observed this in military units and in civilian agencies as well. The Internal Revenue Service, for example, has always struck me as a large enterprise, involved in much routine and unexciting work, but its people have displayed a certain pride in being a part of what they call the Revenue Service. And it is significant to note that this motivational force was kindled more by some commissioners than others (the Blue Ribbon Service).

Finally, the satisfaction, even thrill, these men and women receive from the opportunity to serve the public interest is a motivational force of incalculable value. Ron Pulling, a grade 17 career civil servant in the FAA, told me recently of his pride when the FAA administrator introduced him at a meeting as "the man principally responsible for the new airways legislation." "That means to me," he said, "that I can tell my grandchildren I was largely responsible for the most important bit of aviation legislation in a decade." The man who is responsible for administering social security once turned down the presidency of a private insurance company that paid more than twice his federal salary on the grounds that "it just isn't as important as what I am doing."

I suspect it is wholly apparent to you that I think these motivational forces are real. They cannot be turned on and off as readily as a cash bonus or stock option. Their application requires thought and subtlety. But there are examples over the years as to how they have been recognized and used by the best of political executives who come to Washington.

Public policy is most often the mixture of a bright idea (generated as often from within as from without) tempered with the experience of progressive career people and tested in the fire of pressure group reaction. If political leaders are to get the maximum contribution from the 7,000 top-level career people who can shape, test, and implement the public policies they would introduce, they must understand the environment of the federal service, and even more importantly they must understand what motivates these people and supply the stimuli that will turn them on, not turn them off.

DISCUSSION SUMMARY

In response to a question from the floor about a recent proposal to create an executive service, *Dr. Corson* said he disliked the implication of the proposal that the top level of the career civil service would be limited to grade 15 rather than 18. He, however, found the idea of a contract for civil service executives and a period of time after a reorganization in which the individual preserves his salary to be desirable because it provides protection for the individual who has advanced. He also thought the contract mitigated the reduction to a grade 15, but only for a period of time.

In reply to a second question, Dr. Corson expressed his opinion that consumers were a rapidly developing interest group, with the qualification that consumers were not yet solidified in organizational terms in the way that, for example, the American Federation of Labor is. He also thought that there are fundamental roots for consumerism and that there has been a basic change from the principle of caveat emptor. Because of the complexities of modern products—for example, who can tell the difference between Fortrel and Dacron and the relative qualities of each?—the consumer *cannot* beware. As a consequence, there is an urgent need for aiding the consumer in making choices, and that aid must come from the producer himself and from government. The information that the consumer needs to let him make intelligent choices does not now exist.

Robert Wolfe of the National Archives and Records Service asked whether Dr. Corson accepted the distinction between people in government who want to achieve only in a particular area and are not interested in other areas and others who are willing to achieve and to make a career of whatever comes their way.

Dr. Corson agreed that such differences exist, and he observed that they exist in private business as well as in government.

In answer to a question about the differences between political leaders who remain in jobs only temporarily and civil service employees who are more permanent, Dr. Corson said that he thought the political leaders that come and go in jobs such as secretaryships and assistant secretaryships are much more sensitive to what will be revealed than the career civil servant. He added that the career civil servant becomes accustomed to living an exposed life and to being held to account for what he is doing. On the other hand, one of the first things many secretaries of departments do when they come to Washington is to surround themselves with good public relations men and good lawyers to ensure that they are "protected"—not to see to it that they advance the programs for which they are responsible. The reason for the political leaders' attitude is understandable: they are dependent upon their reputations to a degree that career civil servants are not. Consequently, the political hierarchy at the top tends to be much more careful about what would be revealed than are the career civil servants.

Sidney Baldwin of California State University, Fullerton, asked Dr. Corson to comment on whether he thought the atmosphere in the country had had an impact on the quality of the people who enter public service and on the morale of the public service.

Dr. Corson replied that he was pessimistic about attracting people to public service today, even though he thought that the importance of government in American society was continually growing. He recalled that when he entered federal service in the thirties the opportunities in private business were not great. Government, on the other hand, offered a host of exciting choices: the Works Progress Administration, the National Labor Relations Board, the SEC, the TVA, the administration of social security. At that time the cream of the younger generation was attracted into government.

There have been times since the thirties when that has happened. Recently, however, Dr. Corson had been quite discouraged because students training for government service were not interested in the public service; rather, some were interested in particular programs, but, by and large, most young people can be attracted only to "glamor" programs such as foreign aid, the poverty program, and urban affairs. Such programs are important, but many of the "backbone" programs of government—for example, the Internal Revenue Service, the Foreign Service, Social Security, and the large agricultural programs—require and deserve a larger share of the ablest young people than they have been able to recruit in the late 1960s. Dr. Corson also felt ways had to be found to attract a larger proportion of good talent. He agreed with John Gardner, who earlier had written that it is unfortunate our society is so structured that for each upcoming generation we offer the greatest rewards to the people who will make shoes or underpants and lesser rewards to the people who will run a state school system, a national school system, or a national social security program.

Efforts at Federal Administrative Reform

CHAIRMAN

DWIGHT A. INK

Assistant Director, Office of Management and Budget . . . B.S., Iowa State University; M.A., University of Minnesota . . . local government official, Fargo, N. Dak., and Oak Ridge, Tenn., 1948-52; United States Atomic Energy Commission staff, 1952-66—Assistant to Chairman, 1958-59; Assistant General Manager, 1959-66; Assistant Secretary, Department of Housing and Urban Development, 1966-69; Office of Management and Budget, 1969- . . . recipient of several public service awards.

I am very much interested in the conference that the National Archives is sponsoring here because I think it has a direct bearing upon a major area of concern of the president. I guess all presidents (in recent times, at least) have been interested in discovering how to make the government work better. I think today we see a greater public concern, a greater congressional concern, and a greater presidential concern with actually doing something about the age-old problem of making large, complex governmental organizations function effectively.

We find, however, as we move ahead in this work that we are continually reinventing things that were learned long ago; in one agency we reinvent something that was developed in another agency—something that is susceptible of adaptation from one agency to another —and we continually repeat old mistakes.

Thus, we at the Office of Management and Budget, who are attempting to spearhead the president's efforts at renovating governmental machinery, welcome this kind of conference. I particularly like the word "reform" in the title of this morning's session, because we are very much interested (and, more importantly, the president is interested) in reform, not mere modification or refinement. This is something that one hears over and over again in talking with the president. One hears it in his speeches, in his talks, and this originates with the president himself.

It is our view that in recent years most of the effort within the federal government that has been devoted to improving management has been of the wrong kind. Most of this effort has been devoted and directed toward limited refinements. Now, there is a place for refinement, but in a dynamic society such as ours in the world of today, as one moves along with new and changing programs, there is a widespread need for basic change, for reform. Consequently, I am very pleased with the philosophy of administrative reform which the people designing this session have mapped out as our charter for this morning.

Our first speaker is Richard Polenberg, professor of American history at Cornell University. Dr. Polenberg attended Brooklyn College and Columbia University and taught at Queens and Brooklyn Colleges as well as at Cornell University. He is the author of a book entitled *Reorganizing Roosevelt's Government* and the editor of *America at War: The Home Front.* Some of you have probably seen his articles, which have appeared in a range of publications, particularly the *Journal of American History, Agriculture History, Forest History,* and the *Historian.*

I understand Dr. Polenberg is now working on a book entitled *Franklin Roosevelt and Wartime America,* which is going to be published shortly. He is on leave this academic year and holds a faculty research grant from the Social Science Research Council.

Our second speaker, Dr. Keith Henderson, is going to carry us through more recent history in terms of what has been happening in the area of administrative reform. I will be interested in seeing what kinds of similarities or lack of similarities between early and late efforts will be developed through this discussion.

Dr. Henderson attended Reed College, the University of California, Occidental College, the University of Southern California, and Columbia University. He has had a wide cross-section of experience as well. He has been involved in both the executive and legislative side of activities at the local level; he was in the Civil Service Department of the city of Los Angeles and was a field deputy for the third district councilman in the city of Los Angeles.

Dr. Henderson has also taught at the American University of Beirut and in the Graduate School of Public Administration of New York University. At present he is professor of political science and chairman of the Political Science Department at the State University College at Buffalo.

Relevant to the discussion of this morning, Dr. Henderson was a member of Mayor Lindsay's Reorganization Task Force and of the New York City Department of Labor; he is a member of the advisory committees of the Center for International Studies and the Near Eastern Studies Program and is also a member of Frank O'Connor's State Council of Advisors.

Dr. Henderson has written *The Emerging Synthesis in American Public Administration* and has contributed to several books, including *The Nature of the Non-Western World, Handbook of World History,* and *A New Public Administration.* His list of conference papers and articles is very, very impressive, particularly in the field of local governments in foreign countries, an area in which he has done a great deal of research. Dr. Henderson has also published material in the field of behavioral science and has a wide range of other interests.

We have for our third member of the panel Mr. R. Michael Mc-Reynolds, who studied at the University of Michigan and at the University of Chicago. He was an instructor in the history department of the State University College, Fredonia, New York, and Librarian at the Center for Research Libraries, and he is now at the National Archives, where his work is focused particularly on the Department of Justice; the Supreme Court; that ancient institution, the Bureau of the Budget (which we do not have around any more); and presidential commissions.

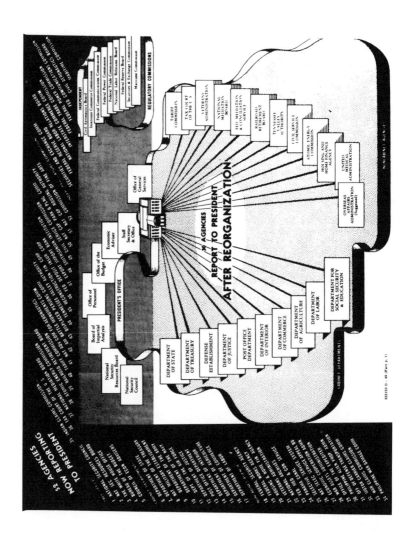

"Concluding Report, A Report to Congress," *The Commission on Organization of the Executive Branch of the Government* (Washington, D.C.: Government Printing Office, 1949).

The New Deal and Administrative Reform

RICHARD POLENBERG

THE ISSUE OF ADMINISTRATIVE reform probably aroused more widespread public concern midway through Franklin Roosevelt's second term than at any other time in the last seventy years. In April 1938, after six weeks of acrimonious debate in the House and Senate, more than one hundred Democratic congressmen deserted President Roosevelt to defeat his plan for executive reorganization. Congressmen who opposed reorganization contended that it would create a presidential dictatorship, and scores of newspapers echoed this sentiment. Disturbed by these allegations, hundreds of thousands of citizens bombarded Washington with letters and telegrams, and, after the Reverend Charles Coughlin denounced the measure in a Sunday radio sermon, a group of persons styling themselves "modern Paul Reveres" descended upon the capital to lobby against it. The recommittal of the bill represented a major setback for the president and dampened prospects for further New Deal reform.

The controversy over executive reorganization poses challenging questions for the historian. Why did Roosevelt attempt to reorganize the government when he did and in the way he did? What was there about the relationship of the federal bureaucracy to the implementation of New Deal policies that seemed to call for reform? What patterns of cooperation, compromise, or conflict emerged between the president and the members of his Committee on Administrative Management, and between that committee and other experts in the field of public administration? What were the major sources of support for, and opposition to, reorganization? In particular, what explains the stance taken by various interest groups and the federal bureaucracy? Still another question concerns public opinion and the reasons the plan provoked so much general indignation. Finally, what accounts for the defeat of the bill, even in a much watered-down form, and how did Roosevelt just a year later manage to put through the Reorganization Act of 1939?

Documentary material in the federal archives goes a long way toward answering some, if not all, of these questions. The relevant holdings fall readily enough into two broad categories. First there are the collections housed at the Franklin D. Roosevelt Library. These include the president's personal and official files as well as the diaries kept by Secretary of the Treasury Henry Morgenthau and Budget Director Harold D. Smith. The Smith diaries, which include regular accounts of conferences with the president, provide insight into Roosevelt's administrative temperament and the role of the Bureau of the Budget after 1939. The Roosevelt Library, moreover, possesses the records of the president's Committee on Administrative Management, which contain correspondence, minutes of meetings, staff memorandums, and drafts of reports. These papers make it possible to trace the origins of the committee, the procedures it followed, and the problems it encountered.

A second category includes the files of government departments and agencies and the records of congressional committees, located in the National Archives and in the federal records centers. Because some departments were more deeply affected by Roosevelt's plan than others, not all collections proved equally useful. Those that yielded the most information were the records of the Bureau of the Budget, the Agriculture and Interior Departments, the National Resources Planning Board, and the Forest Service. The records of the Select Committee on Government Reorganization of the House of Representatives shed light on the legislative approach to administrative reorganization as well as on some of the pressures brought to bear on Congress. Finally, the files of the Senate Special Committee to Investigate Lobbying Activities proved instructive. By subpoenaing the correspondence of various lobbyists, the Senate committee did a great service for historians interested in groups whose desire to disclose their activities has, by the nature of things, been less than overpowering.

What general conclusions about administrative reform under the New Deal can be drawn from these and other source materials? During his first years in the White House the grave problems of the depression had commanded Roosevelt's attention and had led him to adopt unorthodox administrative formulas. Very often the swiftest way to deal with a situation was to bypass the existing administrative apparatus and create a special agency. Moreover, Roosevelt always preferred a competitive approach to administration, and although encouragement of overlapping jurisdictions may have been bad in theory, it often spurred officials to greater achievement. But by early 1936 Roosevelt recognized that administrative reform was necessary to achieve his broad social objectives, and in March he appointed a committee made up of Louis Brownlow, Charles E. Merriam, and Luther Gulick to recommend ways of reorganizing the government. This decision marked something of a turning point in the history of the New Deal. Having fathered the legislation of the welfare state, Roosevelt now wished to give order to the structure of that state.

The report of the president's Committee on Administrative Management, which was issued in January 1937, sought to remove administrative obstacles that were hindering the New Deal. While the proposals were consistent with theories that Brownlow, Merriam, and Gulick had been advocating for years, they also reflected a concern with concrete issues that had arisen during the 1930s. The committee wanted to strengthen the chief executive by creating an administrative structure suited to the requirements of the social welfare state. Perhaps nothing illustrates this more clearly than its recommendations concerning civil service reform, fiscal management, and departmental reorganization.

More than four-fifths of the 250,000 government employees hired during Roosevelt's first term had been exempted from civil service requirements. The administration had deliberately bypassed the civil service because New Deal emergency agencies needed to be organized in a hurry and staffed by personnel sympathetic to Roosevelt's programs. The Civil Service Commission, swamped with applicants, behind in its work and obligated to grant veterans preference, too often failed to recruit men of marked ability. Members of the president's committee believed that the inadequacy of the civil service could, in large measure, be traced to the inherent administrative incompetence of boards and commissions. The much-heralded bipartisanship of such bodies was grossly exaggerated because the minority representative offered no sure protection against partisan control. Commissions spent too much time bickering over trivia; only a single administrator could provide unified, energetic, responsible leadership and make possible a creative civil service program. Replacing the antiquated commission with a highly trained personnel director, Brownlow and his colleagues reasoned, would revitalize the civil service system and at the same time place it at the disposal of the New Deal.

Even more aggravating to the administration were the obstructive tactics employed by the comptroller general, who prescribed the rules and regulations governing expenditures by the executive branch. The comptroller was also expected to provide Congress with an audit of

all government transactions, but in practice much of his power derived from the preauditing function. Government officials frequently requested a preaudit to determine the legality of an expenditure. By deferring administrative action until the comptroller rendered a decision, they could avoid embarrassment of disallowance. The problem was that throughout Roosevelt's first term, the office of comptroller general was held by John R. McCarl, a Republican who had been appointed to a fifteen-year term in 1921. It did not take long for McCarl to conclude that the Roosevelt administration was engaged in an orgy of spending. "Public money was literally flowing in the Washington streets," he exclaimed, and he set out to stem the tide.[1]

New Dealers never tired of denouncing McCarl. They saw him as a petty tyrant who indulged in legal hairsplitting, arbitrarily held up needed funds, and snarled administration in reams of red tape. They muttered that McCarl harassed the TVA, that he was "a reactionary Republican" surrounded by a "group of red-tape artists" whose "officious intermeddling" caused great damage.[2] Brownlow and Merriam shared this estimate of the comptroller's power to do evil. Brownlow once told Roosevelt that "there is grave danger that any spending and recovery program that you may initiate may be quite effectively sabotaged by the present inimical regime in this office."[3] Consequently, the president's committee recommended drawing a sharp line between control and audit. By giving control over expenditures to the executive and providing Congress with an independent postaudit, government fiscal policy would be brought into line with modern accounting practice, and the New Deal would be preserved in the process.

Similarly, the committee's proposals for departmental reorganization represented an attempt to solve administrative dilemmas facing Roosevelt. The Brownlow Committee believed that independent agencies diluted the president's power and in so doing jeopardized the New Deal's social objectives. Its report branded the independent regulatory commissions a "headless 'fourth branch'" of government and provided for transferring their administrative duties to regular departments while permitting them to exercise judicial functions in an independent fashion. Moreover, to rationalize government operations and to give formal recognition to the new functions assumed by the welfare state, the committee suggested creating two new cabinet positions—public works and welfare—changing the name of the Department of the Interior to the Department of Conservation, and giving the president broad authority to transfer agencies.

That the committee's recommendations dovetailed so nicely with Roosevelt's needs was not accidental. Before appointing the committee Roosevelt demanded some assurance that its proposals would be to his liking and that he would not be placed in the awkward position of having to repudiate his own experts. According to Merriam, "the President seemed apprehensive that recommendations might be brought in of a kind which might embarrass him in the development of some alternative plan of his own."[4] Even after Roosevelt's fears on this score were relieved, Brownlow warned his staff that the president could reject any recommendations that he might consider politically inexpedient. "If the President wants to turn down his experts' report because of short-term considerations," Brownlow remarked, "he can not be put in the position of facing a public battle if this results, or else, in order to protect himself, he will never look at a planning report again."[5]

In some ways the very choice of men to serve on the committee ensured that the report would receive presidential blessing. Roosevelt and his appointees had a close personal and political relationship. Brownlow, a lifelong Democrat, shared with Roosevelt the bond of association with Woodrow Wilson. Merriam, formerly a Bull Moose Republican, had turned into a staunch supporter of the New Deal and was always "Uncle Charley" to Roosevelt. Gulick, too, had deserted the Republican party by 1933. All three men sympathized with the New Deal, admired the president, and valued his friendship. Once Roosevelt won reelection in November 1936, they felt free to discuss their report with him and to modify it in some instances to conform with his views.

But not all students of public administration shared the same political assumptions or the same intimacy with the president. In 1936 two congressional committees retained the Brookings Institution to make an independent study of government reorganization. Although at first cordial relations existed between Brownlow's group and Brookings, sharp disagreements eventually came to the surface. The most important difference concerned fiscal management: unlike the president's committee, which held that the comptroller general had proven a sorry failure and that the purely executive function of financial control should be separated from audit, Brookings argued that the defects of the comptroller's office were remediable, and that a distinction could be drawn between executive control to promote efficient management and legislative control to prevent illegal transactions. This dispute, in turn, reflected a broader conflict over the proper balance between executive prerogatives and legislative checks. In March 1937 Brookings released a report that sharply challenged Brownlow's recommendations. Roosevelt's position—that of merely endorsing what "experts" had proposed—was badly undermined by his critics' ability to summon their own "expert" witnesses.

In a last-ditch attempt to head off this split, Brownlow had told the director of Brookings: "In this situation it seems to us of the utmost importance that the 'doctors' do not disagree on technical matters, as this disagreement will be used by oponents [*sic*] of any reform to confuse the issue. . . . It may be that the reputation of government research . . . for scientific impartiality is at stake."[6] In fact, the disagreement revealed that administrative reform was not merely a scientific process. The proper location of a government bureau, the enlargement of presidential power, the role of Congress in controlling expenditures—all of these points, ultimately, involved questions of judgment or governmental philosophy that no science of management could fully answer.

These questions, moreover, involved the interests of organized pressure groups, and it was largely for this reason that reorganization ran into rough sledding. Virtually every pressure group found fault with some aspect of Roosevelt's plan. However much they may have sympathized with the broad aims of reorganization, these groups resisted change because they had established close relationships with the federal agencies serving them and did not want to see those relationships disturbed. Veterans groups, for example, regarded the plan as an attack on veterans preference in the civil service and feared that the independence of the Veterans' Administration would be curtailed and their own influence diminished, if it were transferred to the proposed Department of Welfare. Similarly, the medical profession objected to the probable transfer of the Public Health Service from the Treasury Department, where it was in effect autonomous, to the Department of Welfare. Organized labor, particularly the AFL and the railroad brotherhoods, fought bitterly against moving the Employment Service from the Department of Labor or altering the status of the Railroad Retirement Board and the National Railroad Adjustment Board. Conservationists, forestry groups, lumbermen, and grazing interests worked around the clock to prevent the transfer of the Forest Service from the Department of Agriculture to the proposed Department of Conservation. Their opposition reflected a belief that the Forest Service approach to land management—which stressed commercial use and renewal—could not survive in a department committed to wholesale removal of lands for recreation and aesthetic enjoyment.

Just as various pressure groups sought to preserve their influence over pet bureaus, so federal agencies sought to protect themselves against any abridgement of their autonomy. Officeholders at all levels —cabinet members, White House aides, commissioners of the regulatory agencies, bureau chiefs, and federal employees—lobbied against reorganization with varying degrees of intensity. The chairman of the Interstate Commerce Commission charged that the Brownlow group had made "ill-advised and dangerous recommendations." The head of the Civil Service Commission warned that the appointment of a single administrator would open the door to the return of the spoils system. Among cabinet members, Harold Ickes, Henry A. Wallace, and Frances Perkins proved especially eloquent in defending their prerogatives. Harold Smith noted in his diary that when he informed Secretary Perkins of plans to shift bureaus out of her department, "she wanted to know who was proposing to reduce the Department of Labor to zero, and . . . said that [she considered] the removal of the Employment Service . . . a slap at her. . . . Madam Perkins lectured me for an hour on the historical and philosophical conception of the Labor Department." Smith concluded, "I scarcely got a word in edgewise."[7]

Despite the opposition of pressure groups and important segments of the federal establishment, reorganization might have stood a fair chance if some countervailing force had existed. But unlike other presidential proposals—such as social security, river valley power development, or agricultural aid—administrative reform promised few tangible benefits. Each successful reform associated with the New Deal had enjoyed the support of some social group or geographic region; reorganization lacked any such constituency. Even among Roosevelt's admirers it had less support than any other New Deal measure. What is astonishing, however, is that so many Americans became so hysterical about the issue and took the charge of dictatorship so seriously that the president felt compelled, in the midst of the congressional debate, to disavow publicly any such ambitions.

In part public hysteria was whipped up by enemies of the Roosevelt administration who conducted a massive smear campaign against reorganization. Groups such as the National Committee to Uphold Constitutional Government distorted the bill's provisions beyond recognition and claimed that it would lead to one-man rule. This argument, which Roosevelt's opponents had used in the past with much less success, struck a responsive chord in March and April 1938. The country was then reeling under the impact of a severe recession. For months the president had watched production fall and unemployment rise without offering a solution, and the reorganization bill became a convenient vehicle through which people could express their displeasure with his lack of leadership. Then, too, in March 1938 the Nazis marched into Austria and rapidly absorbed it into the Third Reich. That action tended to stir up fears of executive usurpation and provided ammunition to Roosevelt's critics, who drew misleading parallels between Hitler's and Roosevelt's use of executive authority. Much of the opposition, then, had less to do with the specific provisions of the reorganization bill than with a widespread sense of anxiety and yearning for stability in a particularly troubled period.

It is therefore not entirely surprising that the bill, after squeaking by the Senate, went down to defeat in the House. Many congressmen claimed that a vote against the measure would reaffirm legislative prerogatives, others responded to pressure from their constituents, and still others jumped at the chance to administer a defeat to the president. In addition, Congress's lack of enthusiasm for large-scale bureau shuffling reflected the local basis of its electoral support and the nature of its demands upon the administrative system. Not only were congressmen elected by local interests that favored the status quo but their task was to obtain favors for their constituents. Their ability to secure such consideration often depended upon their familiarity with administrative agencies, and sometimes upon their personal relationship with particular officials. Whereas the president wished to hold agencies to a standard of accountability, many legislators were less interested in this than in preserving the goodwill of administrators. Reorganization threatened to sever the intricate web of personal association so vital to a successful legislative career.

Although the defeat of the bill dismayed Roosevelt, it did not destroy his interest in administrative reform. In 1939 Democratic congressional leaders drafted an extremely modest bill that resembled only faintly the recommendations of the Brownlow Committee. The measure made no effort to modernize the civil service, renovate accounting procedures, create new departments, or restructure the independent regulatory commissions; it simply permitted the president to appoint six assistants and recommend agency transfers subject to a veto by a majority of both houses of Congress. Ironically, the heavy Republican gains in the 1938 elections tended to unify congressional Democrats, and the bill passed with votes to spare. Administrative experts, although they had little to do with drafting the act, were largely responsible for implementing it. Roosevelt, after consulting with Brownlow, Merriam, and the others, proceeded to make imaginative use of his limited powers. Within a few months he created a Federal Security Agency, Federal Works Agency, and Federal Loan Agency and brought related bureaus under them, and he also established the Executive Office of the President, under which were subsumed the White House Office, the Bureau of the Budget, and the National Resources Planning Board. In the end, the administrative experts whose plan had been so roughly treated by Congress in 1938, won at least partial vindication.

Federal Administrative Reorganization
1940-1970

KEITH M. HENDERSON

A TOPIC SUCH AS the thirty years of reorganization history between the 1939 Reorganization Act and the date of this conference provides considerable latitude for treatment. One possible way of handling the subject might be to examine the politics of reorganization within an explicit theoretical context.[1] A variation of this approach, adopted by several public administration textbooks and descriptive studies, is to emphasize the political environment and the tactics of pressure groups without a systematic, explicit framework but using interest group pluralism as an approximate starting point.[2] A somewhat different treatment involves the historical and comparative analysis of formal reorganization acts in a manner that provides a possibly useful perspective on contemporary administrative problems. It is this latter approach which is employed here; its use is determined as much by the needs of practitioners as by the needs of scholars.

This paper will describe federal executive reorganization under the formal reorganization acts—bestowed and extended by Congress, sometimes reluctantly, to the president—and will emphasize documentary source materials available in libraries and archives. The following four basic acts will be examined: the Reorganization Act of 1939 (1939-41), which exempted independent agencies from reorganization and prohibited the creation of new departments; the War Powers Act (1941-45), which exempted the Accounting Office and also prohibited the creation of new departments; the Reorganization Act of 1945 (1945-48), which exempted five or six agencies and prohibited new departments; and the Reorganization Act of 1949, as extended (1949 to present), which provided that the life of an agency cannot be extended and which prohibited the abolishment of departments.

The president's reorganization authority has lapsed three times—

in 1960, 1963-64, and 1969. Mr. Nixon's first legislative request, submitted to Congress on January 30, 1969, was for an extension of the Reorganization Act. A two-year extension was signed into law March 27, 1969.

Of course, the president has recourse to drafting bills that deal with reorganization as well as to formulating reorganization plans for submission to Congress. When proposals are submitted in plan form, Congress cannot amend the plan but can only defeat it in toto by resolution. Plans go to the House Committee on Government Operations.[3]

Regardless of the form in which such proposals are sent to Congress, standard sequences of steps can be discerned in the reorganization process. Frederick C. Mosher has characterized these steps as consisting of "spark"; a study leading to development of a plan; consideration, negotiation, and decision; studies on implementation; and implementation.[4]

Prelude: The Reorganization Act of 1939

In 1939, a reorganization act was passed which authorized the president to "reduce, co-ordinate, consolidate, and reorganize" the executive branch within defined limits, subject to veto by a concurrent resolution of both houses. The number of major departments was not to be increased, and the act placed fifteen of the independent regulatory agencies beyond the president's reorganization power.

Acting under the authority conferred on him by this act, President Roosevelt presented five reorganizations plans during 1939 and 1940 that were approved by Congress. Plans 1 and 2, which went into effect on July 1, 1939, provided for the establishment of three agencies (the Federal Security, Federal Works, and Federal Loan Agencies) to consolidate numerous activities previously separated. The Federal Security Agency, for example, drew the Office of Education from the Interior Department, the Public Health Service and the American Printing House for the Blind from Treasury, and the Social Security Board and the Civilian Conservation Corps from independent agencies. The Bureau of the Budget, as is well known,[5] and also the Central Statistical Board (to be part of BOB), the National Resources Planning Board, and the National Emergency Council were placed in the Executive Office of the President.

Plan 3 related to the Treasury, Interior, Agriculture, and Labor Departments and brought about only minor changes although it provided for the combining of ten divisions of the Treasury Department into a large unit called the Fiscal Service, headed by an assistant secretary and composed of three sections (Office of the Treasurer of the United

States, Bureau of Accounts, and Bureau of Public Debt). Plan 4 proposed moving the Weather Bureau to the Department of Commerce, establishing a Civil Aeronautics Board in the same department, and transferring the Food and Drug Administration from Agriculture to the Federal Security Agency. The final plan, made effective in May 1940, provided solely for transferring the Immigration and Naturalization Service from Labor to the Justice Department.[6]

Reorganization during World War II

Shortly after the United States found itself at war, Congress authorized the president to make such reorganization of the administrative structure as would contribute to national defense. This authority, which extended throughout the war and for six months afterwards, was the basis of most reorganization during this period. Almost at once, President Roosevelt issued executive orders aimed at important changes: the Federal Loan Agency was abolished, and many of its parts, including the Reconstruction Finance Corporation, were transferred to the Department of Commerce; a new National Housing Agency was created to assume responsibility for the work of some sixteen bureaus of the federal government that had been attempting to deal with various aspects of housing; seventeen bureaus of the Department of Agriculture were grouped into four large divisions. Of fundamental significance, in February 1942 the White House announced a sweeping reorganization of the War Department which brought the many subdivisions of that agency under three services designed to handle operations, air warfare, and supplies.

A great deal of documentary material is available on organizational changes during the war. A two-volume guide, compiled by the National Archives, was completed in 1950. Volume 1 covers civilian agencies; volume 2, military. Volume 1 is just over one thousand pages in length and contains detail on over one hundred civilian agencies.[7]

In 1941, the Bureau of the Budget began a project entitled the Administrative History of Defense Organization, the purpose of which was to collect and analyze materials within the bureau and in various other federal agencies on the administrative history of the emergency defense program. During much of its existence, work on the project was done by the War Records Section, headed by Pendleton Herring. Under the general supervision of the Committee on Records of War Administration, documents[8] dealing with war activities of the government were assembled from the various divisions of the bureau, copies were made of relevant documents of other agencies, government officials were interviewed for information about the war program, and reports were prepared on the administrative experience of the government in various fields of war-related activity.

These studies were the basis for the bureau's general administrative history of the government during the war, *The United States at War*.[9] In accordance with policies established by the Committee on Records of War Administration, the War Records Section also encouraged and assisted other agencies in setting up historical units.

The records of the section total about eighty feet and include reports and memorandums on the organization and functioning of war agencies, organization charts, posters, press releases, budget estimates, Budget Bureau interoffice memorandums, and drafts of bills and executive orders containing occasional notations by the president. The materials assembled from other Bureau of the Budget units were considered to be the bureau's most important World War II records. Among other records that came into the custody of the section were minutes, press releases, progress reports, and personnel and fiscal memorandums of the Advisory Commission to the Council of National Defense, 1940-41 (six feet), and staff memorandums, correspondence with government agencies, and other records of the liaison officer for emergency management, 1941-43 (seven feet). The section was abolished in June 1946.[10]

In 1945, President Truman sent a special message to Congress asking for authority, similar to that given his predecessor in 1939, to abolish, consolidate, and reorganize the federal administrative system. Truman pointed out that in 1945 there were 1,141 principal component parts of the executive branch of the government: 13 in the Executive Office of the President; 499 in the 10 departments; 364 in the 23 emergency boards; and 265 in 26 independent establishments, boards, commissions, and corporations.

The Reorganization Acts of 1945 and 1949

Just before recessing for Christmas in 1945, Congress passed an act which authorized the president to make far-reaching changes in the federal administrative structure during the years 1946 and 1947. Provision was made that the ten major departments should be retained and that the several independent agencies could not be abolished. Especially important was the section, also contained in the 1939 act, which provided that changes proposed by the president would become effective unless vetoed within sixty days by a majority vote of both houses of Congress. The 1945 act conferred more sweeping authority on the president to reorganize than had been granted previously. For various reasons—the actions of interest groups, the exercise of a veto by Congress, and so forth— accomplishments during the period 1946-47 were comparatively minor.[11] The national Military Establishment, with the Departments of the Army, Navy, and Air Force as constituent parts, was created, but this change was accomplished by an act of Congress (the National Security Act of 1947) rather than under the Reorganization Act of 1945.[12]

A New Era for Reorganization

The publicity received by the first Hoover Commission report in 1949 probably established a record for anything comparable to that time, with newspapers throughout the country stressing the reduction of $3 billion in annual public expenditures that the commission calculated as feasible. Within the space of a few months, executive orders were issued which resulted in carrying out a major part of the commission recommendations not requiring formal legislation. In addition, by the Reorganization Act of 1949 Congress authorized the creation of the General Services Administration, a reorganization of the State Department, and a new deputy secretary of national defense. After some delay, Congress also conferred on the president limited authority to reorganize; that authority was to last for a period of two years, subject to a veto by an absolute majority vote of either house of Congress within sixty days after the president submitted a plan to Congress. The president promptly sent to Congress seven plans that called for fairly important changes, and all these—except one which would have created a major department in the welfare field—passed the veto hurdle. The Bureau of Employment Security was moved from the Federal Security Agency to the Department of Labor; the Bureau of Public Roads was transferred from the General Services Administration to the Department of Commerce; the postmaster general was given greater authority in managing the Post Office Department; the National Security Council and the National Security Resources Board were placed in the Executive Office of the President; and the chairman of the Civil Service Commission was made chief executive and administrative officer of that agency.

In March 1950, the president sent to Congress twenty-one reorganizations plans. Six proposed to strengthen the authority of the treasury, interior, agriculture, commerce, labor, and justice secretaries; seven made the chairmen of the Interstate Commerce, Federal Trade, Federal Power, Securities and Exchange, and Federal Communications Commissions and the National Labor Relations and Civil Aeronautics Boards the chief executives and administrative officers of their respective agencies. Other plans involved the enlargement of the scope of the Department of Labor, the rearrangement of the functions of the General Services Administration, and the transfer of the work of the Maritime Commission to the Department of Commerce. Sixteen of these became effective late in May 1950, but five plans dealing with the National Labor Relations Board, the Treasury and Agriculture Departments, and the Interstate Commerce and Federal Communications Commissions were vetoed by Congress. A little later the president sent in several other reorganization plans intended to correct defects in proposals Congress had rejected. In September 1950, the president signed an act, largely based on Hoover Commission recommendations, providing for a performance-type budget, the reorganization of the Treasury Department, and a more effective accounting system.

Assessment

The account detailed above does not reveal the conflicts and political problems characteristic of the 1945 and 1949 acts. The 1945 law, although it reduced the number of agencies exempted from the reorganization power, allowed no change in the status of new agencies established by Congress after January 1, 1945, and contained a provision designed to protect the independent regulatory agencies. The intent of the Truman administration, expressed strongly by the Hoover Commission in 1949, was that a new reorganization act should not exempt agencies from the president's control. The commission stated that adequate protection against undesirable reorganization plans "lies both in a sound exercise of the President's discretion and in the reserved power in the Congress by concurrent disapproval of the new proposed plan."

The traditional conflict between the executive and legislative branches over control of agencies was reflected in the debate on the 1949 act. On the surface, the Reorganization Act of 1949 as passed appeared stronger than the 1939 or 1945 acts because it did not exempt agencies. However, it did provide for veto by only one house of Congress rather than by both houses. An informed assessment was offered by Ferrel Heady at the time:

> In estimating the potential of the Reorganization Act of 1949 as a means of achieving needed reorganization, the vital question is whether more was gained by the elimination of exempted agencies than was lost by the substitution of the one-house legislative veto for the two-house veto.
>
> At first glance, the absence of exempted agencies looks like a substantial achievement. Equality of treatment for all executive agencies was one of the objectives sought by the President and the Hoover Commission. When linked with the one-house veto, however, this accomplishment may prove to be more apparent than real. Despite the

laudatory sentiments expressed in the Senate concerning the virtues of a "clean bill," no one need be deceived that the favorite agencies of Congress have been thrown to the wolves by their congressional friends. For the half dozen or so agencies over which Congress has in the past been particularly unwilling to yield reorganization power to the President, the one-house veto will in practice be almost as effective a barrier to reorganization as outright exemption, and probably gives more protection than the "separate package" formula linked with the two-house veto would have provided. No exemptions in an act retaining the two-house veto would have been a pronounced improvement over previous acts. In an act permitting one-house veto, it is debatable whether there has been any gain worthy of mention. It is highly unlikely that a reorganization plan touching any agency to which Congress would have granted exemption will be acceptable to both houses.[13]

The 1949 Act, Extended

After the initial flurry of activity under the 1949 act, Congress began to show increasing reluctance to approve reorganization plans. A tally as of 1963 showed that Congress had rejected eleven of President Truman's forty-one reorganization plans, three of Eisenhower's seventeen, and four of Kennedy's ten. Frequently, defeated plans were attacked as power grabs designed to enhance the role of the executive vis-à-vis the legislative branch.

President Kennedy's poor showing was due largely to the fact that most of his proposals dealt with the federal regulatory agencies—favorites of Congress. Truman, of course, was also defeated on a number of significant measures including Plan 1 (1949), which would have created a cabinet-level department of welfare to absorb most functions of the Federal Security Agency, including the Public Health Service.

Eisenhower's apparent success with his plans was somewhat compromised in the extension of the 1949 Reorganization Act in 1957. The first version of the measure contained a House amendment permitting Congress to veto a reorganization plan by a simple majority vote in either chamber. Previously, such vetoes had required a constitutional majority. Then, too, he had requested a four-year extension.

The Reorganization Act—which lapsed at its expiration on June 1, 1959 (it passed the House but not the Senate)—was reinstated at the beginning of the Kennedy administration in 1961. This extension reestablished the provision that a simple majority of the House or Senate could veto a presidential reorganization plan.

The Reorganization Act of 1949 lapsed again on June 1, 1963, when the Senate failed to act on a House-passed extension bill. In 1964,

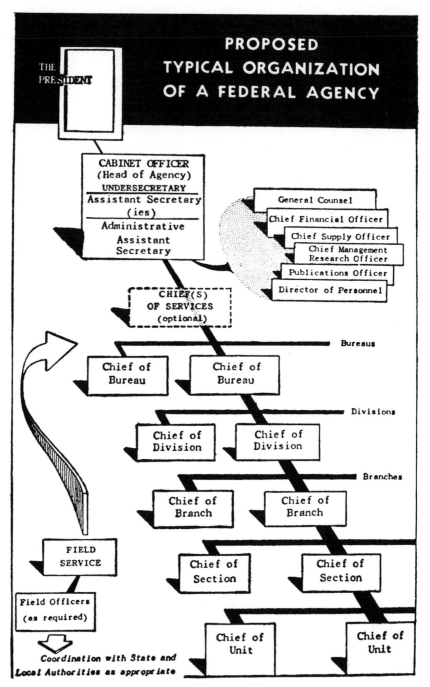

"Concluding Report, A Report to Congress," *The Commission on Organization of the Executive Branch of the Government* (Washington, D.C.: Government Printing Office, 1949), p. 106

however, the Senate did see fit to approve a modified version of the Reorganization Act of 1949. The president was prohibited from creating a new executive department by reorganization plan as in the 1939 and 1945 plans—Congress did not like JFK's idea of creating a department of urban affairs.

Some of the more large-scale reorganizations of the 1950s and 1960s were in plan form, some in bill form. The Kennedy proposal in 1962 to set up a department of urban affairs was submitted in both forms, and Congress killed both, first the bill, then the reorganization plan. Not since the FSA was abolished in April 1953, when another plan created the Department of Health, Education, and Welfare, had a cabinet department been created by a reorganization plan. At that time, the Office of Education, the Food and Drug Administration, the Public Health Service, the Social Security Administration, and so forth were transferred to HEW.

President Johnson was somewhat more circumspect in his dealings with Congress than Kennedy had been and avoided sending to the Hill those proposals which were not likely to receive favorable congressional action. It was not until 1965 that Johnson submitted a reorganization plan. All except one of the seventeen plans Johnson sent up from that time until 1968 went into effect.

Johnson's evident success has been nearly matched by President Nixon's, although those presidents' "administrative styles" of building support differ. Nixon lobbied intensively for the important Plan 2 proposing reorganization of the Executive Office of the President and won by a fairly small margin. A House resolution to disapprove the plan failed on a roll-call vote, 164 to 193. Two months later (July 7, 1970), Plans 3 and 4 were submitted to Congress. Plan 3 established the Environmental Protection Agency and Plan 4 the National Oceanic and Atmospheric Administration in the Department of Commerce.

President Nixon's Advisory Council on Executive Reorganization, headed by Roy L. Ash, has made or will make far-reaching reorganization proposals involving not only the Executive Office of the President, but also the line departments and the major federal regulatory agencies. Four new functional departments (natural resources, human resources, community development, and economic development) would consolidate activities presently conducted by the Agriculture, Interior, Commerce, Labor, Housing and Urban Development, and Transportation Departments and the Department of Health, Education, and Welfare.

Although some of the Ash proposals are old (President Johnson, for example, unsuccessfully attempted to fuse Labor and Commerce), others had not been previously aired. Prospects for successful revamping of line departments and regulatory agencies do not seem good at this time.

Significant structural changes have taken place under the Reorganization Act of 1949, as extended. However, new departments (except HEW), quasi-independent agencies, and units within the Executive Office of the President have been established in recent years without recourse to the act. Examples are the consolidation of the Defense Department in 1958 and the establishment of the National Aeronautics and Space Administration in 1958, the Office of Science and Technology in 1962, the Office of Economic Opportunity in 1964, the Department of Housing and Urban Development in 1965, and the Department of Transportation in 1966.

Perhaps the wholesale shakeups of the 1930s and 1940s ended with the "Wristonization" of the State Department in the mid-1950s (Secretary of State's Public Committee on Personnel, the Wriston Committee) and the publication of the second report of the Hoover Commission. In place of such changes, there has been an institutionalized process of ongoing reorganization and the development of more stable relationships among agencies, support groups, and Congress. Perhaps, too, the deemphasis in public administration thinking on efficiency and economy as final goals means that reorganization is not as important a strategy as formerly. Rather, the stress today is on an *incomes* strategy instead of a *services* strategy, "contracting out" and "performance contracting," and greater reliance than formerly on the business sector or the business model (for example, the Post Office Corporation). This emphasis yields in the minds of many *more* innovations than traditional structural changes.

Records Relating to Presidential Efforts
for Administrative Reform

R. MICHAEL McREYNOLDS

WHEN PRESIDENT NIXON ANNOUNCED the reorganization of the Bureau of the Budget earlier this year, he stated that the test of the reorganization would be whether it provided greater efficiency at the highest level of executive power or whether it only added another level of bureaucracy to the functioning processes of government. The Bureau of the Budget had a reputation for being a lean and highly efficient agency, and the president was obviously confident that the Office of Management and Budget would continue that tradition. Throughout the century, however, presidents have made great efforts to rationalize and reform the executive departments and agencies through reorganization and examination of work methods, and they have appointed groups to study the problem of reorganization.

The National Archives has received large bodies of records from the commissions, committees, and agencies charged with making recommendations to improve government business. Although these records have not been used extensively, they represent a large resource for administrative historians and political scientists. This paper will briefly describe these resources in the context of the commissions of the twentieth century and the commissions' effects on government administrative reform.

Bureau of the Budget

The Bureau of the Budget record group is central to reorganization history, and the bureau has collected many records of its predecessor agencies and commissions. Among bureau files in the National Archives are the records of the Keep Commission, the Taft Commission, the Bureau of Efficiency, and the Central Bureau of Planning and Statistics. The Bureau of the Budget has also had ongoing responsibilities for administrative improvements through its Division of Administrative Management and that division's successors. In addition, the bureau has been involved in the special presidential efforts of the FDR era, the Hoover Commissions, and later groups. Its personnel has been borrowed by the commissions and its advice sought. Most importantly the bureau has often directed or influenced the president's reactions to recommendations and programs emanating from the commissions. Because of the bureau's central role in all reorganizations since its establishment in 1921, the Bureau of the Budget record group has files related to reorganizations in many of its series and is valuable to any history of administrative reforms since the bureau's establishment.

Among bureau records are specific series for some of the commissions and other records pertaining to administrative reform in the series of the central files of the Office of the Director and records of the Division of Legislative Reference.

Keep Commission

President Theodore Roosevelt had a long interest in the improvement of government administration and made the first independent presidential bid to correct administrative weaknesses in the government by commission investigation. In 1905 he appointed the Commission on Departmental Methods and designated Charles H. Keep, assistant secretary of the Treasury Department, to chair the commission. The commission was known as the Keep Commission, but the official name denoted the reform Roosevelt wanted: to bring modern business management techniques and attitudes to government offices. Conflicting views of the president and Congress over control of the federal establishment, however, tended to minimize the administrative reform Roosevelt sought. Thorough reform of government administrative practices met the same fate as many other progressive programs of the Roosevelt era.

The central files of the Keep Commission were acquired by the successor Taft Commission. This series of Keep Commission records is not complete, but it does include reports, inspection tour accounts, questionnaires and some returns, and varied correspondence.

The Keep Commission was composed of departmental officials, and the records which those officials accumulated can be found in the departmental records where the officials were permanently assigned. These records provide additional resources for study of reorganization efforts. This source is also available for later commissions, though not to the extent of the Keep Commission records. There are also many

Keep Commission records accumulated by O. W. Price, the executive secretary of the commission and assistant forester in the Forest Service, which are part of the Forest Service record group.

The departments of the executive branch had their own Keep Commission files within their central files. The central files of the Department of Justice, for example, include correspondence and memorandums on legal questions and Justice Department questionnaires and proposals that the Keep Commission sent to the department in reference to office methods. Some bureaucratic clashes are quite apparent in these records; among the Justice records there is a letter from President Roosevelt asking full cooperation of the Justice Department—a polite indication that the president and the commission were less than satisfied with the responses of the department.

Each investigation of the many commissions appears to have produced records in all departments that are important sources on administrative reform. However, especially in the early commissions, the files vary in their importance and quantity.

The Department of Interior underwent a major reorganization following the investigations and recommendations of the Keep Commission, which gave special attention to that department. Several classes of records within the central classified file of the department contain documents dealing with diverse subjects of the investigation such as the organizational restructuring of the department, contracting procedures, and personnel. These records illuminate the history of the department during a period of investigation and change.

Taft Commission

The active period of the Keep Commission ended in 1907, but its work was continued and broadened in some respects by the Commission on Economy and Efficiency appointed by President Taft in 1910. Taft sought congressional cooperation, and the administrative changes recommended by the Taft Commission enjoyed a friendlier reception from the Senate and House than had suggestions by the Keep Commission. Like the Keep Commission proposals, many of the recommendations of this group involved changes of office operations and the introduction of new business machines and procedures. In some departments modernization brought vastly improved services; few departments were not affected in some manner.

The primary goal of the Commission on Economy and Efficiency was to seek administrative responsibility through increased budget control. There was no national budget, and the estimates submitted to Congress were considered unscientific. Even though the creation of a bureau to control expenditures was not enacted until the Budget Act of 1921, eleven years after the end of the commission, the necessity for such a bureau was documented by the Taft Commission. The files related to the budget inquiry contain records of studies of the budget systems of foreign countries, analyses of the estimates and actual expenses of the departments for 1911 and 1912, and other research data prepared for a report recommending greater budget control.

The commission was centralized under the president, and thus its 144 linear feet of records are not scattered among many record groups. Beyond analyzing the process of budget making, the commission made recommendations on reorganization of departments and bureaus, labor-saving devices, office methodology, and personnel problems.

Records of these commission studies indicate problems within government management that all of the comprehensive commissions sought to rationalize and improve. There are records relating to inquiries for standardizing specifications for purchasing, travel expenditures, and other administrative problems. There are also investigative records and reports of personnel conditions in each department. Special categories of files relate to efficiency records, compensation, and retirement. Labor-saving devices were a particular concern of the Taft Commission, and its records mention machines and processes that had been tested and reported on. Indeed, the wide variety of administrative functions that the Taft Commission studied reflects the comprehensive reforms it sought.

This variety of management reforms, as noted by authorities such as Emmerich, Hobbs, and Merriam in their reviews and reorganization history, is not limited to the Taft Commission or to later commissions, but includes evolutionary change by presidential and intradepartmental directives. The commissions often spawned "little-Keep" or "little-Hoover" commissions within the departments to improve agency administration. Documentation of these administrative changes is found in the records of the departments.

Bureau of Efficiency

The Bureau of Efficiency, established in 1913, was an independent agency from 1916 until its abolishment in 1933. Its small staff made cost and personnel surveys of bureaus and recommended administrative changes to Congress. The bureau tried to provide a continuous service for the president and Congress, as had the Keep and Taft Commissions in their reform attempts. Its work was assumed in the thirties by the Bureau of the Budget.

The Bureau of Efficiency also left a substantial record of its work.

The files, as in the case of the Taft Commission and the Bureau of the Budget, are thoroughly organized. Agencies and commissions charged with improving efficiency—with some consistency to that responsibility—developed for themselves rigorous filing schemes which certainly facilitate research. The classification file entitled "reorganization" contains a series of working papers relating to reorganization plans proposed between 1913 and 1932. (The bureau served as a research agency for congressmen and executive departments on specific questions involved in the reorganization schemes.) After several general classes, the classification system is arranged by executive departments, and the records in these classes relate primarily to the survey work the bureau did for the agencies.

Central Bureau of Planning and Statistics

World War I and its resultant superagencies forced many government offices to streamline their operations. The Central Bureau of Planning and Statistics, working under the War Industries Board, became the focus of efforts to cut duplication in operations and in statistics collecting. Its work was specifically directed to the war effort, and it was liquidated in 1919.

Among the records of the Central Bureau of Planning and Statistics are reports to the president on various war agencies, statistical data, and material sent to the Paris Peace Conference delegation. The records reflect the World War I administrative experience rather than the usual concern for lower administrative costs and greater government office productivity.

New Deal Reforms

The next major presidential reform came in the New Deal era. President Franklin Roosevelt and subsequent presidents pursued the goal of rationalization of government activities. These efforts have been described by the previous speakers at this conference.

The main source of the records of the Committee on Administrative Management, known as the Brownlow Committee, is a collection at the Franklin D. Roosevelt Library. They include records of committee meetings and hearings, reports, bills, correspondence, speeches, and files. The latter category includes administrative histories of several functions of the federal government.

Other archival material can be noted in reference to the Brownlow Committee. Records of congressional reaction to the presidential initiatives are in some cases available to researchers. There were special committees in the House and Senate involved in the reorganization of the late thirties; Professor Richard Polenberg used their records for his book on Roosevelt's reorganization. Other committees such as the Committee on Expenditures in the executive departments and the Committee on Government Operations, with its Subcommittee on Government Reorganization, have created records directly related to presidential administrative reforms. The restrictions set by Congress and its committees can make access difficult at times, but the politics of reform and reorganization can be illumined by both legislative and executive records.

World War II and Postwar Reorganizations

The World War II and the postwar reorganization records are in agency records in the National Archives and in records in the Truman and Roosevelt Libraries. There are also specific files referring to the reorganization plans in the White House official files and in other papers of staff members responsible for the planning and implementation of the war and for transition to peacetime administration.

The Hoover Commissions

The records of the two Hoover Commissions present a vast resource for reorganization history. In the National Archives there are 230 cubic feet of records from the two commissions. From the 1947-49 commission there are the files of the executive director, the Secretary's Office, the Library and Research Section, and nine of the task forces. These task forces studied management problems similar to earlier commissions and committees: agriculture, field services, federal medical services, supply, budgeting, foreign affairs administration, regulatory commissions, national security organization, and personnel. The records of the second commission are similar to the collection of the first commission, with additions of the files of the Office of the Editorial Director, the Office of Legislative Drafting, and several special committees which studied the operations of the Department of Defense.

Three presidential libraries hold papers relating to the Hoover Commissions. The Hoover Library has papers of the commission chairman and of other commission members and staff, and some drafts of reports, clippings files, and other records.

The Truman Library materials include records of the president's Committee on Management Improvement, which was instituted after the close of the first Hoover Commission to investigate the functions of the Bureau of the Budget, the Civil Service Commission, and the new General Services Administration. Other records of reorganization interest are those of the White House related to the unification of the armed forces.

Hoover Commission papers in the Eisenhower Library deal with the liaison between the Hoover Commission and the White House. The president's Advisory Committee on Government Organization chaired by Nelson Rockefeller counseled the president on the recommendations of the Hoover Commission and other administrative matters. Its records and the records of the Commission on Intergovernmental Relations are held by the Eisenhower Library. The library also has the papers of the director of the latter commission, Meyer Kestenbaum. (The presidential libraries programs of obtaining personal papers relevant to White House activities, in many instances, have been successful in collecting the major sources of a presidential program.) In addition, the Eisenhower Library has custody of other staff files and the central files of the White House pertinent to the history of the reorganization in the fifties.

Johnson and Nixon Studies

The various topical commissions of the Johnson presidency did not create great volumes of records, but their studies of budget concepts, the Post Office Department, cost reduction, and the processing time of federal grants-in-aid are a distinct part of the present administrative evolution. This idea was observed recently by John Fischer in his "Easy Chair" column in a recent issue of *Harper's*. Fischer traced the history of the Heinemann study, which was implemented by President Nixon early in his administration. As a result of the Heinemann study, a presidential order was issued to coordinate the districts of four departments to facilitate the granting of monies to state and municipal governments. When the records of this action are available, they will presumably illustrate a major move in the direction of the "new federalism."

The most recent review of executive management was the president's Advisory Council on Executive Organization chaired by Roy Ash. In its records future historians will be able to trace the continuing efforts of administrative reform leading to the creation of the new Office of Management and Budget.

Uses of the Records

This review of National Archives resources relating to presidential administrative reform has been necessarily incomplete. The documentation is broader in content and significance than it has been possible to detail. Yet, few writers have made use of these records. Five articles and one book, however, do exemplify scholarly usage of these archival materials. There are two articles on the Keep Commission, one by Dr. Harold Pinkett in the *Journal of American History* of September 1965, and another by Professor Oscar Kraines in the March 1970 *Western Political Quarterly*. Professor Richard Polenberg in his book, *Reorganizing Roosevelt's Government, 1936-1939*, used legislative and agency records in the National Archives and the Brownlow Committee files at the Roosevelt Library. The agency records included files of the Interior and Agriculture Departments and the National Resources Planning Board. There are also three articles in the *American Archivist* written by former and present National Archives staff members—Ms. Bess Glenn, Dr. Robert Krauskopf, and Dr. Harold Pinkett—that deal with the record-keeping recommendations of the various commissions. These articles were based primarily on National Archives sources.

Most dissertations, articles, and books on federal administrative reform have not used the archival materials described in this paper. Several factors seem to account for this lack of use of archival records. First, many documents and reports have been published by Congress and provide a large resource of information available to libraries. Also, academic interest in reorganization was greatest prior to the transfer of some of the materials to the National Archives. An indication of this fact is that in the *Cumulative Index to the American Political Science Review, 1906-1963*, under the key word "reorganization" there are forty-nine articles listed, and they were all published before 1953.

The question is, what potential uses do the records have for historians and political scientists? Descriptive histories and political analyses of some commissions and presidential administrative reform programs are still to be written. The Hoover Commissions best exemplify this fact: there were critiques published soon after the close of the commissions, and it now may be possible to write a definitive history of the commissions' work with the use of archival sources.

Administrative histories of the departments vis-à-vis the investigations and recommendations of the commissions and the laws subsequently enacted are documented by the records described in this paper. And the determination of the mission, functions, successes, or failures of an agency is highlighted when it comes under the scrutiny of a presidential commission.

There is also abundant documentation for broad functional studies in areas of government management such as budget, personnel, procurement, and natural resources management. Again, the inquiries by the special commissions using contemporary research methods focus on major administrative problems. The development of management theories and practices with each of these functions is recorded in the research files of the commissions and related records of departments.

With the newer econometric techniques, it may be possible to learn what were the actual savings of the administrative changes produced by the commissions. Such research is being done for the present reorganizations and administrative reforms, and it might be possible to relate these techniques to the data of earlier years.

Beyond the specific topic of reorganization, administrative sources have been used to answer questions of political and social importance. In the last year eight to ten doctoral students have used records on administrative matters, primarily records of the Bureau of the Budget, to determine where decisions are made in government that affect a greater populace each year. It is evident that these and related documentary materials offer increasing opportunities for research pertaining to widening areas of public administration.

DISCUSSION SUMMARY

Jerome Finster of the National Archives and Records Service began the discussion by asking to what extent documentation reflects the fact that either overall reorganization of agencies or internal reorganization of agencies is motivated by personalities—by an attempt to put somebody in a particular place, or to get somebody out of a particular place.

Professor Polenberg responded that the documents in the archives might reflect that aspect less than they should because people usually do not write about personalities. Yet he also thought that it may not really be a crucial factor, even though a very controversial figure may occasionally arise. For example, material from the 1930s makes clear the opposition of certain congressmen to giving anything to Harry Hopkins. Congressmen were quite open in saying that as long as Hopkins was to be the man to head a proposed welfare department, they did not want to have any part of it.

But Dr. Polenberg observed that, based on the material he had seen from the 1930s, people were for or against reorganization because of issues—issues such as where a bureau should be located, what policies the bureaus should follow—and it was not essentially a matter of personalities. Even in the case of Comptroller General McCarl, Professor Polenberg thought that Roosevelt wanted to reform the General Accounting Office for reasons that went far beyond simply the existence of McCarl as a roadblock.

Mr. Ink added that in his experience with four administrations he had not seen the personality of incumbents operate as a factor in the design of presidential reorganization plans, but that there had been occasions when it had been a major factor in the salability of a plan. He thought that the prerogatives of the executive versus those of the legislative branch had been much more significant questions when reorganization plans were being examined in Congress.

Sherman L. Ricards, Jr., of Central Michigan University next asked the speakers to comment on whether they thought the major impetus for governmental reform or reorganization derives generally from a desire for rational efficiency (a concept that has developed since the Industrial Revolution and that today is common within our culture) or whether it derives from a desire for specific programs for which the people at the top may feel they have a mandate from an election. In the latter case, the reform is designed to bring about a specific program that can be taken to the people at the end of an administration.

Professor Henderson replied that he thought the second motivation was more significant than the first and that the politics of reorganization should be stressed more than they had been. Dr. Henderson observed that rhetoric remains what it always has been, stressing the logic of structure, but it would be difficult to find any reorganization that did not begin with some sort of spark, some sort of dissatisfaction with things as they are. From that point it progresses into an investigation of some kind, on through to the final implementation.

Dr. Polenberg agreed that specific programs are involved more than any other consideration. He cited the example of Roosevelt, who used the efficiency argument when he presented his 1937 reorganization plan to the country. Roosevelt talked about the "Americanness" of the plan. That is, he argued that Americans like good managers: they want their housewives to be able to balance the budget, and a gas station operator has to know how to run the gas station in the right way. Presenting reorganization in very homey terms, the president said he was simply trying to do in government what the good gas station attendant or a good housewife does. That approach, however, did not work in 1937, even though it did work later with the garden hose analogy for lend-lease. People were unwilling to buy the 1937 reorganization plan as a kind of program in rational efficiency, and it was difficult to sell to the public on the basis of specific programs because people did not feel a great commitment to the programs. In other words, there was no real constituency for reorganization.

Mr. Ink added that of the five reorganization plans President Nixon had sent forward, two had grown out of the Ash Council proposals, a third had been triggered by the Ash Council proposals that were really born within the White House itself, and the others had been generated within his own staff. Thus, the origins of reorganization proposals vary from one administration to another and, within an administration, from one phase of it to another.

Wallace F. Janssen of the Food and Drug Administration urged people who study the history of reorganization to adopt a skeptical approach—to look outside the records of the management experts, study groups, task forces, and so forth, that deal with reorganization, and to look for political motivations, internal power struggles, empire building, interests of pressure groups, popular misconceptions. Mr. Janssen also thought that those who study reorganization history should look for other evidence of organizational shortcomings and problems in order to see whether a reorganization was based on real needs or was undertaken to satisfy a demand to do something that would impress the public. Scholars should look into the origins of slogans such as "the New Federalism" as applied to particular situations, look for vested interests in the reorganization, and finally, look to see if the reorganization really was an improvement and if the commentators had the privilege of revising and extending their remarks for the record.

Robert P. Multhauf of the Smithsonian Institution stated that it was his impression that the pioneer in the use of business machines was the Census Bureau, which began experimenting with the machines in 1890, and he asked if the Census Bureau influenced the Taft Commission's reorganization involving the use of business machines.

Dr. Henderson replied that the commission set up exhibitions of business machines and that commission correspondence files reflect Census Bureau involvement, especially with the exhibitions and the reports on business machines.

Sidney Baldwin of California State University, Fullerton, recalled the distinction Mr. Ink made in his introductory remarks between refinement and reform and asked Mr. Ink whether he had any criteria or indices of measurement he used in determining where a particular plan for change fit on the spectrum between refinement and reform.

Mr. Ink replied that first, he had been talking about emphasis: There is a place for refinement, but the emphasis should be on reform, not on refinement. Second, he was talking in a broad framework of administrative reform, not just reorganization. He felt that reorganization is greatly overstressed in relation to other areas of administrative reform. Reorganization is one of many tools, but all too frequently people become preoccupied with reorganization, and the amount of activity that goes into reorganization tends to obscure other problems that sometimes are really basic. Consequently, reorganization often treats only the symptoms—and sometimes not even the major symptoms—and the basic problems remain.

Mr. Ink continued that because he was speaking in a broad framework he did not have a set of criteria, but he did have two principles he thought basic for considering administrative reform.

First, one should look at the machinery of government, of which organization is only one piece, against the framework of the end objectives as they affect the public, not as they affect the bureaucracy. Next, in order to deliver to the people the kind of service that the legislation contemplated, one must look at the totality of the system. Most of the administrative improvement efforts in the federal government in the past have failed to do this; they have tended to focus in considerable depth on one piece, one segment, of the overall system. A person can consider a part at a time and spend ten years examining the parts before he looks at the whole, but in the meantime the part he considered at the beginning has changed, and the problems the people faced have changed; in reality time has passed him by.

The system therefore should be looked at in its totality. And when it is considered in its totality and from the standpoint of people, citizens who are the government's clients, rather than from the standpoint of the bureaucracy, a different set of priorities is developed. A far greater priority is given to the amount of time that is involved. How long does it take to respond to people, to governors, to mayors? One is much less concerned with some of the relatively minor segments of how this office relates to that, and very often in reforming the overall system, that particular segment is eliminated altogether.

Mr. Ink cited as an illustration of his idea twenty-two programs in the Department of Health, Education, and Welfare that were reduced from several dozen basic steps to essentially two steps, with the average time for delivery of service cut from three to four months to two weeks. About two years had also been eliminated from the planning stage of urban renewal; according to Mr. Ink, previous changes in the urban renewal program had tended to add rather than to cut procedures and processes.

Another member of the audience asked Mr. Ink whether he thought that a good manager can be effective regardless of the organizational structure and whether the best organizational structure will not work under poor management. He also wondered if Mr. Ink believed reorganizations were designed simply to replace persons with rather poor managerial ability.

Mr. Ink responded that personalities are much more of a factor in nonstatutory types of reorganization, particularly within an agency as functions are shifted from one organization to another. As one gets further down in an organization, personalities frequently become a significant factor and sometimes a controlling factor, in industry as well as in government.

He also observed that in principle managers should be able to overcome organizational deficiencies. The extent to which that is possible in practice depends upon the kinds of organizational problems—some are extremely critical, others are not. For example, if one wants to move forward with a high-priority program or project to attain a national goal, time is important and the organizational structure can be absolutely critical. It is generally much less important in the activities which take a relatively long period of time and which are less operational in character.

Mr. Ink continued by stating that he thought the significance of headquarters versus field functions had been underestimated and that far too many field operational activities have been placed in headquarters. Often, however, the answer to the question of which organization should be allocated which functions is not clear-cut; very often it is a reflection of departmental or presidential leadership in determining how the president wants to accomplish a program and where he wants to put the special focus.

Mr. Ink also commented that, in any event, an organizational structure should have built-in flexibility for adaption to new conditions, to new changes, and that he thought this was one of the most frequently violated principles of organization.

Albert L. Sturm of Virginia Polytechnic Institute next requested that a National Archives staff member comment on the materials available on the development of the Military Establishment, the creation of the Department of Defense, and other reorganizations within the military since 1947.

R. Michael McReynolds mentioned the records of one of the task forces of the first Hoover Commission. That task force was established to study the National Security Organization, but Mr. McReynolds said that the records were not available at the time of the conference.

David Rudgers of the National Archives and Records Service added that the Modern Military Division of the archives had among its holdings records concerning the reorganizations of the military services from the beginning of the century when the Office of the Army Chief of Staff was established to about the beginning of World War II. He also observed that virtually all the military records from before World War II in the Modern Military Division deal in some way with military reorganization because reorganization was a very widely discussed topic. The Office of the Chief of Staff has extensive records of General George Marshall's views on reorganization, and the central files of the services all contain discussions concerning the services's missions and roles in the future Department of Defense. He stated that the division possessed these early records and records down to the year 1954, although it does not have naval records from quite that late a period, and that these records are virtually virgin territory because they apparently are not well known in the scholarly community.

Steve Carson of the National Archives and Records Service asked the audience how the National Archives could better serve them in their research.

A member of the audience, noting that the Truman Library periodically publishes lists of its recent acquisitions and sometimes lists of books and articles that have been researched at the library, suggested that other presidential libraries do the same. He also requested that as records are sent by agencies to the federal records centers and are dispersed to the archives branches, a general listing of the locations of records be kept to inform researches where records are.

Harvey Young of Emory University also mentioned that the people who have charge of records in the National Archives Building have had some chance to write record guides and to become familiar with the records, but there are not enough people working in records centers, and records center personnel have not had the opportunity to develop the same kind of service as the National Archives staff has. He asked what steps were contemplated to provide adequate personnel and training so that researchers in the records centers received the kind of help that other researchers receive from the National Archives staff.

Frank B. Evans of the National Archives and Records Service responded by pointing out that the federal records centers are in essence "limbo" depositories; that is, the material in records centers has been transferred to them by active agencies for analysis and for scheduling for ultimate disposition. He estimated that a minimum of 95 percent up to a maximum of 98 percent of that material is ultimately destroyed. Material that eventually will be destroyed is retained at the centers for continuing administrative uses by the agency, but it does not have sufficient historical or other research value to warrant continuing preservation at public expense.

Dr. Evans continued by explaining that the rationale behind the records center is to provide a place to move records from the active operating areas of agencies, where they prevent efficient conduct of current operations. Records centers therefore require a different type of personnel; for the most part, federal records centers are not staffed by professionally trained, historically oriented personnel, but by people who have the talent to, in effect, warehouse the material, to keep it at a minimum cost to the taxpayer, to keep it under the agency's own control, and to make it available to researchers who obtain the agency's permission to use the records. Records at the centers are not in the custody of the National Archives; the archives has not accessioned them. Dr. Evans added that this does not apply to the regional archives branches that are located in records centers. The National Archives has accessioned the records in the branches, and the branches are staffed by professionally trained archivists. He also advised scholars who wish to do research in records centers to work through the current records personnel of the agency whose records they wish to use. These people can help in locating particular files.

Albert U. Romasco of New York University observed that most of the comments at the conference were based on the assumption that research at the National Archives is primarily in depth in the files of one agency. He asked to what extent people who are interested in looking at a series of agencies within one administration can use and can be helped in using the records in the National Archives.

Dr. Evans replied that research across agencies does present a problem because the National Archives acquires and maintains records by the agency of origin. When a researcher works across agency lines, he encounters people who know one block of records but who have very little detailed knowledge of the content of other blocks of records. The Archives's approach to the problem is to attempt to do on paper what it cannot do by physically reshuffling the records to create subject guides across agency lines; it attempts to produce comparative studies, and it has prepared subject guides for the war periods and for Latin American records. He added that the National Archives is currently writing subject guides on records relating to Alaska and on records relating to black studies. It will continue to prepare these guides in other areas as it acquires specialists and as it perfects the other finding aids on which subject guides are based.

New Proposals for Research in the Administration of Public Policy

CHAIRMAN

FRANK B. EVANS

Deputy Assistant Archivist, Office of the National Archives . . . B.A.,
Pennsylvania State University; A.M., University of Pennsylvania;
Ph.D., Pennsylvania State University . . . history faculty, Pennsyl-
vania State University, 1949-58; Associate and State Archivist, Com-
monwealth of Pennsylvania, 1958-63; National Archives and Records
Service staff, 1963- . . . author, *Pennsylvania Politics, 1872-77: A
Study in Political Leadership; Modern Archives: A Select Biblio-
graphic Guide;* and various journal articles.

We are very happy so many of you have come back to share with us
the final session of this conference.

In contrast to previous sessions, our closing session will not attempt to focus on one particular theme. Instead, each of our
speakers, who is thoroughly familiar with the rewards and frustra-
tions of research in federal records and archives, will address himself to a separate aspect of our basic theme and will make suggestions and specific proposals to help overcome the difficulties that we
have touched on throughout this conference. After the presentations
I hope our speakers will respond to each other's proposals and suggestions as well as to questions and comments from the audience.

Our first speaker of the final session, Professor Louis Morton, is a native New Yorker who received his bachelor's and master's degrees from New York University and his doctorate from Duke University. He began his teaching career at the City College of New York and served briefly as a research associate in history at Colonial Williamsburg before he entered military service in World War II. Serving with the United States Army in the Pacific, he became deputy chief historian, Department of the Army, and in that position he wrote two volumes on the war in the Pacific and supervised the preparation of ten other volumes for the army series on World War II. He joined the faculty of Dartmouth College in 1960, where he is currently Daniel Webster Professor and chairman of the Department of History.

A specialist in military history, Dr. Morton's other published works include *Command Decisions in World War II, Total War and Cold War*, and *The Historian and the Diplomat*. Professor Morton is also general editor of a seventeen-volume series entitled *Wars and Military Institutions of the United States*, currently in preparation by the Macmillan Company, and consultant editor of an encyclopedia of World War II, to be published by the Rand-McNally Company.

His continuing services to the scholarly community and to the government are attested to by the numerous professional organizations and agency advisory committees of which he is a member. We are privileged to have the benefit of his knowledge and experience as a member of the National Archives Advisory Council.

Our second speaker is Father Francis Prucha, a native of Wisconsin. Following service in the United States Air Force in World War II, he received his undergraduate degree from Wisconsin State College at River Falls, his master's degree from the University of Minnesota, and his doctorate from Harvard. Entering the Jesuit Order in 1950, he was ordained to the priesthood in 1957. He joined the faculty of Marquette University in 1960, where he has served as chairman of the Department of History and, since 1966, as professor of history. The recipient of research fellowships from the Social Science Research Council, the Guggenheim Foundation, and the National Endowment for the Humanities, Father Prucha is currently on leave of absence as a research fellow at the Charles Warren Center for Studies in American History at Harvard University. A specialist in western military frontier history and in federal Indian policy, his works include *Broadax and Bayonet*, published in 1953, *American Indian Policy in the Formative Years*, published in 1962, and *The Sword of the Republic*, published in 1969.

Our final conference speaker, Professor Sidney Baldwin, is a native of Massachusetts. Reflecting the range of scholarly interests we have attempted to bring together in this conference, Professor Baldwin received his bachelor's degree in history from Wesleyan University, his master's in public administration from Syracuse University, and his doctorate in political science from Syracuse. He has taught at Wesleyan, Northwestern and New York Universities and, since 1967, at California State University, Fullerton, where he is professor of political science. He has also served as an administrative intern in the Department of State, as a research assistant at the Institute for Research and Social Science at Chapel Hill, and as a consultant to the Chicago Citizens' Housing and Planning Council, the New York State Constitutional Revision Commission, and the Republic of Venezuela. He has been assistant editor of the Inter-University Case Program. His publications include *American Government*, which appeared in 1957, and the frequently cited *Poverty and Politics: The Rise and Decline of the Farm Security Administration*, which appeared in 1968.

A Proposal for a Government-Wide Historical Office

LOUIS MORTON

Historical Programs of the Federal Government

ALMOST SINCE ITS INCEPTION, the federal government has supported the publication of historical works related first to its founding and later to its subsequent activities and relations with other nations. Imbued with a sense of history and aware that they were embarked on a great adventure in government, members of the early Congress authorized the printing of *The Journals of the Continental Congress.* In 1818 the government printed *The Journal of the Constitutional Convention* and two years later *The Secret Journals of the Continental Congress,* followed in 1832 by the *Diplomatic Correspondence* prepared by the State Department.[1]

During the next few years, the federal government took a new approach to the publication of historical sources. Instead of having the work done directly by the government, it used the same method employed in the purchase of other goods and services—by contracting out for the work. In 1832 it contracted with Gales and Seaton, publishers of the *Annals of Congress,* and with Matthew St. Clair Clarke and Peter Force for two separate series of documents. The first, completed in 1861, resulted in the *American State Papers* in thirty-eight volumes; the second, completed in 1853, in the nine-volume *Documentary History of the American Revolution,* popularly known as Force's *American Archives.* The *Foreign Relations* series was inaugurated in 1861, the year the *American State Papers* was completed, and has been published continuously since. Other major collections of documents published by the federal government include James D.

This article has also been published in *Prologue: The Journal of the National Archives* (3[Spring 1971]: 3-11), along with a response by Herman Kahn (ibid.:12-14).

Richardson's *Messages and Papers of the Presidents* and *The Official Records of the War of the Rebellion,* the largest and most expensive documentary collection published up to that time. When completed it numbered 128 volumes (not counting the thirty naval volumes) and cost almost $3 million. The *Territorial Papers of the United States* was begun in 1931, first under the aegis of the State Department and later of the National Archives. By 1971 the *Territorial Papers* consisted of twenty-seven volumes, with another scheduled to appear in the near future.

The federal government has also supported in whole or in part the publication of the papers of the Founding Fathers and of some of the most important figures in the nation's history. This program began in 1840 with the publication of James Madison's papers, a new edition appearing after the Civil War. The papers of Adams, Jefferson, and Hamilton followed shortly after. Between 1931 and 1944, thirty-nine volumes of Washington's papers edited by John C. Fitzpatrick were published. Another edition including incoming letters is now in preparation by the University of Virginia with the assistance of the National Historical Publications Commission, a part of the National Archives and Records Service. The commission has also provided guidance and financial support from public and private funds for editing the papers of many of the great figures in American history— Adams, Jefferson, Webster, Calhoun, Clay, and others. More recently, the commission has supported the microfilming of major collections of documents, which, like the Library of Congress microfilms of presidential papers, are available to scholars everywhere on interlibrary loan.

Until fairly recently, virtually all historical works published or sponsored by the federal government consisted of documentary collections. The publication of documents and other source materials rather than narrative histories raised few problems for government officials. Documents that were restricted or confidential in nature could easily be excluded and each reader could draw whatever conclusion he wished from the published documents. Editorial comment could be kept to a minimum; and, allowing for a sufficient period of time between preparation and publication of the documents, little harm could be done by making them available. On the other hand, sponsorship of critical narrative histories by the federal government raised a host of thorny problems.[2] Could historians working for a government agency or under contract to the government write objective history? Would they have access to all the records? Would other historians have equal access so that they could check the work or disagree with the interpretation? For what audience should government history be written—

for officials within the government or for the public? Who would pass on the qualifications of the authors to write history? Who would review the finished manuscript and pass on its publication? Should government history be anonymous, like most government publications, or should authorship be credited? If so, does responsibility for the contents rest with the individual author or with the agency? These and other considerations prompted Secretary of War Newton D. Baker to veto the proposal for a narrative history of American forces in World War I.

The bar to critical narrative history written under government sponsorship was broken by Franklin Roosevelt during the early years of the Second World War when he directed that "an accurate and objective account" of the war be prepared. The military services, which were most directly involved and already had historical offices, responded by organizing historical programs staffed by professional historians in uniform to write a narrative history of the war. Those government agencies that did not already have historical offices followed suit, though not all elected to prepare narrative history. The results achieved by these World War II historical programs, though spotty, warranted their continuation after the war and the establishment of additional programs when new agencies were created. At the present time, nine of the twelve executive departments, and four independent agencies maintain historical programs of some sort.

It would be tedious and quite unnecessary for our purpose to describe each of these programs in detail. Largest, most varied, and perhaps the best known of the government programs are those of the Department of Defense, which include historical offices with the secretary of defense, the Joint Chiefs of Staff, the army, navy, air force, and marines, as well as the major commands of the services in the United States and overseas.

Each of the historical sections of the military services has published narrative histories of its participation in World War II and Korea, some of which is of high professional caliber, and continues to publish histories of past and present operations. In addition, they perform a variety of other services for the staff, some of which is only distantly related to history. Neither the office of the secretary of defense nor the Joint Chiefs of Staff publishes histories, though the historians of the joint chiefs do write narrative histories. These manuscripts are highly classified, however, and their use is restricted to authorized personnel.

The histories of World War II proved that historians working under official sponsorship and even under direct military control could produce objective narrative history equal to the best efforts of academic

138   LOUIS MORTON

historians.[3] Perhaps the best of these is the *U.S. Army in World War II*. This series, produced under the editorship first of Kent Roberts Greenfield and more recently of Stetson Conn and Maurice Matloff, is based on primary sources and maintains a high level of historical scholarship. Numbering now almost seventy volumes, the series includes studies of strategic planning, logistics, manpower, and combat in all theaters. For the student of the Second World War it constitutes an absolutely essential source. The air force series, issued separately though the air force was part of the army during the war, comprises seven volumes published under the editorship of Wesley Frank Craven and James Lea Gate by the University of Chicago Press. Like the army series, it was prepared almost entirely by professional historians who had received their military experience during the war and elected to continue their work after the war.

The navy took a somewhat different tack in preparing its history of World War II. An administrative history, written by professional naval officers under the supervision of the Naval History Division, was published by the Government Printing Office, but the widely read fifteen-volume *History of U.S. Naval Operations* during the war was the work of Samuel Eliot Morison written under contract with a commercial publisher but with full access to the navy's records and support from the Naval History Division.

Nothing comparable to the World War II histories, either in quality or quantity, resulted from the war in Korea, although each of the military services by now had a large and experienced historical staff. The navy and the air force each published a volume on the war, the former under a contract with James A. Field. The army has four volumes planned for Korea, only two of which have been published so far. Each of the services including the marines has published other materials intended for internal use. None has yet published a history of the war in Vietnam, but the army has unveiled plans for an ambitious eight-volume operational series, and the other services have plans of their own.

Second only to the Defense Department's historical program in terms of manpower and publications is that of the State Department. Its major activity continues to be the documentary *Foreign Relations* series, an indispensable source for all students of American foreign policy.[4] The series is up to date through 1945, but with the increased role of the United States in world affairs after World War II and the multiplication of records and functions of the State Department, it is becoming increasingly difficult to keep the series current. This problem is a matter of serious concern for historians since State Department archives are open for research, subject to permission, through those years covered by the series, that is, up to 1945. Records more recent than that year remain closed.

Other executive departments that maintain historical offices are the Departments of Agriculture, the Interior, Health, Education, and Welfare, Labor, and Transportation. The first has had a historical program under a different name since the 1920s and has published several works of importance for agricultural historians—the *Bibliography of the History of Agriculture in the United States,* a history of the Department of Agriculture, and other works. More recently, its duties have been expanded to include the publication of bulletins, staff studies for the secretary, and other materials. It serves also as the secretariat for the Agricultural Historical Society. Interior's historical activity is confined to the National Park Service, which publishes not only handbooks familiar to the thousands of visitors to the various historical and battlefield sites, but also a more scholarly series dealing with historical places and themes such as Indian affairs. Established more recently are the historical offices in the Departments of Labor, Transportation, and HEW, which have published little thus far. Historians in these agencies seem to be concerned mostly with records, bibliography, and oral history and with providing information and background studies for their superiors.

Of the independent agencies, two have developed substantial historical programs: the Atomic Energy Commission and the National Aeronautics and Space Administration. The first, with a very small staff headed by Richard Hewlett, has concentrated on writing a full-scale narrative history of the agency, two volumes of which have appeared so far, both published by a university press. The first of these, *The New World,* is one of the best histories produced in any government historical office; the second volume has only just appeared. The NASA historical office, established in 1959, has published a series of detailed chronologies on space and several historical volumes written under contract with private scholars. The most recent of these is Constance Green's history of the Vanguard project.

In addition to these historical programs and published histories, the federal government supports in one way or another a variety of activities of interest to historians. Certainly the activities and programs of the National Archives and Records Service and of the Library of Congress are of vital concern to all American historians. But these two agencies do more than collect and maintain original sources; they prepare inventories of their holdings, calendars of papers, finding aids to specific collections, and elaborate guides, such as those relating to the Civil War and World War II.[5] Since 1951 the National Archives through its National Historical Publications Commission has been publishing the *Writings on American History*—a task it will soon discontinue. The National Archives also conducts conferences on topics of interest to historians, maintains a publishing program of its own, and publishes the journal *Prologue*. The presidential libraries, which are also under the National Archives, have their own publication programs. The recent three-volume *Franklin D. Roosevelt and Foreign Affairs*, a collection of documents edited by Edgar Nixon and published by the Harvard University Press is an example. The publication of these documents by Harvard has become the focus of a controversy as a result of charges made by Francis L. Loewenheim of Rice University.[6]

The Library of Congress, especially its Manuscript Division, also prepares finding aids and guides, including the multivolume *National Union Catalog of Manuscript Collections*. In addition, the library maintains a center for the coordination of foreign manuscript copying and publishes the *Quarterly Journal* that contains articles of interest to many historians.

The Smithsonian Institution, devoted primarily to science and technology, offers the historian documentation of a different kind, a rich and varied collection of physical, nonliterary sources of the American past. Though it maintains perhaps the most popular tourist attraction in Washington, the Smithsonian's first duty is the advancement of knowledge and for this purpose it has a corps of resident scholars. During the past few years, the Smithsonian has paid increasing attention to history and has expanded its activities in fields of interest to historians, including an American studies program. Recently it has added to its staff Daniel J. Boorstin of Chicago. It has even offered grants and other forms of financial assistance to historians, a practice made possible by the fact that under its charter it is partly a private institution with its own board of regents. In 1966 it began publication of the *Smithsonian Journal of History*, but the venture did not prosper and has since been discontinued. It has also established its own press and now publishes pamphlets on a variety of topics as well as books.

This brief survey of the federal government's support of historical activities hardly does justice to the variety and complexity of goverment history programs or the variety of tasks performed by government historians. If nothing else, it makes clear the commitment of the federal government to history and the importance to the historical profession of ensuring the continuation of these programs while seeking to maintain and raise the quality of historical work produced in these programs.

Historians and the Government

Closely related to this matter of quality is personnel. The problem for all historical agencies in the government is to find qualified historians who are willing to leave academic life for government employment. And even if they do find qualified historians, it is not always possible to hire them under civil service regulations. Aside from the question of numbers—and we do not really know how many "historians" are employed by the federal government—there is the question of nomenclature. It is not at all clear that all those whom the Civil Service Commission classifies as historians would be so regarded by their academic brethren. Moreover, some government historians write for internal consumption rather than for the public on the theory that the expenditure of public funds is justified only if it contributes to the performance of the agency's function. And if the work is classified, it cannot be judged by other historians. Such an arrangement is hardly calculated to attract high caliber professionals whose reputation and mobility rest on the judgment of their peers. It means, further, that historians in the government can be and are assigned all sorts of tasks, useful to the agency perhaps but which bear little relationship to history. It is true that some of the agencies that maintain historical offices have advisory committees consisting of outside scholars, but these meet once or at most twice a year, usually for one day, and they can have little or no effect on day-to-day operations. Finally, there is the problem of security and access. This is not a simple problem, nor is it confined to the military services. Census data since 1890 are barred to outsiders, and so are recent records of the State Department. The United States government has no single rule on access such as a thirty-year rule; each department and agency makes its own rules, and in some instances even congressional records are not open.

There is no doubt that much, if not most, of what is now closed to private scholars could be made available without any damage whatever to national interests or to individuals. But in the mass of classified material there are undoubtedly many documents, perhaps 10 percent, whose disclosure would violate individual rights, reveal vital information to a potential enemy, or inhibit the effective exchange of confidential and private communications between government officials. How to identify and separate this 10 percent from the rest is the nub of the problem; no one has yet found the answer, though a number of proposals have been made.[7] To separate the sensitive material, considering the bulk of the records, would be a vastly expensive and time-consuming operation; to open *all* records twenty or thirty years old is risky. And the tendency of bureaucrats always is to play it safe.

The major impression one is left with after surveying the government's historical programs is the diversity and unevenness of historical activity in Washington. As academicians we are accustomed to finding historians assembled in one place on a campus—a history department, usually in a division of the social sciences or the humanities. Within the government, however, we find historians organized in a variety of ways and allied with activities and functions unrelated to what we regard as the work of the historian—with public relations, intelligence, and records. In some agencies, historians work near the top of the bureaucratic hierarchy; while they profit from this access to the source of power, they are also most exposed in time of crisis. In other agencies, historians are placed in the very bowels of the bureaucracy, safe from interference but far removed from the action.

We are accustomed also, as academicians, to finding historians performing simultaneously two tasks—teaching and research—unless they are unfortunate enough, as so many are, to be called to administration. But government historians, while they perform many administrative chores, do not teach, though perhaps it would be well if they could occasionally give a lesson in history to policy makers. And not all of them do research or write history. In fact, a great many do not function as historians at all. What do they do then? They keep records or assure that proper records are made and preserved, prepare reports for their superiors, provide information for the staff and the public, write speeches, prepare background studies for internal use, and perform a number of other service functions. On occasion, historians may serve in a staff or operating capacity as intelligence or policy analysts, as they do in the Central Intelligence Agency and the State Department.

Historians may even serve in policy-making roles, though it must be admitted that the number who have done so is very small. It is not at all clear, as a matter of fact, that the historian has anything unique to contribute to the solution of current problems, or that he possesses any special qualifications not possessed by others for the analysis of policy and the making of decisions. Moreover, it is doubtful whether the historian in his professional capacity *should* concern himself with current policy issues. After all, how contemporary can the historian be and still retain the perspective and objectivity on which he prides himself—assuming that the records he needs are available to him?[8]

Even when historians function in their professional capacity in government agencies, they may perform quite different tasks. Some may be utilized essentially as editors of documents—the oldest type of historical activity by the government and one that perhaps has greater validity for a government agency than narrative or interpretive history. And even those who write narrative histories for a governmental agency do not always pursue their work in quite the same way historians usually do. Ordinarily, historians work at a slow pace compared to the schedules of government activity, which are established on a weekly or monthly basis. They may work for months or longer with nothing to show but notes. To say the least, this can be terribly frustrating to their administrative superiors, who may insist on written drafts at regular periods. Also, most write with the hope of publication and ultimately of judgment by their peers through reviews in learned journals. This is the way ordinarily that quality is insured and objectivity tested. But much of the history written for the government —how much we do not know—is never tested in this way simply because it is never published, not for lack of a publisher but because it is regarded as a document for internal use rather than to inform the public. How can we judge such work and who profits from it? And some histories, such as those written for the Joint Chiefs of Staff, are so highly classified that they are, in effect, written for the files. So far as we know, literally no one except a handful of officers can read them.

Need for an Office of History

The histories that are ultimately published vary greatly in scope and quality. Some of them are very good, meeting in all respects the standards of the profession; some indifferent and inferior. They range in size from a single volume covering the activities of an entire department over a significant time span to multivolume series covering in the greatest detail the operations of a single office. Sheer bulk is no guarantee of completeness, and often the most important activities of a department or agency, those that would most interest the public, may not be treated at all. Nowhere in this vast array of historical activity is there any sign of a single directing intelligence, any evidence of a plan to produce an integrated history of the whole or to insure that essential matters are covered.

The proposed history of the war in Vietnam by the military services is a case in point. Each of the services has ambitious plans for a history of its operations, and presumably the historians of the Joint Chiefs of Staff will write their own history, which none of us will see. But there will be no overall history on the Defense Department level and, more importantly, none that will treat those aspects of the war that are of greatest interest to the public. Such a history could only

be written at the White House level, or perhaps within the Executive
Office, with access to the files of the National Security Council, State,
Defense, the Joint Chiefs of Staff, the CIA, and other agencies of the
government.

How do we secure such history? How do we assure that important
policies and activities of the government are not neglected or over-
looked, that when new agencies or offices are established a historian
is present to record its birth and to watch its painful growth? How do
we eliminate duplication of effort? How do we make sure that historians are utilized properly and not as speech writers or reference
librarians or public relations officers, that they are given professional
status and adequate compensation? What measures must we take to
guarantee the quality, accuracy, and objectivity of the history written? What can we do to open the records while safeguarding national
interests and individual rights, to ensure that all private scholars are
treated equally in government archives?

There are no easy answers to these questions and I do not pretend
to have any. But I do have a suggestion. The greatest weakness, it
seems to me, is the lack of a single, coordinating body, a historical
office on a high enough level to cut through departmental bureaucracy
and to establish government-wide policy. The creation of such an office, headed by a distinguished (perhaps emeritus) historian, in the
Executive Office of the President or the Office of Management and
Budget would do much to meet some of the problems. It need not be
a large office; perhaps three or four people—an assistant and one or
two secretarial aides. It would have no responsibility for writing history—only ensuring that it is written. It would not review the work of
historians, but would see to it that review procedures were established
and that such review would not be a cloak for censorship. It would attempt to secure quality in the only way that it can be obtained: first,
by finding the best historians possible for the federal government;
second, by creating the conditions necessary for research and writing
and protecting historians from interference; and, finally, by assuring
open publication with authorship credit so that historians can be
judged by their peers.

One man cannot do all this alone, but properly placed in the hierarchy he can do much. His directives concerning general policies would
come from the highest level, backed by the authority of the Executive
Office. If necessary, these directives could be followed by personal
visits. Freedom to deal directly through professional channels with
historians in all departments and on every level would have to be
established. If this were done, information could flow freely both
ways.

A historian on the level of the Executive Office would be a powerful voice for the profession, in and out of government. He would provide historians with direct access to the White House, and perhaps even to the president himself, much as the scientists and economists have been able to do through the Office of the Scientific Adviser and the Council of Economic Advisers. Such an arrangement would undoubtedly raise the prestige of historians everywhere in the government and make government employment more attractive for historians than it now is.

There are many other services a historian in the Executive Office might perform for the profession. He could serve as a link between professional historical organizations and the government. Presumably his relations with the executive secretary of the American Historical Association would be close, and one would expect that the two would work together frequently on a number of matters. He could deal with the Civil Service Commission on the problem of attracting qualified historians into the federal service, with the National Archives, the Library of Congress, and the Smithsonian Institution. One can imagine also that he might very well be helpful in dealing with the Congress on matters of appropriations, and with such departments as HEW in matters of teacher training, research, and educational programs. He could also represent the historians' interest on matters of security, access to records, declassification, and publications policies before the appropriate government agencies. Perhaps he could even urge on the president or his close advisers the advantages of a historical office on the NSC or at the cabinet level to prepare the kind of overarching history we need of such major national efforts as the war in Vietnam, civil rights, and the war on poverty.

I have no illusions about the difficulties of establishing a coordinating historial office on so high a level. Every agency from the Executive Office down could think of a dozen reasons it should not be done, and I doubt very much that the idea would be greeted with enthusiasm by existing historical offices. Historians in a bureaucracy react much the same as other bureaucrats. Nor would I minimize the difficulties facing anyone taking on the task of coordinating the various government historical programs. He would meet opposition in all quarters, even from his fellow historians; he would encounter bureaucratic hurdles that might well throw him; he would have to hack his way through a jungle of rules and regulations. But if he had behind him the support and prestige of the historical profession he might accomplish a great deal. In view of the stake historians have in the historical activities of the federal government, the effort is certainly worth making.

New Approaches to the Study of
the Administration of Indian Policy

FRANCIS PAUL PRUCHA

THIS CONFERENCE, THOUGH ENTITLED simply "Research in the Administration of Public Policy," has a strong historical orientation, and I intend to treat of strictly historical studies, which consider the course of past events, not studies of contemporary or recent situations. Too many of the latter, unfortunately, suffer because they do not rest firmly on a historical background. It seems impossible for anyone to understand a present situation without some knowledge of its past, for anyone to formulate successful administrative policy without some idea of what has been tried before and how well it worked. This presumes, of course, that historians have done their job well. But have they in fact done so?

Historical research in the administration of public policy entails two elements. There is first the formulation and determination of the policy, the definite course or method of action which guides and determines present and future decisions. Then there is the administrative execution of the policy. Neither of these can be studied effectively without the other, for a policy can be fully understood only by watching it unfold in practice; evaluation of the policy depends upon a knowledge of the problems and kinks in its administration; and changes in policy frequently come from faults or difficulties discovered in the field as the policy is applied. On the other hand, the operation, the administration, can hardly be understood unless the rationale behind the policy and its formulation is fully grasped. The intent of the formal legislation of Congress and the regulations from executive agencies needs to be known if one is to judge fairly the administration of a policy.

It may be true that the historical studies of many federal agencies have adequately covered both the formulation of policy and its execution. I do not think it is true in the case of American Indian policy and the Bureau of Indian Affairs.

147

What we find in historical studies is an overwhelming emphasis on investigation of policy and a serious lack of concern for the history of administration. Historians have sought to discover what the United States intended and have argued, sometimes rather heatedly, about the moral implications of the policy. Thus a good many years ago James Malin wrote a prioneering work that he called *Indian Policy and Westward Expansion,* which covered the period 1840 to 1854. In more recent years Reginald Horsman has written *Expansion and American Indian Policy, 1783-1812,* as well as a series of articles dealing with American policy in the decades before the War of 1812. Loring B. Priest's important study on the post-Civil War period has the fancy title *Uncle Sam's Stepchildren,* but the subtitle tells what the book is about: "The Reformation of United States Indian Policy." So with Henry Fritz's *The Movement for Indian Assimilation, 1860-1890,* which in dissertation form was called "The Humanitarian Background of Indian Reform." Elsie Rushmore's monograph was called *The Indian Policy during Grant's Administrations.* To say nothing of my own studies on *American Indian Policy in the Formative Years* and on the Indian policies of Lewis Cass and of Andrew Jackson.

There has been a fascination with investigating and explicating the terms of the relationships between the Europeans who invaded the continent and the Indians who were already here. Contemporary writers of the nineteenth century were intrigued by the same sort of thing—witness, to choose only one example, the rash of articles in such journals as the *Nation* and the *North American Review* in the 1870s, 1880s, and 1890s on "the Indian question," or "the Indian problem." The authors were interested in "what to do about the Indians"—that is, with the development of policy.

And what have we to match against all this on the administration of Indian affairs? Only Laurence F. Schmeckebier's now somewhat outmoded study, *The Office of Indian Affairs: Its History, Activities, and Organization,* in the Brookings Institution's series of monographs. Well, that is not quite fair. There have been some selective studies on aspects of Indian Bureau administration, of which a recent excellent example is Roy E. Meyer's *History of the Santee Sioux,* subtitled "United States Indian Policy on Trial," which shows the application of government law and regulations among a single community of Indians. There have also been a number of doctoral dissertations in recent years which have investigated in depth the working out of some aspect of Indian policy. For example, Robert Whitner's dissertation at the University of Minnesota dealt with the Methodist agencies under Grant's peace policy; and Ronald Satz at the University of Maryland is working on what promises to be a very valuable study of the administration of Indian policy during the Jackson era, 1829 to 1849. The kind of questions Satz is asking indicates the possibilities. What were the duties of the various officials engaged in Indian Affairs? How realistic was the assignment of specific duties to the various echelons in the bureaucracy? What considerations went into the selection of personnel for the Indian office and for posts in the field? What effect did the removal policy have on government agencies hitherto unconnected with Indian affairs? How adequate was the existing bureaucracy for carrying out the removal policy? How responsive was the bureaucracy to crisis situations?

All this is a beginning, but much remains to be done.

The key figure in carrying out Indian policy was the Indian agent. Herbert Welsh, the secretary of the Indian Rights Association, wrote in 1900:

> When it is considered that the Indian Agent is really the key to the proper solution of the Indian problem, the importance of securing good men for these positions and retaining them so long as they faithfully perform their duties will be apparent. As a matter of fact, a great part of the Association's work during the past eighteen years has been to counteract the disastrous results too often caused by placing unworthy, if not dishonest, men in charge of Indian agencies. Had the Government selected the proper kind of agents and other employees, it is safe to say that the Indian problem would have been solved by this time, and the Indian Rights Association would never have been organized.

But where are the historical studies of Indian agents and their operations—not so much biographies of individual agents (although these would have great value), but analytical studies of the office of agent and the effect of the agents on Indian matters? Who has studied the kind of men appointed, their qualifications and character, their skills, their tenure of office? There are suggestive data in Whitner's dissertation on the Methodist agents from 1870 to 1882, and William Unrau in his dissertation at the University of Colorado studied the agents on the southern plains, but these are very little considering the overwhelming resources of the National Archives. Edward Hill's careful brief histories of the agencies from 1824 to 1881 give the names of all the agents. For each one there are files of correspondence in the records of the Bureau of Indian Affairs. The incoming correspondence of the Office of Indian Affairs, arranged by agency or superintendency, is largely composed of letters of agents to the commissioner about problems and activities of the agencies. For the period from 1824 to 1880 alone, these records fill more than five hundred feet of shelf space. The letters received from 1881 to 1907 fill another fifteen hundred feet. Match these statistics with those for the outgoing correspondence, the letters from the commissioner to the agents, passing down to them, as it were, the policy they had to carry out. Add to this the voluminous field office records, which take a whole volume in the preliminary inventory to describe. Can we say that we are satisfied with our knowledge of the administration of Indian affairs while these resources lie largely untouched or at least not systematically exploited?

Take another example: Indian education. Indian reformers and policy makers throughout the whole course of our history of contact between the government and the Indians have placed education of the Indians high on the list of priorities. The commissioner of Indian affairs in 1839, T. Hartley Crawford, asserted that education "is one of the most important objects, if it be not the greatest, connected with our Indian relations. Upon it depends more or less even partial success in all endeavors to make the Indian better than he is." Half a century later Thomas Jefferson Morgan, then the commissioner, declared: "Education is the medium through which the rising generation of Indians are to be brought into fraternal and harmonious relationship with their white fellow-citizens, and with them enjoy the sweets of refined homes, the delights of social intercourse, the emoluments of commerce and trade, the advantages of travel, together with the pleasures that come from literature, science, and philosophy, and the solace and stimulus afforded by a true religion."

But where are our studies of Indian schools, of how the policy was administered? The government's policy of contract schools, in which missionary groups were paid annual per capita sums for the Indian children they instructed, has received limited attention because it resulted in a critical church-state controversy, which some historians claim determined the outcome of the presidential election in 1892. But who has written a detailed scholarly history of a contract school, to say nothing of the system as a whole and its effect on the acculturation of the Indians, on church-state relations, or on educational reform? The standard bibliographies all list Alice C. Fletcher's *Indian Education and Civilization* and Evelyn C. Adams's *American Indian Education*, the first largely a compilation of statistics on Indian schools in the 1880s and the second a very small book. Is that enough?

There is no dearth of materials in the National Archives. There was off and on a special education division in the office of the commissioner of Indian affairs. Letterpress copies of outgoing correspondence on education number a healthy 352 volumes (some eight hundred pages per volume) for the period between 1885 and 1908 alone. And there are innumerable other records of the education division.

And what about the financial or—better—the "business" operations of the agencies? Just take the matter of supplies. The Board of Indian

Commissioners noted in 1890 "the tedious work of receiving, inspecting, assorting, packing 27,425 packages, weighing 4,132,928 pounds and shipping the goods from the [New York] warehouse." Has the distribution of these Indian supplies been studied, and the effect they had on the life of the reservations? I have often had the feeling that the agents and superintendents were so tied up with reports and accounts that they had little time or energy left for anything else. In a famous early imprint from the northwest frontier, Lewis Cass's *Regulations for the Indian Department,* printed in Detroit in 1814, most of the items dealt with the handling of accounts. Should there not be studies on such matters? The records are here. The account books of the agencies, the auditor's vouchers, the contract books, all contain data of immense value in setting the historical balance right. The agents' work was a good deal more than making speeches at Indian councils. And who has investigated in detail the business frauds that made agents rich and infuriated the Indians?

Then there is the history of allotment of land in severalty. This has too often stopped at the policy level. The events and arguments leading up to the eventual passage of the Dawes General Allotment Act in 1887 have been exhaustively studied. The process of allotting the land has been pretty largely neglected. Yet land is the overarching element in many past as well as current Indian matters. Has anyone investigated and evaluated the work of the remarkable ethnologist, Alice Fletcher, who directed the allotment of the lands for the Omahas, the Winnebagos, and the Nez Percés? The Land Division of the Office of the Commissioner of Indian Affairs has records no less voluminous than those for education.

What is the problem? Why are there such gaps in our history of the administration of Indian policy?

In the first place, I suggest, it is the very bulk of the documents. Bureaucracy, after the Civil War especially, really got out of hand. Who has the persistence to dig through such a mass of routine correspondence? Robert Kvasnicka and his staff in the Indian records section of the National Archives will testify that I have been none too courageous myself. I have had several guided tours into the stacks, "surveying" the extent of the Indian office records. I keep hoping that I might get some special inspiration as to how to tackle them—or in my more dicouraged moments, that some of them would simply go away. It will take many researchers, each one digging in some special section of the files, before these riches are properly exploited. Yet books and articles of a purportedly scholarly nature keep appearing on Indian history matters, written by men who have seldom if ever set foot in the National Archives.

Secondly, a mere descriptive or narrative account of the administrative activities these records represent is not enough. Who has the creative skill to write up such a business? Rather, analysis and interpretation are necessary if this sort of administrative investigation is to be fruitful, to say nothing of being interesting. Here is where the social scientists can be of great help to the historians. There is a strong movement among historians to make use of social science concepts and theoretical structures as the framework for the investigation of historical problems. Might not these give the inspiration one needs to gather the data and at the same time supply a framework around which to fashion the study?

One might, for example, consider the theories of bureaucracy advanced by the sociologist Max Weber in order to enhance understanding of the Indian service in its wide connotation, by considering the effect of the groups of expert functionaries on the course of events. At the 1970 meeting of the Organization of American Historians in Los Angeles there was a session devoted to "Bureaucracy and the West." One paper dealt with Indian agents and investigated the reasons for administrative failures. The other treated federal bureaucrats in the West as creative agents of reform. Both authors at least bowed in the direction of Weber. The insights of the sociologist were not fully developed, but the papers pointed in a direction that might prove very fruitful in writing new histories of Indian affairs. They were a significant step beyond the mere recitation of administrative organization and activity with which so much administrative history has been concerned.

I feel a little guilty in asking others to do the work that I myself have shied away from. But it is work that will require many hands and many years. When it is done at last, we will have a sound base on which to build in the present and for the future.

Problems and Opportunities in Research
in the Administration of Federal Policy
and Programs Relating to Poverty

SIDNEY BALDWIN

THE FIRST TIME I ever stepped foot in the National Archives Building was in the winter of 1951. It was a traumatic experience. I was a young graduate student working on a doctoral dissertation in political science, and I had come here to explore the documents and records concerning the Farm Security Administration, an agency in the United States Department of Agriculture now known as the Farmers Home Administration. I was ushered upstairs to see Harold Pinkett, who escorted me out to the stacks and introduced me to several hundred feet of file boxes. He gave me a corner with a desk, offered me whatever assistance I might need, and wished me good luck. Several hundred feet of file boxes! I was stunned. My first impulse was to pack up my things and leave, and to abandon the whole enterprise. But, I was young and I did not know that some things are impossible.

Now that I look back over the intervening years and the long trail down which my research carried me, I feel as President Calvin Coolidge must have felt during one of his apocryphal experiences. During a particularly severe drought in the Southwest during the 1920s, Coolidge went out to witness an Indian rain dance. Called upon to offer a few words, he rose and declared:

> My friends, I want you to know that the Great White Father has come here to tell you that he is going to do everything he can to bring you rain!

Whereupon, a sudden cloud appeared overhead and there was a drenching downpour. Silent Cal ran for cover, and standing with some newsmen he was heard to mutter to himself: "Hmmmm! I didn't know I had it in me!"

As we approach the end of this conference, I have a feeling of impatience which has been described by someone as "a state of annoy-

153

ance when your head is in a hurry but the rest of you keeps it waiting." I have been sitting in these sessions, listening to the discussions
of research problems and of various innovative methods and materials,
and thinking about the data gold mine in this building and other
buildings like it, and my head has been racing ahead of the rest of
me. Of course, I realize that in scholarly work, patience and care are
virtues, but I also remember the story about the famous French marshal Lyautey. Lyautey once instructed his gardner to plant a tree. The
gardener objected that the tree was very slow growing and would not
become full grown for a hundred years. The marshal replied, "In
that case, there is no time to lose, plant it this very afternoon!"

Tree planters, archivists, historians, and other scholars have something in common—they are gamblers. They all perform acts of faith.
The British historian D. G. Hogarth once confessed, "The charm of
guessing ancient motives from the records of ancient deeds fascinated
me—there is much in the pursuit to appeal to a gambler." During the
long time that I spent searching the file boxes in this National Archives, in the Franklin D. Roosevelt Library, and in many other places,
trying to assemble the jigsaw puzzle of rural poverty and the rise and
decline of governmental efforts to cope with it, I frequently sweated
like a gambler, wondering whether the scholarly stakes merited the
great risk of time, energy, resources, and psychological involvement.
Now that it is done, and the critical reviews are in, I do believe that
the gamble was worth it.[1]

What Are Our Problems?

Webster's *New World Dictionary* informs us that the word *problem*
is derived from the Greek terms meaning "to throw forward." The
standard definition is "a question proposed for solution or consideration." Our time is limited here, so I shall restrict myself to three kinds
of questions that seem to be thrown forward for solution or consideration: conceptual problems; problems of jurisdictional and operational
discontinuities; and problems flowing from the politicization of
poverty. I should acknowledge here that some of these problems also
occur in research on other kinds of public policy and programs.

Conceptual Problems

Our conceptual problems involve difficulties of analytical precision
in the very terms that compose the title of this paper—"research,"
"administration," "federal," "policy," "programs," and "poverty."
Agreement on neat and concise verbalizations of such constructs is
probably impossible and undesirable before a gathering as interdis-

ciplinary as this. We may call ourselves archivists, administrators, historians, or social scientists, but many of us are now exploring the same data, learning how to talk with each other, and even beginning to read each other's books and papers. Conceptual clarity remains a problem. "Except ye utter words that are easy to understand," Saint Paul declared, "how shall it be known what is spoken?" But in our search for conceptual clarity and precision, how do we avoid the theoretical closure that characterizes much of the theory building in the separate disciplines of academia?

For instance, what do we mean by *research?* Do we mean simple manhole cover counting, or the careful chronicling of events, or what Charles A. Beard once called "scissors-and-paste" research? Many of the "administrative histories" that have appeared in recent years seem to have been constructed with scissors and staples. They are good reporting, but are they good research? Or, by research do we mean a mode of study and analysis based on empirical data, properly quantified, and organized within an overarching theoretical scheme that seeks to identify and explain patterns and regularities in human affairs? Is research limited to the output of electronic computers?

Similarly, what do we mean by *administration?* Scholars have devoted enormous amounts of time, energy, ingenuity, and resources to the details of pressure politics, legislative process, and the workings of political parties, and the logic of judicial interpretation. However, they have neglected the equally important administrative processes through which laws and ordinances become truly relevant and meaningful. This neglect of the administrative dimension of government and politics, which characterizes much of the history that I have read, implies that Moses was not a lawgiver, but a recording clerk.

Allied to this neglect of administration—especially the neglect of its political and historical implications—is the tendency for historians and other scholars to see everything from the top. It is too frequently assumed, for instance, that the president and the Congress are the sole repositories of political and administrative power. I recall that in my study of the Farm Security Administration the first draft I produced was guilty of this offense. Having dug deeply into the file boxes at Hyde Park, New York, and into many of the papers here in Washington, I told a very warped and misleading story of heroic leadership from on high. It was not until I had spent a great deal of time with the files of many lower-level bureaucrats and other obscure people and had waded through a mass of budgetary, personnel, and other so-called housekeeping documents of the agency that I was able to paint a more authentic picture than earlier.

The terms *policy* and *program* also present some problems. Are they synonymous? Daniel P. Moynihan thinks they are not.[2] He has sharply distinguished between policy actions that "respond to the system in its entirety," such as President Nixon's establishment of the Urban Affairs Council to formulate national urban policy; and program actions that "relate to a single part of the system" and are "directed to a specific situation," such as programs to combat poverty, cancer, and mealybugs. This distinction has led Moynihan to call for greater concern with the careful formulation of national policies and less eagerness to build action programs. Does Moynihan offer us a valid conceptual distinction, or does he present a convenient rationalization for safe talk rather than risky action?

In my opinion, Professor Austin Ranney of the University of Wisconsin has suggested a more useful approach. "Public policy," he has written, "consists of five main components:

(1) A particular object or set of objects;
(2) A desired course of events;
(3) A selected line of action;
(4) A declaration of intent; and
(5) An implementation of intent."[3]

For Ranney, policy embraces program. Legislators and administrators, however, continue to think in terms of programs, which they generally conceive as bundles of administrative objectives, resources, and work schedules. If we are going to make progress, we shall need greater agreement on such terms.

A particularly troublesome conceptual problem involves the meaning, the causes, and the cures of poverty. Almost everyone seems to pay at least lip service to the idea of poverty as a relative concept, but invariably poverty is treated either as an economic problem, a technological problem, a political problem, a racial or ethnic problem, a health problem, or a psychological problem. In my study of the rural poverty that existed during the 1930s and 1940s, for example, I found very little agreement, among both scholars and administrative practitioners, on the nature, causes, and cures of the malady. As each different conception of poverty won popular attention and sufficient bureaucratic and legislative support, a different set of explanations was offered and a different combination of official remedies applied. An important consequence of this syndrome is what Henry S. Kariel of the University of Hawaii has called "the fallacy of closure":

> He [the scholar] closes alternatives the moment he treats immediately observable reality as the only one. Assuming what is real to be "out there," believing that the only problem is to describe it, his focus is then not on what might *conceivably* be observed, not on what moral categories and experimental action might yet establish, but rather on what *is* [Kariel's italics].[4]

For us, as historians, archivists, social scientists, or public administrators, this is not a precious game of definitions. How an ailment is diagnosed largely determines the prescription and prognosis.

Finally, our conceptual problems include the question of what we mean by *federal*. I suppose that at an earlier age, when the United States government had a low profile and did little, when state boundaries meant more than they do now, and before we discovered that our system resembles what the late Professor Morton Grodzins called the "federal marble cake," there was less confusion about the meaning of federal. But, today, with the development of the so-called New Federalism; with the rise of a bewildering array of federal, state, and local agencies of government; with the federal government's development of interface with many commercial consulting firms, community action agencies, and other quasi-public bodies, we can no longer be so certain about the meaning of federal.

If we are going to do meaningful research on the administration of federal policy and programs relating to poverty, if we are going to engage in truly creative scholarship, if we are going to learn from each other, then we shall have to employ constructs that are reasonably free from ambiguity, but reasonably reflective of the real world in all of its bewildering complexity. Plato was right; we should try to "carve at the joints."

The Problems of Jurisdictional and Operational Discontinuities

Even if we resolve or escape our conceptual difficulties, we are faced with problems of jurisdictional and operational discontinuities with the political system, within the national government, and within individual federal agencies. The notion of a mechanistic process permeates much of the thinking about public policy making, public administration, and decision making. Professor William W. Boyer of the University of Delaware, for instance, has offered a model of the public policy making process which consists of "five basic and sequential stages": initiation; preliminary drafting; public participation; final drafting; and reviewing.[5] Similarly, the literature on administrative decision making offers a model resembling a ladder of five rungs: defining the problem; analyzing the problem; developing alternative solutions; deciding upon the one best solution; and converting the decision into effective action. And, of course, there is that traditional model employed by management scientists—nowadays called "systems analysts"—who see administration as a universal process consisting of seven discrete stages: planning; organizing; staffing; direction; coordinating; reporting; and budgeting.

Administration, it is contended, rests upon a pyramidal structure of authority and delegation running downward from *top* management, to *middle* management, to *lower-level* management, and to *operative employees* at the base. To implement this systems scheme, a vast armory of scientific management tools and techniques has been invented, such as systems analysis, automatic data processing, PPBS (planning, programming, and budgeting system), network planning, cost-benefit analysis, and operations research. Simon Ramo, a distinguished scientist-industrialist and a founder of a major systems firm, has argued that through the systems approach we can find a cure for chaos and an escape from the futility of piecemeal solutions to our social problems.[6]

Someday, Simon Ramo's nirvana may come to pass, but the world with which we must deal is to a large extent one of disorder, fragmentation, diffusion, and discontinuity. The poverty warrior, whether he works for Agriculture, HEW, HUD, Justice, Labor, OEO, or any of the state, local, and nongovernmental agencies, is confronted with a bewildering variety of cleavages and hiatuses—constitutional and legal constraints and dilemmas, jurisdictional ambiguities, administrative disjunctions, and human behavioral contradictions and idiosyncrasies. The pathway of public policy making and administration is rough, circuitous, full of unpredictable detours and sudden dead ends.

Furthermore, the management scientists operate from some very tenuous premises. Mathematics, accounting, and statistics are not the only sources of available administrative tools; the social sciences may also be employed. There is not always a one best way of doing everything. Social, cultural, and other situational variables may intervene. It is neither possible nor desirable to formulate a single authoritative ordering of preferences for all of our social needs. Problems do not always get defined, analyzed, decided upon, and resolved in orderly sequence. Delegations of authority and responsibility may jump over constitutional, legal, organizational, and territorial boundaries. Administrative information does not always follow the paths of organizational authority and formal command; there are "rap sessions," the office grapevine, luncheon chats, cocktail party chatter, and golf course dialog in which organizational charts are often ignored. The new breed of management scientists who believe that they are going to save us from chaos are, in the opinion of sociologist Robert Boguslaw, the "New Utopians."[7]

Whether the management scientists are right or wrong in their conception of administration is not the important issue for us here. What does matter is that at an increasing rate, more and more makers and administrators of public policy are producing and using in their work, for good or ill, an ever-mounting mass of data and documents. In 1956, T. R. Schellenberg, then the assistant archivist of the United States, argued that "public records are the grist of the archivist's mill," that "the quality of this grist is determined by the way records are produced," that "public records are the product of activity," and that "much of their meaning is dependent on their relations to the ac-activity."[8] Whether we scholars and archivists like it or not, the administrators' data, computer programs, punch cards, magnetic tapes, and printouts are also becoming the grist of our mills. We are beginning to learn how to cope with it all. The archival trial runs through this ever more tortuous terrain.

The Problems of the Politicization of Poverty

During the years of the Great Depression, chronic poverty was never clearly recognized as requiring the full mobilization of the nation's determination and resources. Poverty was widely believed to be a symptom of economic and technological maladjustment, not an issue of politics and power. The leaders of the Farm Security Administration during the 1930s and 1940s did not have to cope with a Martin Luther King, a Cesar Chavez, a Welfare Rights Organization, CBS documentaries on hunger, poverty marches on Washington, and other political manifestations. Strange as it may seem now to those who lived through that period, the Roosevelt years were comparatively peaceful.

Poverty has now become a thoroughly political problem. The politicization of poverty may have strengthened the thrust toward ameliorative public action, but it also has vastly complicated the work of archivists, administrators, and scholars. Ethnic, race, and class self-consciousness, reflected in the cries for black power, chicano power, and red power, has made it vastly more difficult to carry out empirical research and to document the perceptions and activities of poverty warriors and their clienteles. What has been called the "guinea pig effect," or the "reactive effect of measurement"—i.e., biases related to the awareness of being tested—has become a particularly difficult problem in research among the poor. For example, I have found it enormously difficult to conduct truly candid interviews with local community action leaders who have political involvements with the Black Panthers or the Brown Berets. For these and similar reasons, historians and other scholars working on studies related to poverty will likely have to depend more heavily on archival and other "nonreactive" sources of data.

During the 1930s and 1940s, there were relatively few poverty-related federal programs, and those that did exist were administered within fairly clear organizational lines. The Farm Security Administration, for example, was a highly centralized federal agency that operated through a unified chain of command running from the Washington office through regional and state offices to county offices in hundreds of rural communities. Now that poverty has been politicized, now that we have allegedly gone to war against the problem, every agency of government seems to have joined the struggle. In 1966, for example, the Advisory Commission on Intergovernmental Relations issued a report on intergovernmental relations in the poverty program. The commission reported no fewer than nineteen major federal departments and agencies operating under the umbrella of the Economic Opportunity Act of 1964. To this list must be added literally thousands of local and state governmental agencies, community action councils, neighborhood centers, and other quasi-public bodies. Similarly, in 1967 the Office of Economic Opportunity issued a catalog on federal assistance programs which was the size of the Washington, D.C., telephone directory. It contained detailed descriptions of 459 federal programs designed to help the poor.[9]

This politicization of poverty has provoked virtually all the forces of politics—struggles for power and influence, social conflicts, competing ideologies, and competing notions about something called "human welfare." All these forces present us with enormous challenges.

What Are Our Opportunities?

Opportunity, Webster informs us, is derived from the Latin words meaning "to or toward a port," and is defined as "a combination of circumstances favorable for the purpose." I believe that our opportunities, as our problems, lie in the convergence of several important historical trends:

the expansion of governmental involvement in the life of the people;

the growth of information technology;

a growing concern among historians, especially the younger ones, regarding the meaning and relevance of their work—a sort of "Newer New History";

increasing analytical power in the concepts and methods of the behavioral sciences;

a growing sophistication among archivists regarding the production, preservation, and scholarly use of public records and documents; and

an increasingly more useful and congenial interdisciplinary collaboration and exchange of ideas among scholars.

By encouraging and exploiting these trends, we shall, I believe, find our course toward port. Some examples of our opportunities follow.

The Use of Federal Records Centers and Regional and State Archives

In 1967, Professor William R. Petrowski of the Municipal University of Omaha criticized what he called the "fainthearted and unimaginative use of materials in the National Archives." He pointed to the "exciting materials that open up tremendous opportunities for scholars." Emphasizing that the study of history through the lives and thoughts of the great men who made it is not the only approach available, Professor Petrowski has reminded us that not all of the significant documents on the administration of public policy have found their way to the presidential libraries or to the National Archives at Eighth Street and Pennsylvania Avenue. He informs us, for instance, that the Federal Records Center at Kansas City, Missouri, holds 22,000 cubic feet of unrestricted court records. I wonder what we might learn about the fate of the poor man in federal court by a visit to that records center.[10]

Similarly, Professor G. Q. Flynn of Indiana University recently whetted some appetites when he wrote about the "relevance of local materials available in the Pacific Northwest for a study of the 1930s and the New Deal" from the state's point of view. There in Olympia, Washington, we are told, we shall find the records of the Washington State Department of Public Welfare, and its predecessor agency, the Washington Emergency Relief Administration. This particular gold mine contains files of fruitful correspondence and other records reflecting the state perspective on such federal agencies as the Works Progress Administration, the Social Security Administration, the Rural Resettlement Administration, the Farm Security Administration, and the Civilian Conservation Corps. Those of us who are highly dissatisfied with the formalistic and legalistic treatment of intergovernmental relations that we find in contemporary literature might gain much from a journey to Olympia.[11]

In my own work on the Farm Security Administration, I found materials of great value for the study of poverty in the South generally at the North Carolina Department of Archives and History at Raleigh and at the Library of the University of North Carolina at Chapel Hill. Anyone who reads Ernst Posner's excellent 1964 report, *American State Archives,* will find that North Carolina is not the only state with great archival potentiality.[12] I might also mention that in the Federal Records Center at San Francisco there are operational records on the Farm Security Administration's farm labor camps and the administration of the "bracero" labor program during World War II.

Administrative-Political Case Studies

In the words of Professor Edwin A. Bock of Syracuse University, president of the Inter-University Case Program and a pioneer in the medium, an administrative-political case study might be defined as follows:

> . . . a chronological narrative that portrays how one or more persons (usually officials) went about the business of making (or influencing the making of) a government decision; or how they went about carrying out such a decision; or how they sought to deal with a particular problem of government administration.

"Case studies," Bock explains, are "efforts to wrest significant knowledge and useful understandings from the infinite complexity and tangled interplay of forces and actions that make up the continuity of the real governmental process."[13]

My own study of rural poverty and the Farm Security Administration during the Roosevelt years is illustrative, I believe, of the kind of longitudinal case studies that might be prepared on a great variety of federal agencies and programs related to poverty. The Rural Community Development Service, the Farmers Home Administration, and the Agricultural Stabilization and Conservation Service are waiting for similar treatment. So are the Peace Corps, the Office of Economic Opportunity, the Social Security Administration, and the Manpower Administration. The case studies I have in mind are not simple chronological narratives based on secondary sources and personal recollections. They are attempts to portray "slices of life," as Bock phrases it, to show the flesh quivering.

Professor Douglas G. Montgomery of Case Western Reserve University has prepared a case study, as participant-observer, of the West Oakland (California) Health Center which operated under the sponsorship of the Commerce Department's Economic Development Administration. Professor Murray Seidler of Wayne State University has done a case study, also as participant-observer, of the Federal Concentrated Employment Program of the Department of Labor, which operated in the city of Detroit. Also, Professor Ralph M. Kramer of the University of California, Berkeley, has published a collection of case studies on the participation of the poor in the administration of the Office of Economic Opportunity's Community Action Program in five northern California communities.[14]

Granted that case studies may generate more information and knowledge of an ideographic character than is useful or necessary in theory building and verification, but it is equally true that case studies may force theorists to revise, modify, and perhaps scrap some of their theoretical formulations. I hope that the relevant public records, private documents, and other materials that are available to contemporary case writers will find their ways into archival file boxes. In 1969, a book edited by James L. Sundquist, formerly deputy undersecretary of the United States Department of Agriculture, and a member of President Johnson's poverty task force, was published. It consists of a collection of chapters that are similar to case studies and that were written by various participant-observers of President Johnson's War on Poverty. To a great extent, the strength of the book lies in the intimate knowledge the authors have of the situations and cases they analyze. Available to them was a large body of public documents which are not fully revealed in their footnotes. Will this precious raw material, which was available to them, be equally available to those of us who may sometime in the future seek to retrace their paths and perhaps reinterpret their versions of reality?[15]

Studies of Judicial Administration and the Courts

One of the neglected areas of research on the administration of public policy involves the role of the courts and law enforcement agencies in the administration of poverty-related programs. A large library of reporting and writing by social scientists, working primarily with current survey research data, has accumulated, but official records involved in such administration remain largely untapped. Two recent efforts, which depend on participant-observation and contemporary field research, are a study by Professor Harry P. Stumpf of the University of New Mexico of the politics and administration of the federal program for legal services to the indigent, under the Office of Economic Opportunity, in the San Francisco Bay Area and a study by Professor Martin A. Levin of Brandeis University of the policy impact of criminal court cases in the United States.[16]

Poverty and the law have become a prime focus of attention for scholars interested in the administration of policy and programs relating to the poor. For a few years, during the 1960s, a project on social welfare law at the New York University School of Law compiled a periodic case review and news summary on the legal problems of the poor; it has been continued as the *Clearinghouse Review* by the National Institute for Education in Law and Poverty at the Northwestern University School of Law. These publications have been enormously useful as a key to research opportunities, but the question remains: Will the relevant public documents, the "grist of the archivist's mill," be available to us?

Quantitative and Behavioral Studies

Writing in the January 1965 issue of *The American Archivist,* Professor Samuel P. Hays of the University of Pittsburgh called for more vigorous exploitation of the masses of political, socioeconomic, ethnocultural, sectional, and other data "lying almost unnoticed and relatively unused in county, State, and other archives." By 1969, the American Historical Association, reporting on a survey of its members, revealed that of the 260 responses received, 214 members stated that they were currently using quantitative data. Two hundred fifty-four reported that they planned to do research of this kind in the near future. And the publication, in 1969, of Robert F. Berkhofer's well-reasoned and provocative book, *A Behavioral Approach to Historical Analysis,* signals to me that we are probably on the threshold of important new directions.[17]

Opportunities also lie in the so-called data-bank movement, which is devoted to the collection, retrieval, and classification of vast amounts of machine-readable data. Illustrative are the Inter-University Consortium for Political Research, based at the University of Michigan at Ann Arbor, and the Council of Social Science Data Archives, based at the University of Pittsburgh. A more ambitious variation was proposed several years ago by Professor Robert C. Wood of the Massachusetts Institute of Technology, who called for the creation of a series of "social observatories" that would do for social scientists and historians what Mount Palomar and Mount Wilson have been doing for astronomers.[18]

As the body of archival records and other data grows, it becomes increasingly more difficult to decipher administrative communications. An important methodological innovation, now available to archivists and other scholars, is content analysis, defined as the "systematic study of verbal symbols." Based on the work of Professor Harold D. Lasswell of Yale University during the 1930s and 1940s, content analysis seeks to cut through the "noise" in verbal communications caused by differences in cultural backgrounds, times, languages, and contexts and references.

I am not suggesting that we all must rush out and become social scientists, computer programmers, statisticians, and systems analysts. Nor am I suggesting that conventional archival and historical methods and materials be abandoned. Rather, I am suggesting that those of us who are interested in the past now have greater opportunities to strengthen the power of our generalizations and the evidential verification of our theories. Let each of us employ the methodologies and techniques that we find most productive and congenial, whether they be the quill pen, the stubby yellow pencil, the typewriter, or the computer.

Inscribed over this National Archives Building there is a bold declaration that reads: "This building holds in trust the records of our national life and symbolizes our faith in the permanency of our national institutions." In all candor, I am no longer so certain about the "permanency" of our national institutions, but I am confident that the materials and methods of the people who work in such archival buildings will most certainly change fundamentally in the years to come.

It has become fashionable to lament over our problems, our dilemmas, and our crises. Such a preoccupation reflects as much about our personalities as our scholarly methodologies, as much about our feelings and world views as our intellectual processes. Admittedly, the words *optimism* and *pessimism* are slippery terms, but I fear that James Branch Cabell, the American historical novelist, was probably right when he observed that "The optimist proclaims that we live in the best of all possible worlds; and the pessimist fears this is true." As far as our methodological dilemmas are concerned, I would prefer to stand with the old Negro preacher in North Carolina who, at the depth of the Great Depression, was asked whether he had any hope for the future. His answer, which perhaps applies to our predicament today, went like this:

> I reckon things have stopped getting worse. We are now about half way between "Oh Lord!" and "Thank God!"

DISCUSSION SUMMARY

Professor Baldwin began the discussion by observing that he thought the kind of research Father Prucha suggested might require a joint enterprise among a group of scholars collaborating to be certain they did not duplicate one another's research. He also stated that a consortium approach, in which a group of historians, political scientists, sociologists, and archivists worked together, using whatever computer hardware might be available, might be of help in handling the mass of records available.

In reaction to Dr. Baldwin's presentation, a member of the audience stated that he felt there was a danger in overconceptualization and definition. Dr. Baldwin at first seemed to emphasize conceptualization, but later he mentioned that historians are interested in describing "slices of life." Yet many slices of life do not fit conveniently into conceptualizations or definitions, and there might be a danger in conceptualizing and destroying the authenticity of those details with which historians are concerned.

Martin P. Claussen of Historiconsultants next suggested that the historical office Dr. Morton proposed not be limited to the executive branch but be designed to coordinate historical research in all three branches because all branches have been involved in historical research. Congress especially has been instrumental in generating historical writings of the government—for example, Congress was largely responsible for instituting the *American State Papers* and the *Foreign Relations* series—and the Supreme Court also has been involved in writing some legal history.

Dr. Morton agreed that the other branches were involved in some way in historical writing, but he added that he was not sure it would be possible to coordinate programs for the three branches. He noted, however, that practically all historical activity of the federal government is conducted within the executive branch, even though the legislative branch might initiate many programs and even though the Supreme Court might be engaged in writing some legal history. Because of that fact he thought that a historical office such as he proposed would cover most of the historical programs of the federal government.

Professor Morton also commented that if there were a single office operating through the White House and if a historical program were established for the Supreme Court or the Congress, the coordinator in the executive branch would probably be able to exert a great deal of influence and be of assistance to the legislative and judicial historical offices.

Professor Baldwin mentioned that one of the most useful sources for his study of the Farm Security Administration during the World War II period were unpublished, generally unavailable interviews that had been conducted during the writing of the wartime histories. He emphasized the fact that those sources would not have been created if it had not been for the World War II historical program, and he predicted that the consequences of a national historical program might be very fruitful.

Paul J. Scheips of the Office of the Chief of Military History, Department of the Army, said that he had been interested for a long time in a program such as Dr. Morton suggested and that the idea of a central historical office for the federal government merits consideration by the historical and archival professions. But he also thought that the difficulties would be enormous. For example, each of the services has its own program, as do the Joint Chiefs of Staff, and it is not easy to get the services to cooperate. Dr. Scheips recalled that during the Korean war there was an effort to coordinate about forty agencies to write accounts of the war, but as far as he knew that project had failed. At one time he had tried to bring the lack of interest in the project to the attention of the Committee of Historians in the Federal Government of the American Historical Association, but he did not succeed even in that effort.

On the other hand, Dr. Scheips noted that the services were undertaking a project that might constitute a beginning in the direction of cooperation among historical offices—the writing of the history of integration in the armed forces—but that this was the only cooperative project within the Department of Defense. The Department of Defense historian, however, does possess a rather broad charter that enables him to coordinate the activities of the services more than they are now coordinated. Dr. Scheips thought that this fact offered an opportunity and that the possibilities were endless for joint projects between military and some civilian departments and for projects that could be carried out by historians from the various agencies working together.

Dr. Evans commented in response to Professor Baldwin's presentation that the National Archives had been wrestling with the problem of what to do with the new technology. It had undertaken surveys of all of the machine-readable records being created, particularly the master tapes, in every agency of the government in order to determine where such records were and under what conditions they were being maintained and in order to make certain that tapes with data valuable for a variety of scholarly studies were not erased. He added that the archives was also making progress in acquiring the programs to incorporate as headers on the tapes themselves—the software it is necessary to have if the tapes are to be used.

On another front, the National Archives was trying to apply the new technology to the proliferation of narrative finding aids that had already been created and that were in the process of being created. If the archives can automate its findings aids and put what it does know about the records already in its custody into a data bank and if it can construct that bank in such a way that information about personal papers and manuscript repositories in the state archives throughout the country can be added to it, the time may not be too distant in which the researcher can have on-line access to a data bank that will give him a printout selected in accordance with the chronological period, geographic area, and broad topic in which he is interested.

In response to a question about why it was necessary to take advantage of the new technology, Dr. Evans explained that the volume of data available on National Archives holdings alone was so great that the researcher could spend the better part of several years just reading the preliminary inventories and general and subject guides.

Regarding access to records by researchers who do not live close to Washington, he commented that he foresaw the possibility of communicating information about records in the archives directly to universities located anywhere in the country—in fact, anywhere in the world—and even of transmitting copies of certain files when the researcher can be specific about what he wishes to see.

Professor Baldwin also observed that in his own work he had reached a point at which he realized that the traditional methods of search he used were no longer feasible. He recalled that when he was working on the Farm Security Administration he found more file boxes than he could ever possibly look through; the files were case histories of the hundreds of thousands of families that were helped by the agency, but he did not even try to examine some of them because he knew the task was hopeless.

Keith Henderson of the State University College at Buffalo next asked Professor Baldwin whether historical research involving computers had gone beyond classification to content analysis and whether Dr. Baldwin saw a need for such analysis.

Dr. Baldwin replied that he thought content analysis one of the skills at which historians ought to become adept and that historians ought not to leave it to social scientists. In fact, when historians do research on documentary material, in a sense they are doing content analysis, and they ought to do it in a quantitative way if the material requires it.

James Harvey Young of Emory University introduced the topic of the use of audiovisual materials in writing history. He mentioned a book he had seen entitled *Chicago: Growth of a Metropolis,* coauthored by Harold M. Mayer and Richard C. Wade (1969), in which the text was secondary and the pictures were primary. Dr. Young was very much impressed with the book and believed it was the first work in history he had seen in which a serious, deliberate effort was made to use graphic material as the primary source.

Dr. Evans mentioned that the National Archives has in its custody millions of feet of motion pictures, still pictures, sound recordings, charts, maps, and aerial photographs. He believed that historians needed to develop a research methodology involving the use of audiovisual archives in the course of research rather than as an afterthought for illustration.

Professor Baldwin added that the Farm Security Administration probably did more in pioneering photographic work in the federal government than any agency since. It produced the two documentary films *The River* and *The Plough That Broke the Plains* with Pare Lorenz in addition to an enormous collection of photographic material now at the Library of Congress and the National Archives. One attempt to use this material in the way suggested is represented by Arthur F. Raper's *Tenants of the Almighty* (1943), a photographic narrative essay on Greene County, Georgia. Another such book Professor Baldwin recalled was *Land of the Free* (1938), for which the poet Archibald MacLeish wrote what he called the sound score to accompany the photographs.

Jerome Finster of the National Archives and Records Service commented that the book on Chicago that Professor Young mentioned was well received by urban historians because it represented not so much the use of photographs as an adjunct to the text, but a new technique in historical and social investigation. Mr. Finster added that the staff of the Audiovisual Branch of the Archives had written a report on National Archives holdings of photographic materials for urban research and that the report was available upon request.

Closing Remarks

HERBERT E. ANGEL

THIS CONFERENCE HAS BEEN a continuation of an important effort in the mission of the National Archives and Records Service. That effort involves providing members of academic and governmental institutions an opportunity to learn more about the great volume and variety of major portions of the documentary heritage of the United States. It also entails an attempt to ascertain and develop new and better ways to make this heritage more useful on ever-widening frontiers of research.

This has been the first conference of the National Archives and Records Service devoted to discussions of some representative uses of federal archives for the study of administrative history and the administration of public policy. It was planned not only to attract the interest of historians who have been a major group of our clientele, but also to attract the interest of kindred scholars in political science and public administration. We are pleased that so many members of these disciplines accepted our invitation to participate in the conference.

We have striven to suggest various aspects of federal administration that may be studied profitably in federal archives. Special attention has been directed to actual and potential innovative research in administrative history, in governmental reorganization, and in implementation of certain public policies. Representative classes of archival sources useful for research have also been highlighted.

Our staff has profited from your speeches, questions, and comments, and we hope that the remarks of our staff on some major characteristics of archives has stimulated interest in new research efforts.

We want to thank you, in closing, for your attendance and for your helpful expression of views, and we invite you and your colleagues in your profession to share in our mission to make more available for research the great portions of the nation's recorded experience. We hope that you will come back often—both for formal occasions, such as this, and for the use of materials here in the building.

Appendix

The National Archives and Records

Service and Its Research Resources—

a Select Bibliography

FRANK B. EVANS

THE LISTING THAT FOLLOWS is intended only as an introduction to the National Archives of the United States, their administration, and their research potential. Most of the selections deal with various aspects of accessioned noncurrent official records of the United States government, but also included are works about the record holdings of federal records centers and the variety of documentary materials in the presidential libraries, research resources administered by the National Archives and Records Service but not formally part of the National Archives of the United States.

For those desiring further information about archives, their administration, and their value and use, the most comprehensive listing is the annual classified bibliography published since 1943 in the *American Archivist*, currently under the title "Writings on Archives, Current Records, and Historical Manuscripts." See also National Archives and Records Service, *The Administration of Modern Archives: A Select Bibliographic Guide*, compiled by Frank B. Evans (Washington, D.C., 1970). For a listing of other National Archives and Records Service publications see the current edition of *Select List of Publications of the National Archives and Records Service* (General Information Leaflet no. 3). A limited supply of many of the finding aids listed in that leaflet is available for distribution to government agencies, archives and libraries, educational institutions, and individual scholars.

Record holdings that have been published on microfilm are described in the current edition of *List of National Archives Microfilm Publications*. Inquiries regarding any of the publications of the National Archives and Records Service should be addressed to the Publications Sales Branch (NEPS), National Archives and Records Service (GSA), Washington, D.C. 20408.

In addition to published finding aids, the National Archives Library and the various custodial divisions and branches of the Office of the National Archives have acquired a wide variety of agency-created finding aids and have

An abbreviated version of this bibliography was distributed to conference participants, and an expanded version was published in *Prologue: The Journal of the National Archives* 3 (Fall 1971): 88-112. The bibliography has been updated to include publications through June 1973.

produced numerous typescripts and drafts of specialized finding aids to records on particular geographic areas, subjects, periods, and prominent individuals. Since these finding aids have not been published and are available for use only within the various custodial units, they have not been included in this select bibliography. For information on such research aids and for other information on the availability and location of records relating to any subject of inquiry, the researcher should consult the archival staff.

The place of publication of all books and pamphlets cited in this listing, unless otherwise indicated, is Washington, D.C. Quotation marks have been omitted from the titles of published articles. Because of the frequency with which certain institutions, organizations, periodicals, and serials occur, they have been designated with the following abbreviations and symbols:

AA	American Archivist
AHA	American Historical Association
AHR	American Historical Review
MVHR	Mississippi Valley Historical Review
NA	National Archives
NARS	National Archives and Records Service
PI	Preliminary Inventory
RG	Record Group
RIC	Reference Information Circular
RIP	Reference Information Paper
SIC	Staff Information Circular
SIP	Staff Information Paper
SL	Special List

The National Archives and the National Archives and Records Service: Historical Development*

The Movement for a National Archives

Connor, R.D.W. Our National Archives. *Minnesota History* 17 (1936): 1-19.

---

*Items in this section are arranged, as appropriate, by the period covered or the date of publication.

Bauer, G. Philip. Public Archives in the United States. In *In Support of Clio: Essays in Memory of Herbert A. Kellar*, edited by William B. Hesseltine and Donald R. McNeil. Madison, 1958, pp. 49-76.

Burnette, O. Lawrence, Jr. *Beneath the Footnote: A Guide to the Use and Preservation of American Historical Sources.* Madison, 1969, pp. 3-33.

Leland, Waldo G. American Archival Problems. *Annual Report of the AHA, 1909*, pp. 342-48.

Leland. The National Archives: A Programme. *AHR* 18 (1912): 1-28.

Leland. Recollections of the Man Who Rang the Bell. *AA* 21 (1958): 55-57.

Paullin, Charles O., comp. *History of the Movement for a National Archives Building in Washington, D.C.* Senate Doc. 297, 69th Cong. 2d sess., Serial 6175.

Paltsits, Victor H. An Historical Résumé of the Public Archives Commission from 1899 to 1921. *Annual Report of the AHA, 1922*, 1:152-160.

Shelley, Fred. The Interest of J. Franklin Jameson in the National Archives: 1908-1934. *AA* 12 (1949): 99-130.

The National Archives, 1934-49

Connor, R.D.W. Our National Archives. *Minnesota History* 17 (1936): 1-19.

Boyd, Julian P. Recent Activities in Relation to Archives and Historical Manuscripts in the United States. *Proceedings of the Society of American Archivists, 1936-37,* pp. 13-20.

Child, Sargent B. What Is Past is Prologue. *AA* 5 (1942): 217-27.

Leland, Waldo G.R.D.W. Connor, First Archivist of the United States, *AA* 16 (1953): 45-54.

Posner, Ernst. Some Aspects of Archival Development since the French Revolution. *AA* 3 (1940): 159-72, reprinted in *Archives and the Public Interest: Selected Essays by Ernst Posner,* edited by Kenneth W. Munden. 1967, pp. 23-35.

Campbell, Edward G. The National Archives Faces the Future. *AHR* 49 (1944): 441-45.

Holmes, Oliver W. The National Archives and the Protection of Records in War Areas. *AA* 9 (1946); 110-27.

Brooks, Philip C. Archives in the United States during World War II, 1939-45. *Library Quarterly* 17 (1947): 263-80.

Buck, Solon J. Let's Look at the Record. *AA* 8 (1945): 109-14.

Posner, Ernst. Solon Justus Buck and the National Archives. *AA* 23 (1960): 263-69, reprinted in *Archives and the Public Interest: Selected Essays by Ernst Posner,* edited by Kenneth W. Munden. 1967, pp. 141-47.

Jones, H.G. *The Records of a Nation: Their Management, Preservation, and Use.* New York, 1969, pp. 3-65.

The National Archives and Records Service, 1949-73

Holmes, Oliver W. The National Archives at a Turn in the Road. *AA* 12 (1949): 339-54.

Grover, Wayne C. Recent Developments in Federal Archival Activities. *AA* 14 (1951): 3-12.

Angel, Herbert E. Federal Records Management since the Hoover Commission Report. *AA* 16 (1953): 13-26.

Krauskopf, Robert W. The Hoover Commissions and Federal Record-keeping. *AA* 21 (1958): 371-99.

Grover, Wayne C. The National Archives at Age Twenty. *AA* 17 (1954): 99-107.

Bahmer, Robert H. The National Archives after Twenty Years. *AA* 18 (1955): 195-205.

Posner, Ernst. The National Archives and the Archival Theorist. *AA* 18 (1955): 207-16, reprinted in *Archives and the Public Interest: Selected Essays by Ernst Posner,* edited by Kenneth W. Munden. 1967, pp. 131-40.

Grover, Wayne C. Federal Government Archives. *Library Trends* 5 (1957): 390-96.

Leland, Waldo G. The Creation of the Franklin D. Roosevelt Library: A Personal Narrative. *AA* 18 (1955): 11-29.

Grover, Wayne C. Presidential Libraries: A New Feature of the Archival System of the United States. *Indian Archives* 11 (1957): 1-6.

Kahn, Herman. The Presidential Library—a New Institution. *Special Libraries* 50 (1959): 106-13.

Buck, Elizabeth H. The National Archives and Records Service of the United States. *Archivum* 11 (1961): 121-35.

Bahmer, Robert H. The Management of Archival Institutions. *AA* 26 (1963): 3-10.

Drewry, Elizabeth B. The Role of Presidential Libraries. *Midwest Quarterly* 7 (1965): 53-65.

Grover, Wayne C. Toward Equal Opportunities for Scholarship. *Journal of American History* 52 (1966): 715-24.

Angel, Herbert E. Archival Janus: The Records Center. *AA* 31 (1968): 5-12.

Jones, H.G. *The Records of a Nation: Their Management, Preservation, and Use.* New York, 1969, pp. 66-265, app., 273-95.

Brooks, Philip C. Understanding the Presidency: The Harry S. Truman Library. *Prologue* 1 (Winter 1969): 3-12.

Burnette, O. Lawrence, Jr. *Beneath the Footnote: A Guide to the Use and Preservation of American Historical Sources.* Madison, 1969, pp. 20-33, 147-66.

Cappon, Lester J. The National Archives and the Historical Profession. *Journal of Southern History* 35 (1969); 477-99.

Rhoads, James B. Programs of the National Archives. *Illinois Libraries* 52 (1970): 136-43.

Rhoads. The National Archives and Records Service in 1972. *Prologue* 5 (Spring 1973): 46-49.

O'Neill, James E. Secrecy and Disclosure: The Declassification Program of the National Archives and Records Service. *Ibid.* 5 (Spring 1973): 43-45.

The Appraisal and Disposition of Federal Records

Value and Uses of Federal Records and Archives

Brooks, Philip C. The Historian's Stake in Federal Records. *MVHR* 43 (1956): 259-74.

Brooks. *Research in Archives: The Use of Unpublished Primary Sources.* Chicago, 1969.

Buck, Solon J. The Living Past. *Pennsylvania History* 8 (1941): 47-58.

Burnette, O. Lawrence, Jr. *Beneath the Footnote: A Guide to the Use and Preservation of American Historical Sources.* Madison, 1969, pp. 34-42.

Campbell, Edward G. Old Records in a New War. *AA* 5 (1942): 156-68.

Copeland, Morris A. The Significance of Archives to the Economist and Sociologist. *Proceedings of the Society of American Archivists, 1936-37*, pp. 47-51.

Evans, Luther H. Archives as Material for the Teaching of History. *Indiana Historical Bulletin* 15 (1938): 136:53.

Fishbein, Meyer H. Archival Training for Historians. *AHA Newsletter* 5 (1966): 5-7.

Hays, Samuel P. The Use of Archives for Historical Statistical Inquiry. *Prologue* 1 (Fall 1969): 7-15.

Hyde, Dorsey W., Jr. Public Archives and Public Documents as Aids to Scholarship. American Library Association, *Public Documents, 1936*, pp. 179-86.

Nichols, Roy. Alice in Wonderland. *AA* 3 (1940): 149-58.

Petrowski, William R. Research Anyone? A Look at the Federal Records Centers. *AA* 30 (1967): 581-92.

Rhoads, James B. The Historian and the New Technology. *AA* 32 (1969): 209-13.

Shafer, Boyd C. Lost and Found. *AA* 18 (1955): 217-23.

Smith, Jane F. The Use of Federal Records in Writing Local History: A Case Study. *Prologue* 1 (Spring 1969): 29-51.

Trever, Karl L. Administrative History in Federal Archives. *AA* 4 (1941): 159:69.

White, Gerald T. Government Archives Afield: The Federal Records Centers and the Historian. *Journal of American History* 55 (1969): 833-42.

Wood, Richard G. The National Archives as an Institution for Historical Research. *West Virginia History* 14 (1954): 118-25.

Wright, Almon B. The Scholar's Interest in Personnel Records. *AA* 12 (1949): 271-79.

Appraisal and Disposition Guidelines and Practices

Bahmer, Robert H. Scheduling the Disposition of Records. *AA* 6 (1943): 169-75.

Beers, Henry P. Historical Development of the Records Disposal Policy of the Federal Government Prior to 1934. *AA* 7 (1944): 181-201.

Brooks, Philip C. Archival Procedures for Planned Records Retirement. *AA* 11 (1948): 308-15.

Brooks, Records Section—a Cooperative Task. *Indian Archives* 7 (1953): 79-86.

Brooks. The Selection of Records for Preservation. *AA* 3 (1940): 221-34.

Campbell, Edward G. Records Disposal in the United States. *Archivar* 8 (1955): cols. 107-12.

Drewry, Elizabeth B. Records Disposition in the Federal Government. *Public Administration Review* 15 (1955): 218-21.

Fishbein, Meyer H. Appraisal of Twentieth Century Records for Historical Use. *Illinois Libraries* 52 (1970): 154-62.

Fishbein. A Viewpoint on Appraisal of National Records. *AA* 33 (1970): 175-87.

The General Accessioning Policy of the National Archives. *AA* 8 (1945): 265-68.

Grover, Wayne C. A Note on the Development of Record Centers in the United States. *Indian Archives* 4 (1950): 160-63.

Hall, Sidney R. Retention and Disposal of Correspondence Files. *AA* 15 (1952): 3-14.

Hyde, Dorsey W., Jr. Principles for the Selection of Materials for Preservation in Public Archives. American Library Association, *Public Documents, 1938,* pp. 335-41.

Leahy, Emmett J. Reduction of Public Records. *AA* 3 (1940): 13-38.

Lewinson, Paul. Archival Sampling. *AA* 20 (1957): 291-312.

Lewinson. Toward Accessioning Standards—Research Records. *AA* 23 (1960): 297-309.

NA. *The Appraisal of Current and Recent Records,* by G. Philip Bauer, SIC no. 13. 1946.

NA. *The Appraisal of Modern Public Records,* by T.R. Schellenberg. Bulletin no. 8. 1956.

NARS. *What Records Shall We Preserve?* by Philip C. Brooks. SIP no. 9. 1971.

Perlman, Isadore. General Schedules and Federal Records. *AA* 15 (1952): 27-38.

Pinkett, Harold T. Identification of Records of Continuing Value. *Indian Archives* 16 (1965/1966): 54-61.

Pinkett. Selective Preservation of General Correspondence. *AA* 30 (1967): 33-43.

Schellenberg, T.R. *Modern Archives: Principles and Techniques.* Chicago, 1956, pp. 94-110, 133-60.

Wilson, William J. Analysis of Government Records: An Emerging Profession. *Library Quarterly* 16 (1946): 1-19.

General Descriptions of Federal Archives

General Guides and Lists of Holdings

Carnegie Institution of Washington. *Guide to the Archives of the Government of the United States in Washington,* compiled by Claude H. Van Tyne and Waldo G. Leland. 2d ed. 1907. (Most of the records described in this guide that have survived are now in the National Archives Building.)

NA. *Guide to the Records in the National Archives.* 1948. (This guide superseded an earlier one published in 1937 as part of the *Third Annual Report of the Archivist of the United States,* one published in 1940, and a summary guide published in 1946, intended primarily for the general public. A new edition is now in preparation. For records accessioned since 1948, see *NA Accessions,* published quarterly between January 1940 and June 1952 and irregularly thereafter, and *Prologue: The Journal of the National Archives,* which since January 1969 continues the description of the most important records accessioned since the previous issue.

NA. *List of Record Groups of the National Archives and Records Service.* 1972.

NARS. *Historical Materials in the Herbert Hoover Presidential Library.* 1971.

NARS. *Collections of Manuscripts and Archives in the Franklin D. Roosevelt Library.* 1969.

NARS. *Historical Materials in the Harry S. Truman Library.* 1972.

NARS. *Historical Materials in the Dwight D. Eisenhower Library.* 1970.

Nontextual Records and Archives

NA. *Aerial Photographs in the National Archives,* compiled by Charles E. Taylor and Richard E. Spurr. SL no. 25. 1971.

Baumhofer, Hermine M. Motion Pictures Become Federal Records. *AA* 15 (1952): 15-26.

Cobb, Josephine. The Still Picture Program at the National Archives. *Special Libraries* 45 (1954): 269-73.

NA. *Guide to Cartographic Records in the National Archives.* 1971.

Joerg, W.L.G. Archival Maps as Illustrated by Those in the National Archives. *AA* 4 (1941): 188-93.

Joerg. 175 Years of the Official Mapping of the United States. *Surveying and Mapping* 11 (1951): 271-76.

NA. *List of Selected Maps of States and Territories,* compiled by Janet L. Hargett. SL no. 29. 1971.

Muntz, A. Philip. Federal Cartographic Archives: A Profile. *Prologue* 1 (Spring 1969): 3-7.

NA. *Pre-Federal Maps in the National Archives: An Annotated List,* compiled by Patrick D. McLaughlin. SL no. 26. 1971.

Thomas, Joe D. Photographic Archives. *AA* 21 (1958): 419:24.

Records Relating to
Particular Geographic Areas

Foreign Countries

Alagoa, E.J. Preliminary Inventory of the Records of the United States Diplomatic and Consular Posts in West Africa, 1865-1935. *Journal of the Historical Society of Nigeria* 2 (1960): 78-104.

Basu, Purnendu. Materials Relating to India in the National Archives, Washington. *Indian Archives* 5 (1951): 42-53.

Gustafson, Milton O. State Department Records in the National Archives: A Profile. *Prologue* 2 (1970): 175-84.

Harrison, John P. Opportunities for Inter-American Studies in the National Archives. In *The Caribbean: Peoples, Problems, and Prospects*, edited by A. Curtis Wilgus. Gainesville, 1952, pp. 162-74.

Lokke, Carl L. France in the National Archives. *Bulletin de l'Institut Français de Washington* 5-6 (1957): 16-27.

NA. *Guide to Materials on Latin America in the National Archives*, vol. 1, compiled by John P. Harrison. 1961. (An expanded version of this guide, which will incorporate vol. 2, is currently in preparation.)

NA. *Materials in the National Archives Relating to Cuba*, compiled by Seymour J. Pomrenze. RIC no. 34. 1948.

NA. *Materials in the National Archives Relating to the Dominican Republic*, compiled by Seymour J. Pomrenze. RIC no. 35. 1948.

NA. *Materials in the National Archives Relating to Haiti*. RIP no. 40. 1949.

NA. *Materials in the National Archives Relating to India*. Rip no. 38. 1949.

NA. *Materials in the National Archives Relating to the Mexican States of Sonora, Sinaloa, and Baja California*. RIP no. 42. 1952.

NA. *Materials in the National Archives Relating to the Middle East*, compiled by Elizabeth H. Buck. RIP no. 44. 1955.

NA. *Materials in the National Archives Relating to Rumania*, compiled by James F. Vivian. RIP no. 46. 1970.

NA. Materials in the National Archives of the United States Relating to the Independence of Latin American Nations, compiled by George S. Ulibarri. RIP no. 45. 1968.

NA. *Records in the National Archives Relating to the Russian Empire and the Soviet Union*, compiled by Elizabeth H. Buck. RIP no. 41. 1952.

Rieger, Morris. The National Archives. In *Handbook of American Resources for African Studies*, edited by Peter Duignan. Stanford, 1967, pp. 59-98.

For the complete series of reference information circulars and reference information papers compiled during World War II which describe records at that time in the National Archives relating to various areas of the world, see National Archives Microfilm Publication M248.

United States: General and Regional

Flynn, G.Q. The New Deal and Local Archives: The Pacific Northwest. *AA* 33 (1970): 41-52.

Friis, Herman R. The Documents and Reports of the United States

Congress: A Primary Source of Information on Travel in the West, 1783-1861. In *Travellers on the Western Frontier,* edited by John F. McDermott. Urbana, 1970, pp. 112-67.

Heard, John P. Resource for Historians: Records of the Bureau of Land Management in California and Nevada. *Forest History* 12 (1968): 20-26.

Holmes, Oliver W. Territorial Government and the Records of Its Administration. In *The Frontier Re-examined,* edited by John F. McDermott. Urbana, 1967, pp. 97-109.

Jackson, W. Turrentine. Materials for Western History in the Department of Interior Archives. *MVHR* 35 (1948): 61-76.

Kahn, Herman. The National Archives, Storehouse of National Park History. *Regional Review* 4 (1940): 13-17.

Parker, David W. *Calendar of Washington Archives Relating to the Territories of the United States (to 1873).* 1911.

Peters, Gayle. The Regional Archives System and Its East Point Branch. *Georgia Archive* 1 (1973): 21-30.

Petrowski, William R. Research Anyone? A Look at the Federal Records Centers. *AA* 30 (1967): 581-92.

Schusky, Mary Sue, and Ernest L. Schusky. A Center for Primary Sources for Plains Indian History. *Plains Anthropologist* 15 (1970): 104-8.

Smith, G. Hubert. Some Sources for Northwest History: The Archives of Military Posts. *Minnesota History* 22 (1941): 297-301.

Strong, Dennis F. Sources for Pacific Northwest History: The Federal Records Center in Seattle. *Pacific Northwest Quarterly* 49 (1958): 19-20.

Tutorow, Norman E., and Arthur R. Abel. Western and Territorial Research Opportunities in Tran-Mississippi Federal Records Centers. *Pacific Historical Review* 40 (1971): 501-19.

White, Gerald T. Government Archives Afield: The Federal Records Centers and the Historian. *Journal of American History* 55 (1969): 833-42.

Territories, States, and Cities

Alaska—NA. *Materials in the National Archives Relating to Alaska.* RIC no. 6. 1942.

California—Nasatir, Abraham P., comp. *French Activities in California: An Archival Calendar-Guide.* Stanford, 1945, pp. 511-35.

District of Columbia—Bethel, Elizabeth. Material in the National Archives Relating to the Early History of the District of Columbia. Columbia Historical Society, *Records* 42/43 (1940/41): 169-87.

Colket, Meredith B., Jr. The Public Records of the District of Columbia. Ibid. 48/49 (1949): 281-99.

Florida—Drewry, Elizabeth B. Material in the National Archives Relating to Florida, 1839-1870. *Florida Historical Quarterly* 29 (1944): 97-115.

Iowa—NA. *Cartographic Records Relating to the Territory of Iowa, 1838-46,* compiled by Laura E. Kelsay and Frederick W. Pernell. SL no. 27. 1971.

Louisiana—Maxwell, Richard S. Louisiana and Its History: A Discussion of Sources in the National Archives. *Louisiana History* 13 (Spring 1972): 169-80.

New Hampshire—Owens, James K. Federal Court Records of New Hampshire. *Historical New Hampshire* 25 (Fall 1970): 37-40.

New Mexico—Lounsbury, Ralph G. Materials in the National Archives for the History of New Mexico before 1848. *New Mexico Historical Review* 21 (1946): 247-56.

New York—Morris, Richard B. The Federal Archives of New York City: Opportunities for Historical Research. *AHR* 42 (1937): 256-72.

North Carolina—McConnell, Roland C. Records in the National Archives Pertaining to the History of North Carolina. *North Carolina Historical Review* 25 (1948): 318-40.

Oklahoma—Murphy, Kathryn M. Oklahoma History and the National Archives. *Chronicles of Oklahoma* 30 (1952): 105-20.

Pennsylvania—Connor, R.D.W. The National Archives and Pennsylvania History. *Pennsylvania History* 7 (1940): 63-78.

Hamer, Philip M. The Records of the Federal Government as Materials for the History of Pennsylvania in World War II. *Pennsylvanian* 6 (1949): 45-46.

Wood, Richard G. Research Materials in the National Archives Pertaining to Pennsylvania. *Pennsylvania Magazine of History and Biography* 69 (1945): 89-102.

South Carolina—Dickson, Maxey R. Sources for South Carolina. History in the Nation's Capital. *Proceedings of the South Carolina Historical Association, 1942,* pp. 50-54.

Texas—Evans, Luther H. Texana in the Nation's Capital. *Southwestern Historical Quarterly* 50 (1946): 220-35.

Lounsbury, Ralph G. Early Texas and the National Archives. Ibid. 46 (1943): 203-13.

Vermont—Franklin, W. Neil. Materials in the National Archives Relating to Vermont. *Vermont History* 27 (1959): 240-55.

Gorham, Alan. Federal Court Records Pertaining to Vermont: Sources for Study. Ibid. 36 (1968): 142-43.

Virginia— Gondos, Victor, Jr., and Dorothy Gondos. Materials in the National Archives Relating to Alexandria, Virginia. *Virginia Magazine of History and Biography* 57 (1949): 421-32.

Wisconsin—NA. *Cartographic Records Relating to the Territory of Wisconsin,* 1836-1848, compiled by Laura E. Kelsay and Charlotte M. Ashby. SL no. 23. 1970.

Smith, Jane F. The Use of Federal Records in Writing Local History: A Case Study. *Prologue* 1 (Spring 1969): 29-51.

Wyoming— Jackson, W. Turrentine. Territorial Papers of Wyoming in the National Archives. *Annals of Wyoming* 16 (1944): 45-55.

Records Relating to Administrative, Political, and Military Topics

General

Cain, Robert H. Policy and Administrative Records of the Veterans Administration. *AA* 25 (1962): 455-66.

Hays, Samuel P. Archival Sources for American Political History. *AA* 28 (1965): 17-30.

Hays. The Use of Archives for Historical Statistical Inquiry. *Prologue* 1 (Fall 1969): 7-15.

Hoslett, Schuyler. On the Writing of

Administrative History: Civil and Military Agencies. *Americana* 37 (1943): 527-34.

Stark, Marie C. Policy Documentation in the War Production Board. *AA* 9 (1946): 26-46.

Trever, Karl L. Administrative History in Federal Archives. *AA* 4 (1941): 159-69.

*War Fronts and Home Fronts**

Lokke, Carl L. The Continental Congress Papers: Their History, 1789-1952. *NA Accessions* no. 51 (1954): 1-19.

NA. *Guide to Federal Archives Relating to the Civil War,* compiled by Kenneth W. Munden and Henry P. Beers. 1962.

NA. *Guide to the Archives of the Government of the Confederate States of America,* compiled by Henry P. Beers. 1968.

NA. *Civil War Maps in the National Archives.* 1964.

Irvine, Dallas D. The Genesis of the *Official Records. MVHR* 24 (1937): 221-29.

Rhoads, James B. Civil War Maps and Mapping. *Military Engineer* 49 (1957): 38-43.

Carnegie Endowment for International Peace. *Introduction to the American Official Sources for the Economic and Social History of the World War,* compiled by Waldo G. Leland and Newton D. Mereness. New Haven, 1926.

Lokke, Carl L. A Sketch of the Interallied Organizations of the First World War and Their Records. *AA* 7 (1944): 225-35.

NA. *Handbook of Federal World War Agencies and Their Records,* 1917-1921. 1943.

Kahn, Herman. World War II and Its Background: Research Materials at the Franklin D. Roosevelt Library and Policies Covering Their Use. *AA* 17 (1954): 149-62.

Epstein, Fritz T. Washington Research Opportunities in the Period of World War II. *AA* 17 (1954): 225-36.

Hamer, Philip M. The Records of the Federal Government as Materials for the History of Pennsylvania in World War II. *Pennsylvanian* 6 (1949): 45-46.

NA. *Materials in the National Archives Relating to World War II,* compiled by G. Philip Bauer. RIP no. 39. 1949.

NA. *Federal Records of World War II.* vol. 1, *Civilian Agencies,* 1950. vol. 2, *Military Agencies,* 1951.

NA. *Materials in the National Archives Relating to the Historical Programs of Civilian Government Agencies during World War II.* RIP no. 43. 1952.

Van Riper, Paul P. A Survey of Materials for the Study of Military Management. *Political Science Review* 49 (1955): 828-50.

Postwar Reorganization

NA. *Materials in the National Archives Relating to the Liquidation of Federal Agencies, 1917-44,* compiled by Guy A. Lee. RIC no. 31. 1945.

NA. *Materials in the National Archives Relating to the Termination of Economic Controls by Government Agencies Following World War I,* compiled by G. Philip Bauer. RIC no. 32. 1945.

---

*Arranged by the period covered.

Territorial and Military Government

Holmes, Oliver W. Territorial Government and Records of Its Administration. In *The Frontier Reexamined,* edited by John F. McDermott. Urbana, 1967, pp. 97-109.

NA. *Materials in the National Archives Relating to Military Government by the United States in the Caribbean Area, 1898-1934,* compiled by Kenneth W. Munden and Forrest L. Foor. RIC no. 26. 1944.

Records Relating to Economic Topics

General and Statistical

Copeland, Morris A. The Significance of Archives to the Economist and Sociologist. *Proceedings of the Society of American Archivists, 1936-37,* pp. 47-51.

Fishbein, Meyer H. The Censuses of Manufactures, 1810-1890. *NA Accessions* no. 57 (1963): 1-20.

Fishbein. Early Business Statistical Operations of the Federal Government. Ibid. no. 54 (1958): 1-29.

Holverstott, Lyle J. The General Accounting Office Accession: Its History and Significance. Ibid. no. 52 (1956): 1-11.

Lambert, Robert S. Income-Tax Records as Sources for Economic History. *AA* 24 (1961): 341-44.

NA. *Material in the National Archives Containing Statistical Data on Economic Subjects, 1910-44,* compiled by Guy A. Lee. RIP no. 33. 1945.

Parmalee, J.H. The Statistical Work of the Federal Government. *Yale Review* 19 (1910/11): 289-308, 374-81.

Pumphrey, Lowell J. Materials in the National Archives of Especial Interest for Economists. *American Economic Review* 31 (1941): 344-45.

Statistical Source Materials in the National Archives. *Statistical Reporter* 89 (1945): 82-83.

Ullman, Morris B. The Records of a Statistical Survey. *AA* 5 (1942): 28-35.

Agriculture

Edwards, Everett E. Agricultural Records: Their Nature and Value for Research. *Agricultural History* 13 (1939): 1-12.

Kulsrud, Carl J. The Archival Records of the Agricultural Adjustment Program. Ibid. 22 (1948): 197-204.

Lee, Guy A. The General Records of the United States Department of Agriculture in the National Archives. Ibid. 19 (1945): 242-49.

Pinkett, Harold T. Early Records of the U.S. Department of Agriculture. *AA* 25 (1962): 407-16.

Pinkett. The Archival Product of a Century of Federal Assistance to Agriculture. *AHR* 69 (1964): 689-706.

Pinkett. Records of the First Century of Interest of the United States Government in Plant Industries. *Agricultural History* 29 (1955): 38-45.

Pinkett. Federal Agricultural Records: Preserving the Valuable Core. Ibid. 42 (1968): 139-46.

Commerce, Business, and Industry

Fishbein, Meyer H. Business History Resources in the National Archives. *Business History Review* 38 (1964): 232-57.

Hamer, Elizabeth E. National Archives Aids Businessmen. *Domestic Commerce* 41 (1943): 6-7.

Hancock, Harold B. Materials for Company History in the National Archives. *AA* 29 (1966): 23-32.

Kahn, Herman. Records in the National Archives Relating to the Range Cattle Industry, 1865-1895. *Agricultural History* 20 (1946): 187-90.

Lewinson, Paul. The Industrial Records Division of the National Archives: Economics, Welfare, and Science in United States History. *NA Accessions* no. 55 (1960): 1-7.

NA. *Materials in the National Archives Relating to the Basic Iron, Steel, and Tin Industries,* compiled by Jesse E. Boell. RIC no. 23. 1943.

NA. *Materials in the National Archives Relating to Small Business,* compiled by Forrest L. Foor. RIC no. 20. 1943.

Porter, Patrick G. Source Material for Economic History: Records of the Bureau of Corporations. *Prologue* 2 (1970): 31-33.

Rowland, Buford, and G.B. Snedeker. The United States Court of Claims and French Spoliation Records. *Bulletin of the Business History Society* 18 (1944): 20-27.

Postwar Reconversion

NA. *Materials in the National Archives Relating to the Disposition of Surplus Property Following the First World War,* compiled by Guy A. Lee. RIC no. 27. 1944.

NA. *Materials in the National Archives Relating to the Termina-tion of Economic Controls by Government Agencies Following World War I,* compiled by G. Philip Bauer. RIP no. 32. 1945.

NA. *Materials in the National Archives Relating to the Termination or Modification of Contracts and the Settlement of Claims Following the First World War,* compiled by Guy A. Lee. RIP no. 24. 1944.

Labor

Cannon, M. Hamlin, and Herbert Fine. Repository of Labor Records. *American Federationist* 50 (1943): 29.

Fishbein, Meyer H. Labor History Resources in the National Archives. *Labor History* 8 (1967): 330-51.

Harvey, O.L. Inventory of Department of Labor Archives. Ibid. 4 (1963): 196-98.

NA. *Materials in the National Archives Relating to Labor and Labor Problems.* RIC no. 10. 1942.

NA. *Materials in the National Archives Relating to Labor Migration during the First World War and the Post-War Period.* RIC no. 15. 1943.

NA. *Materials in the National Archives Relating to the Demobilization of the Armed Forces and to the Relief, Rehabilitation, and Employment of Veterans Following World War I,* compiled by Evangeline Thurber. RIC no. 28. 1944.

Forests

NA. *Materials in the National Archives Relating to Forest Products.* RIC no. 19. 1943.

NA. *Materials in the National Archives Relating to the Work of* the Civilian Conservation Corps, compiled by Evangeline Thurber. RIC no. 30. 1944.

Pinkett, Harold T. The Forest Service, Trail Blazer in Recordkeeping Methods. *AA* 22 (1959): 419-26.

Pinkett. Records of Research Units of the United States Forest Service in the National Archives. *Journal of Forestry* 45 (1947): 272-75.

Pinkett. Forest Service Records as Research Material. *Forest History* 13 (1970): 18-29.

Public Lands

Gates, Paul W. Research in the History of American Land Tenure. *Agricultural History* 28 (1954): 121-26.

Gumm, Clark. The Foundation of Land Records. *Our Public Lands* 7 (1957): 12-14.

Harrison, Robert W. Public Land Records of the Federal Government. *MVHR* 41 (1954): 277-88.

Heard, John P. Resource for Historians: Records of the Bureau of Land Management in California and Nevada. *Forest History* 12 (1968): 20-26.

Thomas, Earl J. From Old Records to New. *Our Public Lands* 7 (1957): 6-7, 15.

Select Subjects

Doeringsfeld, Walter W., and Dwight L. Greene. Exploring the Sea: Riches from Government Files. *Ocean Industry* 4 (1969): 44-50.

Guthrie, Chester L. The United States Grain Corporation Records in the National Archives. *Agri-*

cultural History 12 (1938): 347-54.

NA. *Materials in the National Archives Relating to the Dehydration of Foods.* RIC no. 21. 1943.

NA. *Materials in the National Archives Relating to Food Production and Distribution, 1917-40.* RIC no. 17. 1943.

NA. *Materials in the National Archives Relating to Nutrition and Food Conservation by Consumers, 1917-1941,* compiled by Lillie A. Bontz and Max Levin. RIC no. 25. 1944.

NA. *Materials in the National Archives Relating to Rubber,* compiled by Robert H. Lando. RIC no. 29. 1944.

NA. *Materials in the National Archives Relating to Transportation.* RIC no. 16. 1943. rev. ed. RIC no. 36. 1948.

Wright, Almon B. Food and Society: War Time Archives of the United States Food Administration. *American Scholar* 7 (1938): 243-46.

Wright. Records of the Food Administration: New Field for Research. *Public Opinion Quarterly* 3 (1939): 278-84.

Wright. World War Food Controls and Archival Sources for Their Study. *Agricultural History* 15 (1941): 72-73.

Records Relating to
Social and Cultural Topics

General

Copeland, Morris A. The Significance of Archives to the Economist and Sociologist. *Proceedings of the Society of American Archivists, 1936-37,* pp. 47-51.

Crawford, William R. Sociological Research in the National Archives. *American Sociological Review* 6 (1941): 203-16.

Pinkett, Harold T. Records in the National Archives as Sources for Research in the Social Sciences. *Social Studies* 43 (1952): 147-51.

Tucker, Sarah J. Archival Materials for the Anthropologist in the National Archives, Washington, D.C. *American Anthropologist* 43 (1941): 617-44.

U.S. Social Security Administration, Office of Research and Statistics. *Social Security Sources in Federal Records, 1934-1950,* by Abe Bortz. 1969.

National, Ethnic, and Racial Groups

Calkin, Homer L. The United States Government and the Irish. *Irish Historical Studies* 9 (1954): 28-54. (Valuable for records dealing with all immigration.)

Forman, Grant. A Survey of Tribal Records in the Archives of the United States Government in Oklahoma. *Chronicles of Oklahoma* 11 (1932): 625-34.

Hill, Edward E. The Tucson Agency: The Use of Indian Records in the National Archives. *Prologue* 4 (Summer 1972): 77-82.

Lewinson, Paul, comp. *A Guide to Documents in the National Archives: For Negro Studies.* American Council of Learned Societies, Committee on Negro Studies Publication no. 1. 1947.

Litton, Gaston. The Resources of the National Archives for the Study of the American Indian. *Ethnohistory* 2 (1955): 191-208.

McConnell, Roland C. Importance of the Records in the National Archives on the History of the Negro. *Journal of Negro History* 34 (1949): 135-52.

Mock, James R. The National Archives with Respect to the Records of the Negro. Ibid. 23 (1938): 49-56.

NA. *Calendar of Negro-Related Documents in the Records of the Committee for Congested Production Areas in the National Archives,* compiled by Elaine E. Bennett for the American Council of Learned Societies, Committee on Negro Studies. 1949.

Pinkett, Harold T. Recent Federal Archives as Sources for Negro History. *Negro History Bulletin* 30 (1967): 14-17.

Reingold, Nathan. Resources on American Jewish History in the National Archives. *Publications of the American Jewish Historical Society* 47 (1958): 186-95.

Select Subjects

Atkins, James A. Resource Materials and Agencies for Adult Education. *Journal of Negro Education,* Summer 1945, pp. 494-508.

Kulsrud, Carl J. Sampling Rural Rehabilitation Records for Transfer to the National Archives. *AA* 10 (1947): 328-34.

Lewinson, Paul. The Industrial Records Division of the National Archives: Economics, Welfare, and Science in United States History. *NA Accessions* no. 55 (1960): 1-7.

Pinkett, Harold T. Records in the National Archives Relating to the Social Purposes and Results of the Operation of the Civilian Conservation Corps. *Social Service Review* 22 (1948): 46-53.

Records Relating to Science and Technology

General

Buck, Solon J. The National Archives and the Advancement of Science. *Science* 83 (1936): 379-85.

Grover, Wayne C. The Role of the Archivist in the Preservation of Scientific Records. *Isis* 53 (1962): 55-62.

Lewinson, Paul. The Industrial Records Division of the National Archives: Economics, Welfare, and Science in United States History. *NA Accessions* no. 55 (1960): 1-7.

Reingold, Nathan. The National Archives and the History of Science in America. *Isis* 46 (1955): 22-28.

Records of Specific Agencies

Collier, Clyde M. The Archivist and Weather Records. *AA* 26 (1963): 477-85.

Darter, Lewis J., Jr. History and Records of the Weather Bureau and Its Predecessor Agencies. *Bulletin of the American Meterological Society* 23 (1942): 172.

Hogan, Donald W. Unwanted Treasures of the Patent Office. *American Heritage* 9 (1958): 16-19, 101-3.

Jackson, Joseph G. Records of Research. *Patent Office Society Journal* 35 (1953): 239-58.

Reingold, Nathan. Research Possibilities in the U.S. Coast and Geodetic Survey Records. *Archives internationales de l'Histoire des Sciences* 11 (1958): 337-46.

Reingold. Science in the Civil War: The Permanent Commission of the Navy Department. *Isis* 49 (1958): 307-18.

Reingold. U.S. Patent Office Records as Sources for the History of Invention and Technological Property. *Technology and Culture* 1 (1960): 156-67.

Rubincam, Milton. Charles J. Wister's Weather Reports in the National Archives. *Pennsylvanian* 4 (1956): 5.

Records Containing Data on Individuals

Alldredge, Everett O. The Federal Records Center, St. Louis: Personnel Files and Fiscal Records. *AA* 18 (1955): 111-22.

Bethel, Elizabeth. Records in the National Archives, Washington, D.C., of Significance for Genealogists. *American Genealogist* 18 (1945): 193-201.

Carroll, Mrs. Kieran J. Sources for Genealogical Research in State Department Records. *National Genealogical Society Quarterly* 52 (1964): 189-98.

Franklin, W. Neil. Availability of Federal Census Schedules in the States. Ibid. 50 (1962): 19-25.

Lathrop, Barnes F. History from the Census Returns. *Southwestern Historical Quarterly* 51 (1948): 293-312.

NA. *Civilian Personnel Records in the National Archives,* compiled by Seymour J. Pomrenze. RIC no. 37. 1948. (These records are now in the National Personnel Records Center, St. Louis, Mo.)

NA. *Guide to Genealogical Records in the National Archives,* compiled by Meredith B. Colket, Jr., and Frank E. Bridgers. 1964.

Owen, Thomas M., Jr. How the National Archives Can Aid Genealogists. *National Genealogical Society Quarterly* 36 (1948): 37-41, reprinted from *Alabama Historical Quarterly* 8 (1946): 25-34.

Rubincam, Milton. Genealogical Research in the National Archives: Historical Background and Facilities for Research. *New England Historical and Genealogical Register* 105 (1951): 42-48.

Smith, Jane F. The Use of Federal Records in Writing Local History: A Case Study. *Prologue* 1 (Spring 1969): 29-51.

U.S. Social Security Administration, Office of Research and Statistics. *Social Security Sources in Federal Records, 1934-1950,* by Abe Bortz. 1969.

Wright, Almon B. The Scholar's Interest in Personnel Records. *AA* 12 (1949): 271-79.

Recordkeeping Practices and Published Finding Aids for Accessioned Records of Individual Agencies*

General United States Government

Records of the Continental and Confederation Congresses and the Constitutional Convention (RG 360)

Lokke, Carl L. The Continental Congress Papers: Their History, 1789-1952. *NA Accessions* no. 51 (1954): 1-19.

War Department Collection of Revolutionary War Records (RG 93)

NA. *Preliminary Inventory of the War Department Collection of Revolutionary War Records,* compiled by Mabel E. Deutrich, revised by Howard H. Wehmann. PI no. 144. 1970.

General Records of the United States Government (RG 11)

NA. *Preliminary Inventory of United States Government Documents Having General Legal Effect,* compiled by Ralph E. Huss. PI no. 159. 1964.

Records of the Legislative Branch

Records of the United States Senate (RG 46)

NA. *Preliminary Inventory of the Records of the United States Senate,* compiled by Harold E. Hufford and Watson G. Caudill. PI no. 23. 1950.

NA. *Preliminary Inventory of the Records of Certain Committees of the Senate Investigating the Disposal of Surplus Property, 1945-48,* compiled by George P. Perros and Toussaint L. Prince. PI no. 59. 1953.

NA. *Preliminary Inventory of the Records of the Senate Committee on Appropriations: Subcommittee on Inquiry in re Transfer of Employees, 1942,* compiled by Theodore J. Cassady and Harold E. Hufford. PI no. 12. 1948.

NA. *Preliminary Inventory of the Records of the Senate Committee on Education and Labor: Subcommittee on Wartime Health and Education, 1943-46,* compiled by George P. Perros. PI no. 42. 1952.

NA. *Preliminary Inventory of the Records of the Senate Committee on Interstate Commerce: Subcommittee to Investigate Interstate Railroads, 1935-43,* compiled by Albert U. Blair and John W. Porter. PI no. 75. 1954.

NA. *Preliminary Inventory of the Records of the Special Committee of the Senate on Atomic Energy, 1945-46,* compiled by George P. Perros. PI no. 62. 1953.

NA. *Preliminary Inventory of the Records of the Special Committee of the Senate to Investigate Air-Mail and Ocean-Mail Contracts, 1933-35,* compiled by Watson G. Caudill, Toussaint L. Prince, and Albert U. Blair. PI no. 63. 1953.

NA. *Preliminary Inventory of the Records of the Special Committee of the Senate to Investigate the National Defense Program, 1941-48,* compiled by Harold E. Hufford and Toussaint L. Prince. PI no. 48. 1952.

NA. *Preliminary Inventory of the Records of the Special Committee of the Senate to Investigate Petroleum Resources, 1944-46,* compiled by George P. Perros. PI no. 61. 1953.

NA. *Papers of the United States Senate Relating to Presidential Nominations, 1789-1901,* compiled by George P. Perros, James C. Brown, and Jacqueline A. Wood. SL no. 20. 1964.

NA. *Hearings in the Records of the U.S. Senate and Joint Committees of Congress,* compiled by Charles E. South and James C. Brown. SL no. 32. 1972.

Records of the United States House of Representatives (RG 233)

Rowland, Buford. Recordkeeping Practices of the House of Representatives. *NA Accessions* no. 53 (1957): 1-19.

NA. *Preliminary Inventory of the Records of the United States House of Representatives, 1789-1946,* compiled by Buford Rowland, Handy B. Fant, and Harold E. Hufford. PI no. 113, 2 vols., 1959.

NA. *Preliminary Inventory of the Records of the Appropriations Committee of the House of Representatives: Subcommittee on the Works Progress Administration, 1939-41,* compiled by George P. Perros. PI no. 107. 1958.

NA. *Preliminary Inventory of Certain Committees of the House of Representatives Investigating the Disposal of Surplus Property, 1946-48,* compiled by George P. Perros. PI no. 65. 1954.

NA. *Preliminary Inventory of the Records of the House Committee on the Civil Service Pertaining to the Investigation of Civilian Employment in the Federal Government, 1942-46,* compiled by George P. Perros. PI no. 69. 1954.

NA. *Preliminary Inventory of the Records of the House of Representatives Select Committee of Inquiry into Operations of the United States Air Services, 1924-25,* compiled by George P. Perros. PI no. 108. 1958.

NA. *Preliminary Inventory of the Records of the House of Representatives Select Committee to Investigate Real Estate Bondholders' Reorganizations, 1934-38,* compiled by José D. Lizardo. PI no. 96. 1956.

NA. *Preliminary Inventory of the Records of the Military Affairs Committee of the House of Representatives Relating to an Investigation of the War Department, 1934-36,* compiled by

George P. Perros. PI no. 80. 1955.

NA. *Preliminary Inventory of the Records of the Select Committee of the House of Representatives Investigating National Defense Migration, 1940-43*, compiled by George P. Perros. PI no. 17. 1954.

NA. *Preliminary Inventory of the Records of the Select Committee of the House of Representatives on Foreign Aid, 1947-48*, compiled by George P. Perros. PI no. 111. 1958.

NA. *Preliminary Inventory of the Records of the Select Committee of the House of Representatives on Post-War Military Policy, 1944-46*, compiled by George P. Perros. PI no. 70. 1954.

NA. *Preliminary Inventory of the Records of the Select Committee of the House of Representatives to Investigate Acts of Executive Agencies Beyond the Scope of Their Authority, 1943-46*, compiled by George P. Perros. PI no. 84. 1955.

NA. *Preliminary Inventory of the Records of the Select Committee of the House of Representatives to Investigate Air Accidents, 1941-43*, compiled by George P. Perros. PI no. 67. 1954.

Records of Joint Committees of Congress (RG 128)

NA. *Hearings in the Records of the U.S. Senate and Joint Committees of Congress*, compiled by Charles E. South and James C. Brown. SL no. 32. 1972.

NA. *Preliminary Inventory of the Records of the Joint Congressional Aviation Policy Board, 1947-48*, compiled by Watson

G. Caudill and George P. Perros. PI no. 74. 1954.

Records of the United States General Accounting Office (RG 217)

Holverstott, Lyle J. The General Accounting Office Accession: Its History and Significance. *NA Accessions* no. 52 (1956): 1-11.

Records of the Judicial Branch

Campbell, William J. A Jurist's View of the Legal History Contained in Federal Court Records. *Chicago Bar Record* 53 (March 1972): 261-63.

Glenn. The Supreme Court Collection at the National Archives. *American Journal of Legal History* 4 (1960): 241-56.

Records of the Supreme Court of the United States (RG 267)

Browning, James R., and Bess Glenn. The Supreme Court Collection at the National Archives. *American Journal of Legal History* 4 (1960): 241-56.

NA. *Preliminary Inventory of the Records of the Supreme Court of the United States*, compiled by Marion M. Johnson. PI no. 139. 1962.

NA. *Index to the Manuscript and Revised Printed Opinions of the Supreme Court of the United States in the National Archives, 1808-73*, compiled by Marion M. Johnson, Elaine C. Everly, and Toussaint L. Prince. SL no. 21. 1965.

Records of District Courts of the United States (RG 21)

NA. *List of Pre-1840 Federal District and Circuit Court Records*, compiled by R. Michael McReynolds. SL no. 31. 1972.

NA. *Preliminary Inventory of the Records of the United States District Court for the Eastern District of Pennsylvania,* compiled by Marion M. Johnson, Mary J. Grotenrath, and Henry T. Ulasek. PI no. 124. 1960.

NA. *Preliminary Inventory of the Records of the United States District Court for the Southern District of New York,* compiled by Henry T. Ulasek and Marion M. Johnson. PI no. 116. 1959.

Records of the United States Court of Claims (RG 123)

Cox, Henry B. A Nineteenth-Century Archival Search: The History of the French Spoliation Claims Papers. *AA* 33 (1970): 389-401.

Rowland, Buford, and G.B. Snedeker. The United States Court of Claims and Spoliation Records. *Bulletin of the Business History Society* 18 (1944): 20-27.

NA. *Preliminary Inventory of the Records of the United States Court of Claims,* compiled by Gaiselle Kerner. PI no. 58. 1953.

Records of the Executive Branch
GENERAL

Chatfield, Helen L. The Development of Record Systems. *AA* 13 (1950): 259-67.

Glenn, Bess. The Taft Commission and the Government's Record Practices. *AA* 21 (1958): 277-303.

Gondos, Victor, Jr. The Era of the Woodruff File. *AA* 19 (1956): 303-20.

Krauskopf, Robert W. The Hoover Commissions and Federal Recordkeeping. *AA* 21 (1958): 371-99.

Pinkett, Harold T. Investigations of Federal Recordkeeping, 1887-1906. *AA* 21 (1958): 163-92.

Pinkett. New York as the Temporary National Capital, 1785-1790: The Archival Heritage. *NA Accessions* no. 60 (1967): 1-11.

RECORDS OF PRESIDENTIAL AGENCIES

Records of the Bureau of the Budget (RG 51)

NA. *Preliminary Inventory of the Records of the Central Bureau of Planning and Statistics,* compiled by Gaiselle Kerner. PI no. 98. 1957.

Records of Presidential Committees, Commissions, and Boards (RG 220)

NA. *Preliminary Inventory of the Records of the American War Production Mission in China,* compiled by John E. Maddox. PI no. 88. 1955.

NA. *Preliminary Inventory of the Records of the Commission on the Renovation of the Executive Mansion,* compiled by Bess Glenn. PI no. 117. 1959.

NA. *Preliminary Inventory of the Records of the President's Air Policy Commission,* compiled by Henry T. Ulasek. PI no. 49. 1952.

NA. *Preliminary Inventory of the Records of the President's Commission on Migratory Labor,* compiled by Hardee Allen. PI no. 86. 1955.

NA. *Inventory of the Records of the Rubber Survey Committee,* compiled by Philip P. Brower. 1947.

NA. *Preliminary Inventory of the Records of the War Refugee Board,* compiled by Henry T.

Ulasek and Ira N. Kellogg, Jr. PI no. 43. 1952.

Records of the President's Organization on Unemployment Relief (RG 73)

NA. *Preliminary Inventory of the Records of the President's Organization on Unemployment Relief,* compiled by Leo Pascal. PI no. 137. 1962.

Records of the National Resources Planning Board (RG 187)

NA. *Preliminary Inventory of the Central Office Records of the National Resources Planning Board,* compiled by Virgil E. Baugh. PI no. 50. 1953.

NA. *Preliminary Inventory of the Records of the Regional Offices of the National Resources Planning Board,* compiled by Virgil E. Baugh. PI no. 64. 1954.

NA. *Preliminary List of Published and Unpublished Reports of the National Resources Planning Board, 1933-43,* compiled by Lester W. Smith, Estelle Rebec, and Mary F. Handley. 1946.

Records of the Office of Government Reports (RG 44)

NA. *Preliminary Inventory of the Records of the Office of Government Reports,* compiled by H. Stephen Helton. PI no. 35. 1951.

DEPARTMENT OF STATE

General Records of the Department of State (RG 59)

Allen, Andrew H. The Historical Archives of the Department of State. *Annual Report of the AHA, 1894,* pp. 281-98.

Gustafson, Milton, O. Foreign Relations Research in the National Archives. Depart-

ment of State *SHAFR Newsletter* 1 (1970): 17-18.

Gustafson. State Department Records in the National Archives: A Profile. *Prologue 2 (1970): 175-84.*

Helton, H. Stephen, *Recordkeeping in the Department of State, 1789-1956. NA Accessions* no. 56 (1961): 1-24.

Wright, Almon B. Archival Sources for the study of War-Time Relations of Latin America with the United States, 1917-1920: Illustrations of Their Use. *Inter-American Bibliographical Review* 1 (1941): 23-35.

NA. *Preliminary Inventory of the General Records of the Department of State,* compiled by Daniel T. Goggin and H. Stephen Helton. PI no. 157. 1963.

NA. *List of Documents Relating to Special Agents of the Department of State, 1789-1906,* compiled by Natalia Summers. SL no. 7. 1951.

Records of the Foreign Service Posts of the Department of State (RG 84)

Beers, Henry P. The American Consulate in California: Documents Relating to Its Establishment. *California Historical Society Quarterly* 37 (1958): 1-17.

Colket, Meredith B., Jr. The Preservation of Consular and Diplomatic Post Records of the United States. *AA* 6 (1943): 193-205.

Harrison, John P. The Archives of United States Diplomatic and Consular Posts in Latin America. *Hispanic American Historical Review* 33 (1953): 168-83.

Miller, Hunter. Transfer to the Department of State of the Older Archives of Certain American Embassies, Legations, and Consulates. *AHR* 39 (1933): 184-85.

NA. *Preliminary Inventory of the Records of Selected Foreign Service Posts,* compiled by Alexander P. Mavro. PI no. 60. 1953.

NA. *List of Foreign Service Post Records in the National Archives,* compiled by Mark G. Eckhoff and Alexander P. Mavro, revised by Mario D. Fenyo and John Highbarger. SL no. 9. 1967.

Records of Boundary and Claims Commissions and Arbitrations (RG 76)

Stark, Charlotte. Materials for Research in the Files of International Claims Commissions. *American Neptune* 3 (1943): 48-54.

NA. *Preliminary Inventory of Records Relating to Civil War Claims: United States and Great Britain,* compiled by George S. Ulibarri and Daniel T. Goggin. PI no. 135. 1962.

NA. *Preliminary Inventory of the Records Relating to International Boundaries,* compiled by Daniel T. Goggin. PI no. 170. 1968.

NA. *Preliminary Inventory of Records Relating to United States Claims against the Central Powers,* compiled by George S. Ulibarri and Francis J. Heppner. PI no. 143. 1962.

NA. *Preliminary Inventory of the Records of United States and Mexican Claims Commissions,* compiled by George S. Ulibarri. PI. no. 136. 1962.

Records of International Conferences, Commissions, and Expositions (RG 43)

NA. *Preliminary Inventory of the Records of United States Participation in International Conferences, Commissions, and Expositions,* compiled by H. Stephen Helton. PI no. 76. 1955.

Records of the American Commission to Negotiate Peace (RG 256)

NA. *Preliminary Inventory of the Records of the American Commission to Negotiate Peace,* compiled by H. Stephen Helton. PI no. 89. 1955.

NA. *Preliminary Inventory of the Cartographic Records of the American Commission to Negotiate Peace,* compiled by James B. Rhoads. PI no. 68. 1954.

DEPARTMENT OF THE TREASURY

Strobridge, Truman R. Archives of the Supervising Architect, Treasury Department, *Journal of the Society of Architectural Historians* 20 (1961): 198-99.

Records of the Bureau of the Public Debt (RG 53)

NA. *Preliminary Inventory of the "Old Loan" Records of the Bureau of the Public Debt,* compiled by Philip D. Lagerquist, Archie L. Abney, and Lyle J. Holverstott. PI no. 52. 1953.

Records of the Bureau of Customs (RG 36)

Morison, Samuel E. The Customhouse Records in Massachusetts as a Source of History. *Proceedings of the Massachusetts Historical Society* 54 (1920/21): 324-31.

NA. *Preliminary Inventory of the Records of the Collector of Customs, Puget Sound District, in the Federal Records Center, Seattle, Washington,* compiled by Elmer W. Lindgard. PI no. 122. 1960.

NA. *List of American-Flag Merchant Vessels That Received Certificates of Enrollment or Registry at the Port of New York, 1789-1867,* compiled by Forrest R. Holdcamper. SL no. 22, 2 vols., 1968.

Records of the Bureau of the Mint (RG 104)

NA. *Preliminary Inventory of the Records of the United States Mint at Philadelphia,* compiled by Lyle J. Holverstott and Jean McNiece. PI no. 40. 1952.

Records of the United States Secret Service (RG 87)

NA. *Preliminary Inventory of the Records of the United States Secret Service,* compiled by Lyle J. Holverstott. PI no. 16. 1949.

Records of the Internal Revenue Service (RG 58)

Lambert, Robert S. Income-Tax Records as Sources for Economic History. *AA* 24 (1961): 341-44.

NA. *Preliminary Inventory of the Records of the United States Direct Tax Commission for the District of South Carolina.* PI no. 14. 1948.

DEPARTMENT OF DEFENSE

Deutrich, Mabel E. Decimal Filing: Its General Background and an Account of Its Rise and Fall in the U.S. War Department. *AA* 28 (1965): 199-218.

Grover, Wayne C. War Department Records in the National Archives. *Journal of the American Military History Foundation* 1 (1937): 122.

Huber, Elbert L. War Department Records in the National Archives. Ibid. 6 (1942): 247-54.

Records of International Military Agencies (RG 333)

NA. *Preliminary Inventory of the Records of the Headquarters, United Nations Command,* compiled by Paul Taborn and Andrew Putignano. PI no. 127. 1960.

DEPARTMENT OF THE ARMY

Records of the Headquarters of the Army (RG 108)

NA. *Records of the Headquarters of the Army,* compiled by Aloha South. Inventory no. 1. 1970.

Records of the War Department General and Special Staffs (RG 165)

Bethel, Elizabeth. Early Records of the War Department General Staff in National Archives. *AA* 8 (1945):241-47.

Records of the Adjutant General's Office, 1780s-1917 (RG 94)

NA. *Preliminary Inventory of the Records of the Adjutant General's Office,* compiled by Lucille H. Pendell and Elizabeth Bethel. PI no. 17. 1949.

Records of the Office of the Chief of Engineers (RG 77)

Beers, Henry P. Records of the Office of the Chief of Engineers, War Department Archives. *Journal of the American Military History Foundation* 2 (1938): 94.

Records of the Office of the Inspector General (RG 159)

Owen, Arthur F. Opportunities for Research: The Early Records of the Office of the Inspector General, 1814-48. *Military Affairs* 7 (1943): 195-96.

Records of the Office of the Paymaster General (RG 99)

NA. *Preliminary Inventory of the Records of the Office of the Paymaster General,* compiled by Roland C. McConnell. PI no. 9. 1948.

Records of the Office of the Chief of Finance (Army) (RG 203)

NA. *Preliminary Inventory of the Records of the Office of the Chief of Finance (Army),* compiled by Richard W. Giroux, revised by Mazie H. Johnson. PI no. 142. 1962.

Records of the Office of the Chief Signal Officer (RG 111)

Phillips, Helen C. Signal Corps Historical Collection. *Military Affairs* 18 (1954): 88-89.

NA. *Preliminary Inventory of the Records of the Office of the Chief Signal Officer,* compiled by Mabel E. Deutrich. PI no. 155. 1963.

NA. *List of World War I Signal Corps Films,* compiled by K. Jack Bauer. SL no. 14. 1957.

Records of the Bureau of Refugees, Freedman, and Abandoned Lands (RG 105).

NA. *Preliminary Inventory of the Records of the Bureau of Refugees, Freedmen, and Abandoned Lands, Washington Headquarters,* compiled by Elaine Everly. PI no. 174. 1973.

Records of the Chemical Warfare Service (RG 175)

NA. *Preliminary Inventory of the Records of the Chemical Warfare Service,* compiled by Raymond P. Flynn. PI no. 8. 1948.

FIELD COMMANDS AND INSTALLATIONS

Smith, G. Hubert. Some Sources for Northwest History: The Ar-

chives of Military Posts. *Minnesota History* 22 (1941): 297-301.

Records of United States Army Continental Commands, 1821-1920 (RG 393).

NA. *Preliminary Inventory of the Records of the United States Army Continental Commands, 1821-1920.* Vol. 1, compiled by Elaine Everly et al. PI no. 172. 1973.

Records of the Military Government of Cuba (RG 140)

NA. *Preliminary Inventory of the Records of the Military Government of Cuba,* compiled by Margareth Jorgensen. PI no. 145. 1962.

Records of the Provisional Government of Cuba (RG 199)

NA. *Preliminary Inventory of the Records of the Provisional Government of Cuba,* compiled by Roland Rieder and Charlotte M. Ashby. PI no. 146. 1962.

Records of the Dominican Customs Receivership (RG 139)

NA. *Preliminary Inventory of the Records of the Dominican Customs Receivership,* compiled by Kenneth W. Munden. PI no. 148. 1962.

Records of the Military Government of Veracruz (RG 141)

NA. *Preliminary Inventory of the Records of the Military Government of Veracruz,* compiled by Kenneth W. Munden. PI no. 138. 1962.

Records of the American Expeditionary Forces (World War I), 1917-23 (RG 120)

NA. *Preliminary Inventory of the Cartographic Records of the American Expeditionary Forces, 1917-21,* compiled by Franklin W. Burch. PI no. 165. 1966.

NAVY DEPARTMENT

Bartlett, Kenneth F. Early Correspondence Filing Systems of the Office of the Secretary of the Navy. *NA Accessions* no. 58 (1964): 1-11.

Darter, Lewis J., Jr. Federal Archives Relating to Matthew Fontaine Maury. *American Neptune* 1 (1941): 149-58.

Fishwick, Marshall W. A Note on World War II Naval Records. *AHR* 55 (1949): 82-85.

Glenn, Bess. Navy Department Records in the National Archives. *Military Affairs* 7 (1943): 247-60.

Merrill, James M. The Naval Historian and His Sources. *AA* 32 (1969): 261-68.

Ray, Thomas W. Naval Aviation Photographs in the National Archives. *Military Affairs* 15 (1951): 207-9.

Reingold, Nathan. Science in the Civil War: The Permanent Commission of the Navy Department. *Isis* 49 (1958): 307-18.

Wood, Richard G. Records of the United States Naval Home, Philadelphia. *Pennsylvanian* 4 (1947): 31.

Records of the Office of the Chief of Naval Operations (RG 38)

NA. *Preliminary Inventory of the Cartographic Records of the Office of the Chief of Naval Operations*, compiled by Charlotte M. Ashby. PI no. 85. 1955.

Records of the United States Marine Corps (RG 127)

NA. *Records of the U.S. Marine Corps*, compiled by Mazie Johnson. Inventory no. 2. 1970.

NA. *Preliminary Inventory of the Cartographic Records of the United States Marine Corps*,

compiled by Charlotte M. Ashby. PI no. 73. 1954.

Records of the Bureau of Medicine and Surgery (RG 52)

NA. *Preliminary Inventory of the Records of the Bureau of Medicine and Surgery*, compiled by Kenneth F. Bartlett. PI no. 6. 1948.

Records of the Bureau of Ordnance (RG 74)

NA. *Preliminary Inventory of the Records of the Bureau of Ordnance*, compiled by William F. Shonkwiler. PI no. 33. 1951.

Records of the Bureau of Ships (RG 19)

NA. *Preliminary Inventory of the Records of the Bureau of Ships*, compiled by Elizabeth Bethel et al. PI no. 133. 1961.

Records of the Bureau of Yards and Docks (RG 71)

NA. *Preliminary Inventory of the Records of the Bureau of Yards and Docks*, compiled by Richard G. Wood. PI no. 10. 1948.

Records of the Bureau of Naval Personnel (RG 24)

NA. *Preliminary Inventory of the Records of the Bureau of Naval Personnel*, compiled by Virgil E. Baugh. PI no. 123. 1960.

Records of the Hydrographic Office (RG 37)

NA. *Inventory of the Records of the Hydrographic Office*, compiled by Mazie Johnson and William J. Heynen. Inventory no. 4. 1971.

Records of the Bureau of Aeronautics (RG 72)

NA. *Preliminary Inventory of the Records of the Bureau of Aeronautics*, compiled by William F. Shonkwiler. PI no. 26. 1951.

Records of Naval Districts and Shore Establishments (RG 181)

NA. *Preliminary Inventory of the*

Records of the Naval Establishments Created Overseas during World War II, compiled by Richard G. Wood. PI no. 13. 1948.

DEPARTMENT OF THE AIR FORCE

Atkinson, Gloria L. The Archives of the USAF Historical Division. *Special Libraries* 59 (1968): 444-46.

DEPARTMENT OF JUSTICE

Litton, Gaston L. Enrollment Records of the Eastern Band of Cherokee Indians. *North Carolina Historical Review* 17 (1940): 199-231.

Records of the United States Court for China. *American Journal of Legal History* 1 (1957): 234-35.

Records of the Office of the Pardon Attorney (RG 204)

NA. *Preliminary Inventory of the Records of the Office of the Pardon Attorney,* compiled by Gaiselle Kerner. PI no. 87. 1955.

Records of the Court of Claims Section (Justice) (RG 205)

NA. *Preliminary Inventory of the Records of the Court of Claims Section of the Department of Justice,* compiled by Gaiselle Kerner and Ira N. Kellogg, Jr. PI no. 47. 1952.

Records of the Solicitor of the Treasury (RG 206)

NA. *Preliminary Inventory of the Records of the Solicitor of the Treasury,* compiled by George S. Ulibarri. PI no. 171. 1968.

POST OFFICE DEPARTMENT

Tingley, Ralph R. United States

Government Documents as Source of Postal History. *American Philatelist* 63 (1949): 55-57.

Records of the Post Office Department (RG 28)

NA. *Preliminary Inventory of the Records of the Post Office Department,* compiled by Arthur Hecht et al., revised by Forrest R. Holdcamper. PI no. 168. 1967.

DEPARTMENT OF THE INTERIOR

Dewing, Charles E. The Wheeler Survey Records: A Study in Archival Anomaly. *AA* 27 (1964): 219-27.

Jackson, W. Turrentine. Materials for Western History in the Department of Interior Archives. *MVHR* 35 (1948): 61-76.

Records of the Office of the Secretary of the Interior (RG 48)

NA. *Preliminary Inventory of the Cartographic Records of the Office of the Secretary of the Interior,* compiled by Laura E. Kelsay. PI no. 81. 1955.

NA. *Index to Appropriation Ledgers in the Records of the Office of the Secretary of the Interior, Division of Finance, 1853-1923,* compiled by Catherine M. Rowland. SL no. 18. 1963.

Records of the Bureau of Land Management (RG 49)

Gates, Paul W. Research in the History of American Land Tenure. *Agricultural History* 28 (1954): 121-26.

Harrison, Robert W. Public Land Records of the Federal Government. *MVHR* 41 (1954): 277-88.

Heard, John P. Resource for Historians: Records of the Bureau of Land Management in California and Nevada. *Forest History* 12 (1968): 20-26.

Smith, Jane F. The Use of Federal Records in Writing Local History: A Case Study. *Prologue* 1 (Spring 1969): 29-51.

NA. *Preliminary Inventory of the Land-Entry Papers of the General Land Office,* compiled by Harry P. Yoshpe and Philip P. Brower. PI no. 22. 1949.

NA. *List of Cartographic Records of the General Land Office,* compiled by Laura E. Kelsay. SL no. 19. 1964.

Records of the Bureau of Indian Affairs (RG 75)

NA. *Preliminary Inventory of the Records of the Bureau of Indian Affairs,* compiled by Edward E. Hill. PI no. 163, 2 vols., 1965.

NA. *List of Cartographic Records of the Bureau of Indian Affairs,* compiled by Laura E. Kelsay. SL no. 13. 1954.

NA. *List of Documents Concerning the Negotiation of Ratified Indian Treaties, 1801-1869,* compiled by John H. Martin. SL no. 6. 1949.

Records of the National Park Service (RG 79)

Kahn, Herman. The National Archives Storehouse of National Park History. *Regional Review* 4 (1940): 13-17.

NA. *Preliminary Inventory of the Records of the National Park Service,* compiled by Edward E. Hill. PI no. 166. 1966.

Records of the Office of Territories (RG 126)

NA. *Preliminary Inventory of the Records of the Office of Territories,* compiled by Richard S. Maxwell and L. Evans Walker. PI. no. 154. 1963.

NA. *Preliminary Inventory of the*

Records of the Office of the U.S. High Commissioner of the Philippine Islands, compiled by Richard S. Maxwell. PI no. 151. 1963.

NA. *Preliminary Inventory of the Records of the United States Antarctic Service,* compiled by Charles E. Dewing and Laura E. Kelsay. PI no. 90. 1955.

Records of the Bureau of Reclamation (RG 115)

NA. *Preliminary Inventory of the Records of the Bureau of Reclamation,* compiled by Edward E. Hill. PI no. 109. 1958.

NA. *List of Photographs of Irrigation Projects of the Bureau of Reclamation,* compiled by Emma B. Haas, Anne H. Henry, and Thomas W. Ray. SL no. 15. 1959.

Records of the Commissioner of Railroads (RG 193)

NA. *Preliminary Inventory of the Records of the Commissioner of Railroads,* compiled by Marion M. Johnson. PI no. 158. 1964.

Records of the Bureau of Insular Affairs (RG 350)

NA. *Records of the Bureau of Insular Affairs,* compiled by Richard S. Maxwell. Inventory no. 3. 1971.

NA. *Records of the Bureau of Insular Affairs Relating to Puerto Rico, 1898-1934: A List of Selected Files,* compiled by Kenneth W. Munden and Milton Greenbaum. SL no. 4. 1943.

NA. *List of Records of the Bureau of Insular Affairs Relating to the Dominican Customs Receivership, 1905-1940,* compiled by Kenneth W. Munden. SL no. 5. 1943.

NA. *Records of the Bureau of Insular Affairs Relating to the*

Philippine Islands, 1898-1935: A List of Selected Files, compiled by Kenneth W. Munden. SL no. 2. 1942.

NA. *Records of the Bureau of Insular Affairs Relating to the United States Military Government of Cuba, 1898-1902, and the United States Provisional Government of Cuba, 1906-1909: A List of Selected Files,* compiled by Kenneth W. Munden. SL no. 3. 1943.

Records of the Puerto Rico Reconstruction Administration (RG 323)

NA. *Preliminary Inventory of the Records of the Puerto Rico Reconstruction Administration,* compiled by Mary J. Schmittou and Mario D. Fenyo. PI no. 152. 1963.

Records of the National Bituminous Coal Commission, 1935-36 (RG 150)

NA. *Preliminary Inventory of the Records of the National Bituminous Coal Commission, 1935-36,* compiled by Wallace B. Goebel, revised by Charles Zaid. PI no. 156. 1963.

Records of the Solid Fuels Administration for War (RG 245)

NA. *Preliminary Inventory of the Records of the Solid Fuels Administration for War,* compiled by Edward F. Martin. PI no. 34. 1951.

For Records of the Dominican Customs Receivership (RG 139), Records of the Military Government of Cuba (RG 140), and Records of the Provisional Government of Cuba (RG 199), see DEPARTMENT OF THE ARMY.

DEPARTMENT OF AGRICULTURE

Edwards, Everett E. Agricultural Records: Their Nature and Value for Research. *Agricultural History* 13 (1939): 1-12.

Kulsrud, Carl J. The Archival Records of the Agricultural Adjustment Program. Ibid. 22 (1948): 197-204.

Lee, Guy A. The General Records of the United States Department of Agriculture in the National Archives. Ibid. 19 (1945): 242-49.

Pinkett, Harold T. The Archival Product of a Century of Federal Assistance to Agriculture. *AHR* 69 (1964): 689-706.

Pinkett. Early Records of the U.S. Department of Agriculture. *AA* 25 (1962): 407-16.

Pinkett. Federal Agricultural Records: Preserving the Valuable Core. *Agricultural History* 42 (1968): 139-46.

Records of the Office of the Secretary of Agriculture (RG 16)

NA. *Preliminary Inventory of the Records of the Office for Agricultural War Relations,* compiled by Harold T. Pinkett. PI no. 37. 1952.

Records of the Forest Service (RG 95)

Pinkett, Harold T. The Forest Service, Trail Blazer in Recordkeeping Methods. *AA* 22 (1959): 419-26.

Pinkett. Records of Research Units of the United States Forest Service in the National Archives. *Journal of Forestry* 45 (1947): 272-75.

Pinkett. Forest Service Records as Research Material. *Forest History* 13 (1970): 18-29.

NA. *Preliminary Inventory of the Records of the Forest Service,* compiled by Harold T. Pinkett, revised by Terry W. Good. PI no. 18. 1969.

NA. *Preliminary Inventory of the Cartographic Records of the Forest Service*, compiled by Charlotte M. Ashby. PI no. 167. 1967.

NA. *Materials in the National Archives Relating to Forest Products*. RIC no. 19. 1943.

Records of the Commodity Exchange Authority (RG 180)

NA. *Preliminary Inventory of the Records of the Commodity Exchange Authority*, compiled by Stanley W. Brown and Virgil E. Baugh. PI no. 112. 1959.

Records of the Federal Extension Service (RG 33)

NA. *Preliminary Inventory of the Records of the Extension Service*, compiled by Virgil E. Baugh. PI no. 83. 1955.

Records of the Farmers Home Administration (RG 96)

NA. *Preliminary Inventory of the Records of the Farmers Home Administration*, compiled by Stanley W. Brown and Virgil E. Baugh. PI no. 118. 1959.

Records of the Bureau of Animal Industry (RG 17)

NA. *Preliminary Inventory of the Records of the Bureau of Animal Industry*, compiled by Harold T. Pinkett. PI no. 106. 1958.

Records of the Bureau of Plant Industry, Soils, and Agricultural Engineering (RG 54)

Pinkett, Harold T. Records of the First Century of Interest of the United States Government in Plant Industries. *Agricultural History* 29 (1955): 38-45.

NA. *Preliminary Inventory of the Records of the Bureau of Plant Industry, Soils, and Agricultural Engineering*, compiled by Harold T. Pinkett. PI no. 66. 1954.

Records of the Bureau of Agricultural Engineering (RG 8)

NA. *Preliminary Inventory of the Records of the Bureau of Agricultural Engineering*, compiled by Nathan Reingold. PI no. 53. 1953.

Records of the Bureau of Agricultural and Industrial Chemistry (RG 97)

NA. *Preliminary Inventory of the Records of the Bureau of Agricultural and Industrial Chemistry*, compiled by Helen T. Finneran. PI no. 149. 1962.

Records of the Bureau of Entomology and Plant Quarantine (RG 7)

NA. *Preliminary Inventory of the Records of the Bureau of Entomology and Plant Quarantine*, compiled by Harold T. Pinkett. PI no. 94. 1956.

Records of the Bureau of Agricultural Economics (RG 83)

NA. *Preliminary Inventory of the Records of the Bureau of Agricultural Economics*, compiled by Vivian Wiser. PI no. 104. 1958.

NA. *Writings Relevant to Farm Management in the Records of the Bureau of Agricultural Economics*, compiled by Vivian Wiser. SL no. 17. 1963.

NA. *Cartographic Records of the Bureau of Agricultural Economics*, compiled by William J. Heynen. SL no. 28. 1971.

Records of the Office of Labor (War Food Administration) (RG 224)

NA. *Preliminary Inventory of the Records of the Office of Labor of the War Food Administration*, compiled by Harold T. Pinkett. PI no. 51. 1953.

DEPARTMENT OF COMMERCE

Fishbein, Meyer H. Business History Resources in the National Archives. *Business History Review* 38 (1964): 232-57.

Fishbein. Early Business Statistical Operations of the Federal Government. *NA Accessions* no. 54 (1958): 1-29.

Hancock, Harold B. Materials for Company History in the National Archives. *AA* 29 (1966): 23-32.

Lewinson, Paul. The Industrial Records Division of the National Archives: Economics, Welfare, and Science in United States History. *NA Accessions* no. 55 (1960): 1-7.

NA. *Materials in the National Archives Relating to the Basic Iron, Steel, and Tin Industries,* compiled by Jesse E. Boell. RIC no. 23. 1943.

NA. *Materials in the National Archives Relating to Small Business,* compiled by Forrest L. Foor. RIC no. 20. 1943.

Porter, Patrick G. Source Material for Economic History: Records of the Bureau of Corporations. *Prologue* 2 (1970): 31-33.

Records of the Bureau of the Census (RG 29)

Fishbein, Meyer H. The Censuses of Manufactures, 1810-1890. *NA Accessions* no. 57 (1963): 1-20.

Lathrop, Barnes F. History from the Census Returns. *Southwestern Historical Quarterly* 51 (1948): 293-312.

NA. *Preliminary Inventory of the Records of the Bureau of the Census,* compiled by Katherine H. Davidson and Charlotte M. Ashby. PI no. 161. 1964.

NA. *Preliminary Inventory of the Cartographic Records of the Bureau of the Census,* compiled

by James B. Rhoads and Charlotte M. Ashby. PI no. 103. 1958.

NA. *Population Schedules, 1800-1870: Volume Index to Counties and Major Cities.* SL no. 8. 1951.

NA. *Federal Population and Mortality Schedules, 1790-1890, in the National Archives and the States: Outline of a Lecture on Their Availability, Content, and Use,* compiled by W. Neil Franklin. SL no. 24. 1971.

Records of the Patent Office (RG 241)

Hogan, Donald W. Unwanted Treasures of the Patent Office. *American Heritage* 9 (1958): 16-19, 101-3.

Jackson, Joseph G. Records of Research. *Journal of the Patent Office Society* 35 (1953): 239-58.

Reingold, Nathan. U.S. Patent Office Records as Sources for the History of Invention and Technological Property. *Technology and Culture* 1 (1960): 156-67.

Records of the Coast and Geodetic Survey (RG 23)

Reingold, Nathan. Research Possibilities in the U.S. Coast and Geodetic Survey Records. *Archives internationales de l'Historie des Sciences* 11 (1958): 337-46.

NA. *Preliminary Inventory of the Records of the Coast and Geodetic Survey,* compiled by Nathan Reingold. PI no. 105. 1958.

Records of the Weather Bureau (RG 27)

Collier, Clyde M. The Archivist and Weather Records. *AA* 26 (1963): 477-85.

Darter, Lewis J., Jr. History and

Records of the Weather Bureau and Its Predecessor Agencies. *Bulletin of the American Meteorological Society* 23 (1942): 172.

NA. *Preliminary Inventory of the Climatological and Hydrological Records of the Weather Bureau,* compiled by Harold T. Pinkett, Helen T. Finneran, and Katherine H. Davidson. PI no. 38. 1952.

NA. *List of Climatological Records in the National Archives,* compiled by Lewis J. Darter, Jr. SL no. 1. 1942.

Records of the Bureau of Marine Inspection and Navigation (RG 41)

Holdcamper, Forrest R. Registers, Enrollments, and Licenses in the National Archives. *American Neptune* 1 (1941): 275-94.

NA. *List of American-Flag Merchant Vessels That Received Certificates of Enrollment or Registry at the Port of New York, 1798-1867,* compiled by Forrest R. Holdcamper. SL no. 22, 2 vols., 1968.

DEPARTMENT OF LABOR

Cannon, M. Hamlin, and Herbert Fine. Repository of Labor Records. *American Federationist* 50 (1943): 29.

Fishbein, Meyer H. Labor History Resources in the National Archives. *Labor History* 8 (1967): 330-51.

Harvey, O.L. Inventory of Department of Labor Archives Ibid. 4 (1963): 196-98.

NA. *Materials in the National Archives Relating to Labor and Labor Problems.* RIC no. 10. 1942.

Records of the Wage Adjustment Board (RG 236)

NA. *Preliminary Inventory of the Records of the Wage Adjustment Board,* compiled by Leonard Rapport. PI no. 72, 1954.

DEPARTMENT OF HEALTH, EDUCATION, AND WELFARE

Records of the Public Health Service (RG 90)

NA. *Preliminary Inventory of the Records of the National Board of Health,* compiled by Charles Zaid. PI no. 141. 1962.

Records of the Social Security Administration (RG 47)

U.S. Social Security Administration, Office of Research and Statistics. *Social Security Sources in Federal Records, 1934-1950,* by Abe Bortz. 1969.

DEPARTMENT OF HOUSING AND URBAN DEVELOPMENT

General Records of the Department of Housing and Urban Development (RG 207)

NA. *Preliminary Inventory of the General Records of the Housing and Home Finance Agency,* compiled by Katherine H. Davidson. PI no. 164. 1965.

Records of the Federal Housing Administration (RG 31)

NA. *Preliminary Inventory of the Cartographic Records of the Federal Housing Administration,* compiled by Charlotte Munchmeyer. PI no. 45. 1952.

DEPARTMENT OF TRANSPORTATION

Records of the Bureau of Public Roads (RG 30)

NA. *Preliminary Inventory of the Records of the Bureau of Public Roads,* compiled by Truman R. Strobridge. PI no. 134. 1962.

Independent Agencies

CURRENT AGENCIES

Records of the Commission of Fine Arts (RG 66)

NA. *Preliminary Inventory of the Records of the Commission of Fine Arts,* compiled by Richard S. Maxwell. PI no. 79. 1955.

Records of the Federal Communications Commission (RG 173)

NA. *Preliminary Inventory of the Records of the Federal Communications Commission,* compiled by Albert W. Winthrop. PI no. 93. 1956.

Records of the Federal Trade Commission (RG 122)

NA. *Preliminary Inventory of the Records of the Federal Trade Commission,* compiled by Estelle Rebec. PI no. 7. 1948.

Records of the Panama Canal (RG 185)

NA. *Preliminary Inventory of the Textual Records of the Panama Canal,* compiled by Richard W. Giroux, revised by Garry D. Ryan. PI no. 153. 1963.

NA. *Preliminary Inventory of the Cartographic Records of the Panama Canal,* compiled by James B. Rhoads. PI no. 91. 1956.

Records of the Public Buildings Service (RG 121)

Strobridge, Truman R. Archives of the Supervising Architect, Treasury Department. *Journal of the Society of Architectural Historians* 80 (1961): 198-99.

NA. *Preliminary Inventory of the Records of the Public Buildings Service,* compiled by W. Lane Van Neste and Virgil E. Baugh. PI no. 110. 1958.

NA. *Title Papers of the Public Buildings Service,* compiled by W. Lane Van Neste and Virgil E. Baugh; revised by Stanley W. Brown. SL no. 30. 1972.

Records of the Selective Service System, 1940- (RG 147)

NA. *Preliminary Inventory of the Records of the Selective Service System, 1940-1947,* compiled by Richard G. Wood. PI no. 27. 1951.

Records of the Veterans Administration (RG 15)

NA. *Preliminary Inventory of the Administrative Records of the Bureau of Pensions and the Pension Service,* compiled by Thayer M. Boardman, Myra R. Trever, and Louise W. Southwick. PI no. 55. 1953.

DISCONTINUED AGENCIES— FROM WORLD WAR I TO 1933

Records of the Allied Purchasing Commission (RG 113)

NA. *Preliminary Inventory of the War Industries Board Records.* PI no. 1. 1941.

Records of the Council of National Defense (RG 62)

NA. *Preliminary Inventory of the Council of National Defense Records, 1916-1921.* PI no. 2. 1942.

Records of the National War Labor Board (World War I) (RG 2)

NA. *Preliminary Inventory of the Records of the National War Labor Board,* compiled by Herbert Fine. PI no. 5. 1943.

Records of the United States Food Administration (RG 4)

LaFuze, G. Leighton. The Puerto Rico Food Administration: Its Organization and Papers. *His-*

204   RESEARCH IN THE ADMINISTRATION OF PUBLIC POLICY

panic American Historical Review 21 (1941): 499-504.

Wright, Almon B. Food and Society: War Time Archives of
the United States Food Administration. American Scholar 7
(1938): 243-46.

Wright. Records of the Food Administration: New Field for Research. Public Opinion Quarterly 3 (1939): 278-284.

Wright. World War Food Controls and Archival Sources for
Their Study. Agricultural History 15 (1941): 72-73.

NA. Preliminary Inventory of the
Records of the United States
Food Administration, 1917-
1920. pt. 1, The Headquarters
Organization. PI no. 3. 1943.

Records of the United States Grain
Corporation (RG 5)

Guthrie, Chester L. The United
States Grain Corporation Records in the National Archives.
Agricultural History 12 (1938):
347-54.

Records of the United States Housing Corporation (RG 3)

NA. Preliminary Inventory of the
Records of the United States
Housing Corporation, compiled
by Katherine H. Davidson. PI
no. 140. 1962.

Records of the United States Shipping Board (RG 32)

NA. Preliminary Inventory of the
Records of the United States
Shipping Board, compiled by
Forrest R. Holdcamper. PI no.
97. 1956.

Records of the War Industries
Board (RG 61)

NA. Preliminary Inventory of the
War Industries Board Records.
PI no. 1. 1941.

Records of the War Labor Policies
Board (RG 1)

NA. Preliminary Inventory of the
War Labor Policies Board Records, compiled by Mary Walton
Livingston and Leo Pascal. PI
no. 4. 1943.

Records of the War Trade Board
(RG 182)

NA. Preliminary Inventory of the
Records of the War Trade
Board, compiled by Alexander
P. Mavro. PI no. 100. 1957.

DISCONTINUED AGENCIES—
SINCE 1933

Records of the Board of Investigation and Research—Transportation (RG 198)

NA. Preliminary Inventory of the
Records of the Board of In-
vestigation and Research,
Transportation, compiled by
Leo Pascal. PI no. 19 1949.

Records of the Civilian Conservation Corps (RG 35)

Pinkett, Harold T. Records in the
National Archives Relating to
the Social Purposes and Results of the Operation of the
Civilian Conservation Corps.
Social Service Review 22
(1948): 46-53.

NA. Preliminary Inventory of
the Records of the Civilian
Conservation Corps, compiled
by Harold T. Pinkett. PI no. 11.
1948.

Records of the Committee for Congested Production Areas (RG 212)

NA. Preliminary Inventory of the
Records of the Committee for
Congested Production Area,
compiled by Leo Pascal and
Jeanette McDonald. PI no. 128.
1960.

NA. Calendar of Negro-Related
Documents in the Records of
the Committee for Congested

Production Areas in the National Archives, compiled by Elaine E. Bennett for the American Council of Learned Societies, Committee on Negro Studies. 1949.

Records of the Committee on Fair Employment Practice (RG 228)

NA. *Preliminary Inventory of the Records of the Committee on Fair Employment Practice,* compiled by Charles Zaid. PI no. 147. 1962.

Records of the Foreign Broadcast Intelligence Service (RG 262)

NA. *Preliminary Inventory of the Records of the Foreign Broadcast Intelligence Service,* compiled by Walter W. Weinstein. PI no. 115. 1959.

Records of the Foreign Economic Administration (RG 169)

NA. *Preliminary Inventory of the Records of the Foreign Economic Administration,* compiled by H. Stephen Helton. PI no. 29. 1951.

Records of the Maritime Labor Board (RG 157)

NA. *Preliminary Inventory of the Records of the Maritime Labor Board,* compiled by Caroline W. Hiatt and Salvatore D. Nerboso. PI no. 20. 1949.

Records of the National Recovery Administration (RG 9)

NA. *Preliminary Inventory of the Records of the National Recovery Administration,* compiled by Homer L. Calkin, Meyer H. Fishbein, and Leo Pascal. PI no. 44. 1952.

NA. *Select List of Documents in the Records of the National Recovery Administration,* compiled by Homer L. Calkin and Meyer H. Fishbein. SL no. 12. 1954.

Records of the National War Labor Board (World War II) (RG 202)

NA. *Preliminary Inventory of the Records of the National War Labor Board (World War II),* compiled by Estelle Rebec. PI no. 78. 1955.

NA. *Lists of Wage Stabilization Cases Acted on by the Headquarters Offices of the National War Labor Board, 1942-45.* pt. 1, *Cases Arranged by Issue Involved.* pt. 2, *Cases Arranged by Industry Involved,* compiled by Estelle Rebec, Arthur Hecht, and Paul Flynn. SL no. 10. 1953.

Records of the Office of Censorship (RG 216)

NA. *Preliminary Inventory of the Records of the Office of Censorship,* compiled by Henry T. Ulasek. PI no. 54. 1953.

Records of the Office of Community War Services (RG 215)

NA. *Preliminary Inventory of the Records of the Office of Community War Services,* compiled by Estelle Rebec. PI no. 132. 1960.

Records of the Office for Emergency Management (RG 214)

NA. *Prelininary Inventory of the Records of the Office for Emergency Management,* compiled by Henry T. Ulasek. PI no. 92. 1956.

Records of the Office of Inter-American Affairs (RG 229)

NA. *Preliminary Inventory of the Records of the Office of Inter-American Affairs,* compiled by H. Stephen Helton. PI no. 41. 1952.

Records of the Office of Price Administration (RG 188)

NA. *Preliminary Inventory of the Records of the Accounting De-*

partment .of the Office of Price Administration, compiled by Meyer H. Fishbein and Elaine E. Bennett. PI no. 32. 1951.

NA. *Preliminary Inventory of the Records of the Enforcement Department of the Office of Price Administration,* compiled by Meyer H. Fishbein and Betty R. Bucher. PI no. 120. 1959.

NA. *Preliminary Inventory of the Records of the Information Department of the Office of Price Administration,* compiled by Betty R. Bucher. PI no. 119. 1959.

NA. *Preliminary Inventory of the Records of the Price Department of the Office of Price Administration,* compiled by Meyer H. Fishbein, Walter W. Weinstein, and Albert W. Winthrop. PI no. 95. 1956.

NA. *Preliminary Inventory of the Records of the Rationing Department of the Office of Price Administration,* compiled by Meyer H. Fishbein et al. PI no. 102. 1958.

Records of the Office of War Information (RG 208)

NA. *Preliminary Inventory of the Records of the Office of War Information,.* compiled by H. Stephen Helton. PI no. 56. 1953.

NA. *List of Photographs Made by the Office of War Information at the United Nations Conference on International Organization, San Francisco, 1945,* compiled by Emma B. Haas, Anne Harris, and Thomas W. Ray. SL no. 11. 1953.

Records of the Office of War Mobilization and Reconversion (RG 250)

NA. *Preliminary Inventory of the Records of the Office of War*

Mobilization and Reconversion, compiled by Homer L. Calkin. PI no. 25. 1951.

Records of the Petroleum Administration for War (RG 253)

NA. *Preliminary Inventory of the Records of the Petroleum Administration for War,* compiled by James R. Fuchs and Albert Whimpey. PI no. 31. 1951.

Records of the Price Decontrol Board (RG 251)

NA. *Preliminary Inventory of the Records of the Price Decontrol Board,* compiled by James J. Fleischmann and Victor Gondos, Jr. PI no. 46. 1952.

Records of the Public Works Administration (RG 135)

NA. *Preliminary Inventory of the Records of the Public Works Administration,* compiled by L. Evans Walker. PI no. 125. 1960.

Records of the Retraining and Reemployment Administration (RG 244)

NA. *Preliminary Inventory of the Records of the Retraining and Reemployment Administration,* compiled by Thayer M. Boardman. PI no. 28. 1951.

Records of the Shipbuilding Stabilization Committee (RG 254)

NA. *Preliminary Inventory of the Records of the Shipbuilding Stabilization Committee,* compiled by Leo Pascal. PI no. 121. 1959.

Records of the Smaller War Plants Corporation (RG 240)

NA. *Preliminary Inventory of the Records of the Smaller War Plants Corporation,* compiled by Katherine H. Davidson. PI no. 160. 1964.

Records of the United States War Ballot Commission (RG 230)

NA. *Preliminary Inventory of the*

Records of the United States War Ballot Commission, compiled by Robert W. Krauskopf. PI no. 24. 1951.

Records of the War Production Board (RG 179)

NA. *Preliminary Inventory of the Records of the War Production Board,* compiled by Fred G. Halley and Josef C. James. PI no. 15. 1948.

Records of the War Relocation Authority (RG 210)

NA. *Preliminary Inventory of the Records of the War Relocation Authority,* compiled by Estelle Rebec and Martin Rogin. PI no. 77. 1955.

Records of the War Shipping Administration (RG 248)

NA. *Preliminary Inventory of the Records of the War Shipping Administration,* compiled by Allen M. Ross. PI no. 30. 1951.

Records of the Work Projects Administration (RG 69)

NA. *Preliminary Inventory of the Records of the Federal Writers' Projects, Work Projects Administration, 1935-44,* compiled by Katherine H. Davidson. PI no. 57. 1953.

Smiley, David L. A Slice of Life in Depression America: The Records of the Historical Records Survey. *Prologue* 3 (Winter 1971): 153-59.

National Archives Collection of World War II War Crimes Records (RG 238)

NA. *Preliminary Inventory of the United States Counsel for the Prosecution of Axis Criminality,* compiled by Fred G. Halley. PI no. 51. 1949.

General Records of the Economic Stabilization Agency (RG 296)

NA. *Preliminary Inventory of the*

General Records of the Economic Stabilization Agency, compiled by Charles Zaid. PI no. 129. 1960.

Records of or Relating to Other Governments

Records of the National Capital Planning Commission (RG 328).

NA. *Preliminary Inventory of the National Capital Planning Commission,* compiled by Dorothy S. Provine. PI no. 175. 1973.

War Department Collection of Confederate Records (RG 109)

Cappon, Lester J. A Note on Confederate Ordnance Records. *Journal of the American Military History Foundation* 4 (1940): 94-102.

Irvine, Dallas D. The Archive Office of the War Department: Repository of Captured Confederate Archives, 1865-1881. *Military Affairs* 10 (1946): 93-111.

Irvine. The Fate of Confederate Archives. *AHR* 44 (1939): 823-41.

Lokke, Carl L. The Captured Confederate Archives under Francis Lieber. *AA* 9 (1946): 277-319.

NA. *Preliminary Inventory of the War Department Collection of Confederate Records,* compiled by Elizabeth Bethel. PI no. 101. 1957.

Treasury Department Collection of Confederate Records (RG 365)

NA. *Preliminary Inventory of the Treasury Department Collection of Confederate Records,* compiled by Carmelita S. Ryan. PI no. 169. 1967.

Records of the Government of the Virgin Islands (RG 55)

NA. *Preliminary Inventory of the Records of the Government of the Virgin Islands of the United States,* compiled by H. Donn Hooker. PI no. 126. 1960.

National Archives Collection of Foreign Records Seized, 1941- (RG 242)

NA. *Supplement to the Guide to Captured German Documents.* 1959.

NA. *Index of Microfilmed Records of the German Foreign Ministry and the Reich's Chancellery Covering the Weimar Period.* 1958.

Other Holdings

National Archives Collection of Records of Inaugural Committees (RG 274)

NA. *Preliminary Inventory of the Records of Inaugural Committees,* compiled by Hardee Allen. PI. no. 131. 1960.

NA. *Preliminary Inventory of the Records of the 1961 Inaugu-* ral *Committee,* compiled by Marion M. Johnson. PI no. 162. 1964.

NA. *List of Motion Pictures and Sound Recordings Relating to Presidential Inaugurations,* compiled by E. Daniel Potts. SL no. 16. 1960.

National Archives Gift Collection (RG 200)

NA. *Preliminary Inventory of the Sir Henry S. Wellcome Papers in the Federal Records Center, Seattle, Washington,* compiled by Elmer W. Lindgard. PI no. 150. 1963.

NA. *Guide to the Ford Film Collection in the National Archives,* compiled by Mayfield Bray. 1970.

National Archives Gift Collection of Materials Relating to Polar Regions (RG 401).

Wilson, Alison. The Center for Polar Archives, Washington, D.C. *Polar Record* 16 (1973): 541-52.

*Listed generally under NA record group titles within the organizational framework of the government.

Notes

Archival Sources for Studies of Federal Administration, pages 23-30

1. James Madison, *The Writings of James Madison*, ed. Gaillard Hunt, 9 vols. (New York: G. P. Putnam's Sons, 1900-1910), 8:304.

2. U.S., *United States Code*, Title 44, sec. 3101 (1970).

3. Leonard D. White, *Introduction to the Study of Public Administration*, 4th ed. York: Macmillan Co., 1955), p. 35.

4. Samuel P. Hays, *Conservation and the Gospel of Efficiency: The Progressive Conservation Movement, 1890-1920.* (Cambridge: Harvard University Press, 1959), p. 279.

5. Richard G. Hewlett and Oscar E. Anderson, Jr., *The New World, 1939/1946*, vol. 1, *A History of the United States Atomic Energy Commission* (University Park: Pennsylvania State University Press, 1962), p. 657.

6. Paul H. Appleby, *Big Democracy* (New York: Alfred A. Knopf, 1945), p. 42.

7. See Helen L. Chatfield, "The Development of Record Systems," *American Archivist* 13 (July 1950): 260.

8. See Paul Lewinson, "Archival Sampling," *American Archivist* 20 (October 1957): 243-94.

9. Charles A. Beard and William Beard, *The American Leviathan: The Republic in the Machine Age* (New York: Macmillan Co., 1930), p. vii.

10. Carl J. Friedrich, "Public Policy and the Nature of Administrative Responsibility," in *Public Policy: A Yearbook of the Graduate School of Public Administration, Harvard University*, ed. Carl. J. Friedrich and Edward S. Mason (Cambridge: Harvard University Press, 1940), p. 16.

11. Rexford G. Tugwell, *The Democratic Roosevelt: A Biography of Franklin D. Roosevelt* (Garden City, N.Y.: Doubleday, 1957), p. 351.

12. Arthur M. Schlesinger, Jr., "The Historian and History," *Foreign Affairs* 41 (April 1963): 493.

13. Allan Nevins, *The Gateway to History*, rev. ed. (Garden City, N.Y.: Anchor Books, 1962), p. 134.

14. William Anderson and John M. Gaus, *Research in Public Administration* (Chicago: Public Administration Service for the Committee on Public Administration of the Social Science Research Council, 1945), p. 12.

Saccharin: A Bitter Regulatory Controversy, pages 39-49

1. Harvey Washington Wiley, "Why I Support Wilson and Marshall," pencil draft, box 192, Harvey W. Wiley Papers, Manuscript Division, Library of Congress, Washington, D.C.

2. The indispensable work on Wiley is Oscar E. Anderson, Jr.'s biography, *The Health of a Nation: Harvey W. Wiley and the Fight for Pure Food* (Chicago: University of Chicago Press, 1958). See also, James Harvey Young, "The Science and Morals of Metabolism: Catsup and Benzoate of Soda," *Journal of the History of Medicine and Allied Sciences* 23 (1968): 86-104.

3. Wiley, "Why I Support Wilson and Marshall."

4. Clemens Kleber, "Twenty-five Years in the Service of the Saccharin Industry" (an abbreviated version of a lecture given by Fahlberg at the Fifth International Congress for Applied Chemistry in Berlin, 1903), *Pharmaceutical Review* 21 (1903): 467-71; Frederick H. Getman, *The Life of Ira Remsen* (Easton, Penn.: Journal of Chemical Education, 1940), pp. 61-67.

5. Hugh McGuigan, "Some Facts about Saccharin and Food," *Dietetic and Hygienic Gazette* 22 (1906): 193-96.

6. *Ibid.;* "Saccharin in Diabetes," a typed document citing from the literature, Solicitor's File F&D 7304, Office of the General Counsel, Records of the Office of the Secretary of Agriculture, Record Group 16, Archives Branch, Washington National Records Center, Suitland, Maryland. Records in the Archives Branch, Washington National Records Center, are hereafter indicated by the symbols AB, WNRC.

7. "Saccharin in Diabetes"; McGuigan, "Some Facts about Saccharin and Food"; R. G. Eccles, "The Influence of Antiseptics on Digestion," *Dietetic and Hygienic Gazette* 22 (1906): 134-37.

8. Anderson, *Health of a Nation*, passim; Young, "Science and Morals of Metabolism."

9. Wiley to Secretary of Agriculture, December 6, 1911, carbon, file 1 for 1911, and Wiley to McCabe, January 13, 1908, carbon, file 4 for 1908, both in Bureau of Chemistry General Correspondence, Records of the Bureau of Agricultural and Industrial Chemistry, Record Group 97, National Archives Building, Washington, D.C.; Wiley to L. Craigen Coyle, June 7, 1906, copy, Solicitor's file 817, RG 16, National Archives Building. Records in the National Archives Building are hereafter indicated by the symbol NA.

10. Anderson, *Health of a Nation*, p. 204.

11. Letters between Wiley and McCabe, especially McCabe to Wiley, March 30, 1907, file 8 for 1907, Bureau of Chemistry General Correspondence, RG 97, NA.

12. Anderson, *Health of a Nation*, pp. 210-11; Young, "Science and the Morals of Metabolism."

13. *American Food Journal* 3 (August 15, 1908): 13; Harvey W. Wiley, *Harvey W. Wiley, an Autobiography* (Indianapolis: Bobbs-Merrill, 1930), p. 242.

14. Wiley to R. G. Eccles, January 31, 1910, carbon, box 85, Wiley Papers, Library of Congress.

15. Wiley to H. E. Barnard, August 30, 1910, copy, box 85, Wiley Papers, Library of Congress.

16. Anderson, *Health of a Nation*, passim; Young, "Science and Morals of Metabolism."

17. U.S., Department of Agriculture, Referee Board of Consulting Scientific Experts, *Influence of Saccharin on the Nutrition and Health of Man*, Department of Agriculture Report no. 94 (Washington, D.C.: Government Printing Office, 1911), p. 7.

18. Ibid., pp. 7-8.

19. U.S., Department of Agriculture, *Saccharin under the Food and Drugs Act of June 30, 1906* (Washington, D.C.: Government Printing Office, 1911), pp. 61-76, contains briefs by Wiley, W. D. Bigelow, chief of the bureau's Division of Foods, and L. F. Kebler, chief of the bureau's Division of Drugs. Those who served under Wiley agreed with his position.

20. Food Inspection Decision 135, April 29, 1911, Food Inspection Board Records, Records of the Food and Drug Administration, Record Group 88, NA.

21. Testimony of John F. Queeny, transcript, pp. 535-36, Monsanto Chemical Works case, I.S. no. 10132-L, RG 88, Washington National Records Center, Suitland, Maryland. Records in the Washington National Records Center are hereafter indicated by the symbol WNRC.

22. FID 138, July 12, 1911, Food Inspection Board Records, RG 88, NA.

23. Hearing Accorded to Manufacturers of Saccharin, May 23, 1911, in Department of Agriculture, *Saccharin under the Food and Drugs Act,* pp. 8-16; Hough quotation from his reply brief, ibid., p. 97.

24. Hough to Taft, February 26 and 27, 1912, FID 142, Food Inspection Board Records, RG 88, NA.

25. Hearings, May 23 and November 22, 1911, in Department of Agriculture, *Saccharin under the Food and Drugs Act,* pp. 8-16, 18-32.

26. FID 142, March 11, 1912, Saccharin file for 1912, RG 16, NA. Secretary Franklin MacVeagh wrote Secretary James Wilson a letter of dissent, February 27, 1912, printed copy, Saccharin file for 1912, RG 16, NA.

27. Ira Remsen et al. to Secretary of Agriculture, January 13, 1912, printed copy, Saccharin file for 1912, RG 16, NA.

28. *American Food Journal* 7 (September 15, 1912): 7; ibid. 9 (May 1914): 217.

29. FID 142, March 11, 1912, Saccharin file for 1912, RG 16, NA.

30. Anderson, *Health of a Nation,* pp. 252-53.

31. Saccharin Hearing 1460, July 1, 1913, Food Inspection Board Records, RG 88, NA.

32. Alsberg to Secretary of Agriculture, July 17, 1913, Saccharin file for 1913, RG 16, NA. Alsberg to Houston, January 5, 1915, Saccharin file for 1914, RG 16, NA.

33. *American Food Journal* 12 (March 1917): 127; transcript, p. 15, Monsanto Chemical Works case, I. S. no. 10132-L, RG 88, WNRC.

34. New York *Evening World,* November 10, 1919, in Saccharin file for 1919, RG 16, NA.

35. *American Food Journal* 14 (November 1919): 23; original copy for intended press release, 1919, Accession 66A1020, box 149, RG 88, WNRC.

36. Transcript, pp. 40-126, Monsanto Chemical Works case, I. S. no. 10132-L, RG 88, WNRC.

37. Ibid., pp. 282-97 for Solomon Solis Cohen. Haven Emerson's testimony, which should appear in ibid., pp. 357-83, is missing from the file, a note saying it was removed and sent to Dr. Emerson. Dr. Emerson's testimony, along with that of the other key government witnesses, is summarized in a thirteen-page mimeographed document, "Abstract of Testimony," prepared in 1921 for mailing to state and municipal food and drug officials, Saccharin file for 1921, RG 16, NA.

38. Transcript, pp. 158-245, 1360-407, Monsanto Chemical Works case, I. S. no. 10132-L, RG 88, WNRC.

39. Ibid., pp. 411-64, 543-605, 632-840.

40. Ibid., pp 478-511, 606-32.

41. Ibid., pp. 1272-94.

42. Ibid., pp. 1185-207, 1221.

43. *Monthly Review of the Bureau of Chemistry* 3 (December 1919): 32-33; *Food and Drug Review* 8 (June 1924): 13.

44. McCabe to Secretary of Agriculture Edward Meredith, April 14, 1920; Meredith to McCabe, June 16, 1920, carbon; both in Saccharin file for 1920, RG 16, NA.

45. *Food and Drug Review* 8 (June 1924): 13-18; W. W. Skinner to Senator E. F. Ladd, May 24, 1924; carbon, decimal file 482.3 for 1924, RG 88, AB, WNRC.

46. Secretary of Agriculture Henry C. Wallace to John F. Queeny, May 21, 1924, carbon, Monsanto Chemical Works case jacket, I. S. no. 10132-L, RG 88, WNRC; Walter G. Campbell to Solicitor, November 4, 1924, carbon, Saccharin file for 1924; RG 16, NA; Secretary of Agriculture Howard M. Gore to Attorney General, December 4, 1924, carbon, Solicitor's file F&D 7304, Office of the General Counsel, RG 16, AB, WNRC.

47. Attorney General Harlan Stone to Secretary of Agriculture Gore, December 9, 1924; Gore to Stone, December 29, 1924, carbon; Assistant Attorney General William J. Donovan to Allen Curry, United States Attorney in Saint Louis, January 5, 1925, carbon; Curry to Attorney General, January 6, 1925, photostat; Donovan to Curry, January 9, 1925, copy; Donovan to Gore, January 9, 1925; all in Solicitor's file F&D 7304, Office of the General Counsel, AB, WNRC. *St. Louis Globe-Democrat*, April 21, 1925, clipping in decimal file 428.3 for 1925, RG 88, AB, WNRC.

48. M. D. Moore to Charles A. McAvoy, December 30, 1926, carbon, decimal file 482.3 for 1926, RG 88, AB, WNRC.

49. M. D. Moore to M. M. Goldschein, November 27, 1935, carbon, decimal file 482.3 for 1935, RG 88, AB, WNRC.

50. FDA press release, November 20, 1959, decimal file 003.52 for 1959, RG 88, AB, WNRC. More recent concerns that have prompted the reconsideration of saccharin's status rest not on the kinds of hazards to health which the government sought to establish in the Monsanto trials, but in the fear that saccharin might be carcinogenic, might be teratogenic, and might interact adversely with other drugs. The latest review of the data, *Safety of Saccharin for Use in Food,* was prepared for the Food and Drug Administration at its request by the Ad Hoc Subcommittee on Non-Nutritive Sweeteners of the Food Protection Committee, Food and Nutrition Board, National Academy of Sciences-National Research Council. Delivered in July 1970, the report presented the judgment of the scientists that "the present and projected use of saccharin in the United States does not pose a hazard." They nonetheless recommended six types of studies, some of them long-range, to evaluate saccharin's safety more scientifically than had thus far been done. They also recommended a maximum daily safe intake. This level the FDA included as a ceiling in a regulation, issued on February 1, 1972, which removed saccharin from the GRAS list, provisionally declared it a food additive, set levels for its use, and required labeling as to quantity on beverages, intermediate mixes, and final food products. In a June 22, 1971, press release, the FDA had pointed to recent research revealing that "when cholesterol pellets containing saccharin were implanted directly into mouse bladders an increased incidence of bladder cancers resulted." Long-term feeding studies in animals were announced as under way "to assess by more relevant tests the potential hazards [of saccharin] to man." In May 1973 the FDA extended its interim food additive regulation, stated that the feeding studies were continuing, and announced that a contract had been made with NAS-NRC to review the results of the experiments for any possible carcinogenicity of saccharin. A more conclusive regulatory decision on saccharin awaited the outcome of this review. FDA press release, May 24, 1973.

51. McCann, "Records Disposal and Reporting," mimeographed text of speech before Station Chiefs Clerks Conference, 1948, in decimal file 047.3 for 1948, RG 88, AB, WNRC.

The Attempt of the National Recovery Administration to
Raise Bituminous Coal Prices, pages 51-61

1. Franklin D. Roosevelt, *The Public Papers and Addresses of Franklin D. Roosevelt,* ed. Samuel I. Rosenman, 13 vols. (New York: Random House, 1938-50), 2:246.

2. F. E. Berquist et al., "Economic Survey of the Bituminous Coal Industry under Free

Competition and Code Regulation," National Recovery Administration Work Materials no. 69, 2 vols., mimeographed (Washington, D.C., 1936), 1:ii; Newell W. Roberts, R. C. Brown, and S. E. Burt, "History of the Code of Fair Competition for the Bituminous Coal Industry," 4 vols., 1:14, 42, in Records of the Division of Review, Code Histories for Industries under Approved Codes, Records of the National Recovery Administration, Record Group 9, National Archives Building, Washington, D.C. Records in the National Archives Building are hereafter indicated by the symbol NA.

3. Berquist, "Economic Survey," 1:8-9; 2:548-51; Appendix III. It is impossible to determine average per ton mine levels just prior to the effective establishment of the code prices in November 1933. The Bureau of Mines reported $1.34 as the average mine price for all coal during 1933. The Coal Unit of NRA's Division of Review calculated that the average price for commercial as opposed to captive coal mined by railroads, steel mills, or utility companies sagged to $1.03 between January and September 1933. There are no monthly price figures for pre-NRA 1933. The last month during the life of the code for which monthly figures are available is January 1935. U.S., Bureau of the Census, *Historical Statistics of the United States, Colonial Times to 1957* (Washington, D.C.; Government Printing Office, 1960), p. 356. Berquist, "Economic Survey," 1:8.

4. Glen Lawhon Parker, *The Coal Industry: A Study in Social Control* (Washington, D.C.: American Council on Public Affairs, 1940), p. 74. At the conclusion of the first of these wage agreements, the United Mine Workers of America joined the operators' committee in calling it the "greatest in magnitude and importance ever to have been negotiated in the history of collective bargaining in the United States." They agreed that it marked the "beginning of a new era in the task of stabilizing and modernizing the economic processes of this basic industry." *New York Times,* September 22, 1933.

5. Pittsburgh Coal Company, *Annual Report, 1934,* p. 4; Berquist, "Economic Survey," 1:8-9.

6. U.S., National Recovery Administration, "Production, Prices, Employment and Payrolls in Industry, Agriculture, and Railway Transportation," National Recovery Administration Work Materials no. 15, mimeographed (Washington, D.C., 1935), p. 19.

7. Ibid., p. 21; *Cleveland Trust Company Business Bulletin* 22 (June 15, 1941); Bureau of the Census, *Historical Statistics,* p. 356, gives the following production figures for bituminous coal: 1935, 372,373,000 tons; 1934, 359,368,000 tons; 1933, 333,631,000 tons; and 1932, 309,710,000 tons.

8. U.S., National Recovery Administration, Committee of Industrial Analysis, *Report,* mimeographed (Washington, D.C., 1937), p. 168.

9. U.S., *Statutes at Large,* vol. 48, p. 195.

10. James P. Johnson, "Reorganizing the United Mine Workers of America in Pennsylvania During the New Deal," *Pennsylvania History* 37 (April 1970): 117-32.

11. Carroll Lawrence Christenson, *Economic Redevelopment in Bituminous Coal* (Cambridge: Harvard University Press, 1962), pp. 31, 66-72, and 295, n. 26.

12. Christenson, *Economic Redevelopment,* pp. 191-92. Christenson's study offers solid evidence of the important impact of geography on both wages and prices.

13. Reed Moyer, *Competition in the Midwestern Coal Industry* (Cambridge: Harvard University Press, 1964), p. 178 and passim. Clair Wilcox, *Public Policies toward Business* (Chicago: Richard D. Irwin, 1955), p. 466; Berquist, "Economic Survey," 2:505. Adam Thomas Shurick, *The Coal Industry* (Boston: Little, Brown & Co., 1924), pp. 271-72.

14. Ralph Hillis Baker, *The National Bituminous Coal Commission* (Baltimore: Johns Hopkins Press, 1941), p. 21; Moyer, *Competition,* pp. 101-2; Parker, *Coal Industry,* p. 24; Berquist, "Economic Survey," 2:504.

15. Sidney A. Hale, "Behind the Bituminous Code: A Move from Chaos to Order,"

New York Times, September 24, 1933, sec. IX, p. 3; Blaine Davis, "Marketing Problems of Bituminous Coal," *Harvard Business Review* 11 (November 1932): 99; Moyer, *Competition,* pp. 69, 160-61; Shurick, *The Coal Industry,* pp. 205-6; Wilcox, *Public Policies toward Business,* p. 465.

16. Christenson, *Economic Redevelopment,* p. 89; Moyer, *Competition,* pp. 36-37, 200-205.

17. Bureau of the Census, *Historical Statistics,* p. 356.

18. National Industrial Conference Board, Inc., *The Competitive Position of Coal in the United States* (New York: National Industrial Conference Board, 1931), p. 249.

19. Baker, *National Bituminous Coal Commission,* p. 7; Parker, *Coal Industry,* p. 36.

20. Bureau of the Census, *Historical Statistics,* p. 356.

21. National Industrial Conference Board, *Competitive Position,* pp. 28-30.

22. Bureau of the Census, *Historical Statistics,* p. 356.

23. *New York Times,* October 4, 1933. Many realistic businessmen understood, of course, that the NRA could not revolutionize American business practices. Yet the spirit of the time is indicated by Fordham University's rush to offer a new course on industrial relations under NRA and by Eleanor Roosevelt's speeches on the new social order. Hugh S. Johnson, administrator of the NRA, often exuded a messianic fervor. *New York Times,* September 7 and 24, 1933.

24. U.S., *Statutes at Large,* vol. 48, pp. 195 ff.

25. *New York Times,* July 23 and 24, 1933.

26. Ellis W. Hawley, *The New Deal and the Problem of Monopoly* (Princeton: Princeton University Press, 1966), pp. 33-34. The confusions among New Dealers and in the act itself are discussed in Broadus Mitchell, *Depression Decade: From New Era through New Deal* (New York, Rinehart & Co., 1947), pp. 228, 253, and passim; see also Charles F. Roos, *NRA Economic Planning* (Bloomington: Indiana University Press, 1937), p. 472; *New York Times,* October 17 and July 4, 1933.

27. James P. Johnson, "Drafting the NRA Code of Fair Competition for the Bituminous Coal Industry," *Journal of American History* 53 (December 1966): 521-41.

28. *Code of Fair Competition for the Bituminous Coal Industry,* art. VI (copy in author's possession). Berquist, "Economic Survey," 2:500, 506.

29. Hawley, *New Deal and the Problem of Monopoly,* p. 65; Mitchell, *Depression Decade,* p. 247; "Development of the Code Authority" (typescript study, no author, no date), Records of the NRA history Unit, RG 9, NA, pp. 1-2; Robert Connery, *The Administration of an N.R.A. Code: A Case Study of the Men's Clothing Industry* (Chicago: Committee on Public Administration, Social Science Research Council, 1938), p. 22.

30. George A. Blackford to N. W. Roberts, NRA Assistant Deputy Administrator, July 11, 1934, in Northern Panhandle of West Virginia Subdivisional Code Authority, Reports; David C. Reay to C. E. Adams, NRA Division Administrator, August 1, 1934, Northern Panhandle of West Virginia Subdivisional Code Authority, Code Authority Meetings; memorandum, E. Kendall Bragg, NRA Assistant Counsel, to Mr. Sherman Burt, March 4, 1935, in Ohio Subdivisional Code Authority, Administration Members; James Burnes, Jr., to Clarence Darrow, June 12, 1934, Northern Panhandle of West Virginia Subdivisional Code Authority, Code Authority Meetings; Kelleys Creek Colliery Company telegram to Wayne Ellis, NRA Deputy Administrator, June 29, 1934, in Southern Subdivisional Code Authority, Code Authority—all in Consolidated Files on Industries Governed by Approved Codes (hereafter cited as CF), RG 9, NA.

31. Roberts, "History of the Code of Fair Competition," 1:14.

32. *Code of Fair Competition;* Berquist, "Economic Survey," 2:501-2.

33. "Report of Presidential Member for the Northern Panhandle of West Virginia Sub-

divisional Code Authority, June 10, 1935," in Roberts, "History of the Code of Fair Competition," 3:B8. A similar situation existed in the men's clothing industry. Connery, *Administration of an N.R.A. Code*, p. 28.

34. "Report of the Presidential Member of the Eastern Subdivisional Code Authority, June 6, 1935," in Roberts, "History of the Code of Fair Competition," 3:B8. Frank Haas, NRA Technical Advisor on Coal, to William Emery, Jr., November 23, 1933, in Northern Panhandle of West Virginia Subdivisional Code Authority, Code Authority Meetings, CF, RG 9, NA.

35. Fred Berquist, who compiled the NRA work materials on the coal code, wrote to Leon Henderson that this lack of central authority was "the biggest problem in the coal code." Berquist to Henderson, March 16, 1934, General, CF, RG 9, NA.

36. Because Johnson feared having too many hard-and-fast rules during the first months of NRA, confusion and delays became characteristic of the entire operation. Hawley, *New Deal and the Problem of Monopoly*, pp. 63-65; Connery *Administration of an N.R.A. Code*, p. 123; Hugh S. Johnson to Kenneth M. Simpson, Deputy Administrator, October 6, 1933, Division I, Administrative Members, CF, RG 9, NA.

37. Telegram, David C. Reay, Secretary of the Northern West Virginia Subdivisional Code Authority, to Franklin D. Roosevelt, November 14, 1933, Northern Panhandle of West Virginia Subdivisional Code Authority, Code Authority, Meetings; NRA Press Release 1845, November 21, 1933, Division I, Administration Members, CF, RG 9, NA. By November 10 Johnson had appointed only about one-tenth of the governmental representatives on the approved code agencies. Special Industrial Recovery Board, "Proceedings of the Special Industrial Recovery Board," November 20, 1933 (mimeographed copy in the Columbia University School of Business Administration), pp. 8-9.

38. *Coal Age* 39 (February 1934), p. 71.

39. Berquist, "Economic Survey," 2:518-20; "Record of Conference of Representatives of Coal Producers from Iowa, Illinois, Indiana, Western Kentucky, and Eastern Representatives, December 7, 1933," Division I, Prices, Conferences, CF, RG 9, NA, pp. 1-4, 10, 18; *Coal Age* 38 (December 1933), pp. 428-29; ibid. (November 1933), pp. 390-91.

40. Although Johnson admitted that the failure to bring "good men" into NRA was "the greatest handicap" the administration suffered, he offered erratic leadership himself. (Johnson tried to get Harold Ickes to administer coal and failed.) The general vainly hoped that the codes would work as some sort of Marquis of Queensbury rules—that public opinion could force compliance. Even NRA General Counsel Donald Richberg, who would later oppose Johnson inside NRA, exhorted the 10 percent who refused to comply: "But the blue eagle is an honest bird. He is an honest American. He will not protect a 10 percent. And when the blue eagle has once flown away he will not return." Hugh S. Johnson, *The Blue Eagle from Egg to Earth* (New York: Doubleday, Doran & Co., 1935), p. 206; *New York Times*, August 1 and 31 and September 21, 1933; Mitchell, *Depression Decade*, p. 238.

41. *Coal Age* 37 (November 1933), pp. 391-92; Johnson to Simpson, October 6, 1933, Division I, Administrative Members, CF, RG 9, NA.

42. One concerned operator wrote the White House that Simpson "lacks knowledge of coal, oil, and steel, is a completely disorganized intellect, weak, vacillating, uniformed and syncophantic." Ben Grey to Steve Early, September 14, 1933, Official File 175, Franklin D. Roosevelt Library, Hyde Park, New York (hereafter cited as FDRL).

43. David C. Reay to Wayne P. Ellis, February 17, 1934, Northern Panhandle of West Virginia Subdivisional Code Authority, Code Authority, CF, RG 9, NA; Herbert Harris, *American Labor* (New Haven: Yale University Press, 1938), p. 141; "Hearing Held before the National Bituminous Coal Industrial Board, January 19, 1934," Code Authority, CF, RG, 9, NA, pp. 10-11.

44. Memorandum, George Hadesty, Presidential Member Northern Panhandle of West Virginia, June 10, 1935, in Roberts, "History of the Code of Fair Competition," 3:B8; "Hearing Held before the National Bituminous Coal Industrial Board, January 16, 1934," Transcripts of Hearings, CF, RG 9, NA, p. 24.

45. "Record of Conference," p. 23.

46. *Coal Age* 39 (February 1934), p. 71.

47. Berquist, "Economic Survey," 2:520; Stephen P. Burke, *"Price Fixing" in the Bituminous Coal Industry* (Fairmont, W. Va.: Northern West Virginia Subdivisional Code Authority, 1935), pp. 15, 21, 29.

48. "Hearing Held before the Presidential Member Code Authority of Western Pennsylvania, June 13, 1934," Western Pennsylvania Subdivision, Hearings, CF, RG 9, NA, pp. 11-14.

49. *Coal Age* 39 (July 1934), p. 258.

50. George A. Blackford to Wayne P. Ellis, May 17, 1934, Northern Panhandle of West Virginia Subdivisional Code Authority, Reports, CF, RG 9, NA. The *New York Times* wrote on August 26, 1934, that Pittsburgh operators and miners were in "general agreement" that the NRA was "the most effective answer yet given to the troubles of that industry." A *Coal Age* survey found that except for the smaller mining areas of the West and Southwest, the industry "indorses the code as a distinct benefit to the industry and wishes to see the code control continued. . . ." *Coal Age* 39 (October 1934), p. 380.

51. *New York Times,* January 13, 1934; *Coal Age* 39 (February 1934), p. 32.

52. *New York Times,* January 19, 1934; "Hearing Held before the National Bituminous Coal Industrial Board, January 16, 1934," Transcripts of Hearings, CF, RG 9, NA, pp. 1-3, 4, 14.

53. "Hearing Held before the National Bituminous Coal Industrial Board, January 16, 1934," pp. 10-11. "Report of Committee No. Four on Planning, National Bituminous Coal Industrial Board Meeting, January 16-19, 1934"; "Report of Committee No. Two on a Definite Plan of Enforcement, National Bituminous Coal Industrial Board Meeting, January 18, 1934," Transcripts of Hearings, CF, RG 9, NA.

54. *Coal Age* 39 (July 1934), p. 291.

55. "Minutes of Meeting of Representatives of Code Authorities of Divisions I, II, III, held June 1, 1934, Netherlands-Plaza Hotel, Cincinnati, Ohio," Transcripts of Hearings, CF, RG 9, NA; Berquist, "Economic Survey," 2:524; *Coal Age* 39 (July 1934), p. 257.

56. *Coal Age* 39 (July 1934), p. 291.

57. Berquist, "Economic Survey," 2:523-25; *Coal Age* 39 (July 1934), p. 291, ibid. (August 1934), p. 325.

58. "Hearing on the Bituminous Coal Industry, Presidential Members and Chairmen of Code Authorities, June 25, 1934," Transcripts of Hearings, CF, RG 9, NA, pp. 16, 18, 38, and passim; "Hearing of the Administrative Advisory Committee of Division I, December 20, 1934," Transcripts of Hearings, CF, RG 9, NA, pp. 11-35.

59. In October 1934, *Coal Age* noted that the proposed executive order which would have extended the Adams plan to all the divisions of the code was "temporarily held up because the Department of Justice already is studying the question of price relationships" (p. 400).

60. Hawley, *New Deal and the Problem of Monopoly,* pp. 87-138; John P. Miller, *Unfair Competition: A Study in Criteria for the Control of Trade Practices* (Cambridge: Harvard University Press, 1941), pp. 336-49.

61. Henderson was supported in the NRA by Donald Richberg. Richberg to Marvin McIntyre, September 5, 1934, Donald Richberg Papers, box 45, Library of Congress, Washington, D.C.; Schlesinger, *Coming of the New Deal,* pp. 13-32; Hugh S. Johnson, *Blue Eagle,* pp. 382-85.

62. *New York Times,* October 6, 1934.

63. Northern West Virginia Subdivisional Code Authority, Circular no. 78, October 13, 1934, Northern Panhandle of West Virginia Subdivisional Code Authority, Code Authority, Meetings, CF, RG 9, NA.

64. *New York Times,* October 6, 1934.

65. David C. Reay to Wayne P. Ellis, October 8, 1934, Northern Panhandle of West Virginia Subdivisional Code Authority, Code Authority, Meetings, CF, RG 9, NA.

66. John L. Lewis to Wayne P. Ellis, December 17, 1934, Hearings, CF, RG, 9, NA.

67. Docket File, National Coal Board of Arbitration, CF, RG 9, NA; Berquist, "Economic Survey," 2:529; "Hearing before the National Bituminous Coal Industrial Board, January 3-16, 1935," CF, RG 9, NA, passim.

68. Berquist, "Economic Survey," 2:512. The *Chicago Tribune* called for an organization of consumers to retaliate against the effectiveness of the market prices in coal for Chicago. "Burn Less Coal," May 28, 1934.

69. Berquist, "Economic Survey," 2:280, 343, Tables V and XVII; U.S., Congress, Senate, Committee on Interstate Commerce, *Stabilization of the Bituminous Coal Mining Industry,* Hearings before a Subcommittee of the Committee on Interstate Commerce, 74th Cong., 1st sess., February 19-March 7, 1935, p. 137. Miners often struck operators who were chiseling on prices, because they realized that cutting prices inevitably led to wage cuts. *New York Herald Tribune,* December 14, 1934.

70. *New York Times,* August 26, 1934. For other similar views see U.S., Congress, Senate, Committee on Interstate Commerce, *Hearings on S. 4668, a Bill to Regulate Interstate Commerce in Bituminous Coal and for Other Purposes,* 74th Cong., 2d sess., June 3, 12, 13, 1936, p. 233; and "Record of Conference," p. 44.

71. 21 (March 1935), p. 14.

72. 39 (October 1934), pp. 380-82.

73. Quoted in "The Coordinator," *Newsletter of Smokeless Code Authority Bureau* 6 (July 26, 1934) Code Authority, CF, RG 9, NA, p. 2.

74. Sidney Hale, in George Galloway, *Industrial Planning under the Codes* (New York York: Harper & Bros., 1935), p. 183.

Address: Deepening the Wellsprings of Public Policy, pages 83-89

1. John Kenneth Galbraith cites four motivational forces—compulsion, pecuniary compensation, identification, and adaptation—that find their illustrations in the federal service. See Galbraith, *The New Industrial Society* (Boston: Houghton Mifflin, 1967), chap. 11, "The General Theory of Motivation," pp. 128-39.

2. New York: Van Nostrand-Reinhold, 1961.

The New Deal and Administrative Reform, pages 97-104

1. John R. McCarl, "Government-Run Everything," *Saturday Evening Post,* October 3, 1936, pp. 8-9, 52, and October 17, 1936, pp. 8-9.

2. Fred A. Ironside, Jr., to Donald R. Richberg, September 18, 1934, President's Committee on Administrative Management files, box 9, Franklin D. Roosevelt Library, Hyde Park, New York, hereafter cited as FDRL; Harold L. Ickes, *The Secret Diary of Harold L. Ickes,* 3 vols. (New York: Simon & Schuster, 1954), 2:354; David E. Lilienthal, *The Journals of David E. Lilienthal,* 2 vols. (New York: Harper & Row, 1964), 1:345.

3. Brownlow to Roosevelt, April 11, 1938, Franklin D. Roosevelt Papers, Official File 285C, box 7, FDRL.

4. Merriam to Brownlow, February 20, 1936, President's Committee on Administrative Management files, box 1, FDRL.

5. "Minutes of the New York Conference," May 9-10, 1936, President's Committee on Administrative Management files, box 1, FDRL.

6. Brownlow to Harold G. Moulton, March 11, 1937, President's Committee on Administrative Management files, box 2, FDRL.

7. Harold D. Smith Diary, April 27 and May 6, 1939, Harold D. Smith Papers, FDRL.

Federal Administrative Reorganization, 1940-1970, pages 105-114

1. See Louis C. Gawthrop, *Bureaucratic Behavior in the Executive Branch* (New York: Free Press, 1969).

2. Examples of this variation are found in Sidney Baldwin, *Poverty and Politics: The Rise and Decline of the Farm Security Administration* (Chapel Hill: University of North Carolina Press, 1968); Edith T. Carper, "The Reorganization of the Public Health Service," in *Governmental Reorganizations: Cases and Commentary,* ed. Frederick C. Mosher (Indianapolis, Ind.: Bobbs-Merrill, 1967); R. G. Hewlett, *The New World, 1939/1946, a History of the United States Atomic Energy Commission* (University Park: Pennsylvania State University Press, 1962); Louis M. Kohlmeier, *The Regulators: Watchdog Agencies and the Public Interest* (New York: Harper & Row, 1970); Harvey C. Mansfield, *A Short History of O.P.A.* (Washington, D.C.: Government Printing Office, 1949); Robert L. Rosholt, *An Administrative History of NASA, 1958-1963* (Washington, D.C.: National Aeronautics & Space Administration, 1966); Gilbert Y. Steiner, *Social Insecurity: The Politics of Welfare* (Chicago: Rand McNally, 1966); Harold Wolman, *Politics of Federal Housing* (New York: Dodd Mead, 1971).

3. Thomas Henderson, *Congressional Oversight of Executive Agencies* (Gainesville: University of Florida, 1970).

4. "Some Notes on Reorganization in Public Agencies," in *Public Administration and Democracy: Essays in Honor of Paul H. Appleby,* ed. Roscoe C. Martin (Syracuse: Syracuse University Press, 1965).

5. Officially, Executive Order 8248 of September 8, 1939, specifies the bureau's functions as part of the Executive Office of the President in accordance with Reorganization Plan 1 of 1939 which transferred the bureau.

6. See U.S., National Archives and Records Service, *Federal Register* (Washington, D.C.: Government Printing Office), April 11, May 22, and June 2, 1940, for details on Plans 3, 4, and 5.

7. U.S., National Archives and Records Service, *Federal Records of World War II,* 2 vols. (Washington, D.C.: Government Printing Office, 1950-51).

8. The committee was composed of the director of the Bureau of the Budget, the librarian of Congress, the archivist of the United States, and representatives of the American Political Science Association, the American Society for Public Administration, the American Historical Association, and the Social Science Research Committee.

9. U.S., Bureau of the Budget, *The United States at War: Development and Administration of the War Program by the Federal Government* (Washington, D.C.: Government Printing Office, 1946).

10. See Henry Venneman, "Records of War Administration," *Military Affairs 6* (Fall 1942) 191-96; idem, "The Recording of World War," *American Political Science Review 38* (April 1944); U.S., Bureau of the Budget, "Federal Historical Reports; a Summary of Publications, Manuscripts, and Plans" processed (June 12, 1947). See also Luther Gulick, "War Organization of the Federal Government," *American Political Science Review 38* (December 1944); E. P. Herring, *The Impact of War: Our American Democracy under Arms* (New York: Farrar & Rinehart, 1941); Earl Latham, "Executive Management and the Federal Field Service," *Public Administration Review 5 (1945).*

11. Ferrel Heady, "The Reorganization Act of 1949," *Public Administration Review* 9 (1949).

12. R. H. Connery, "Unification of the Armed Forces—The First Year," *American Political Science Review* 43 (February 1949); Elias Huzar, "Reorganization for National Security," *Journal of Politics* 12 (May 1950).

13. Ferrel Heady, "The Reorganization Act of 1949," pp. 74.

A Proposal for a Government-Wide Historical Office, pages 135-145

1. For a detailed description of the history and organizaiton of the historical programs of the various agencies of the federal government, see Walter Rundell, Jr., "Uncle Sam the Historian: Federal Historical Activities," *Historian* 33 (November 1970): 1-20. The author has drawn heavily in the survey that follows on this excellent summary as well as his own personal knowledge and interviews with participants in these programs.

2. Louis Morton, "The Writing of Official History," *Army* 11 (May 1961): 38-39; Martin Blumenson, "Can Official History Be Honest History?" *Military Affairs* 26 (Winter 1962-63): 153-61.

3. Louis Morton, *Writings on World War II*, American Historical Association, Service Center for Teachers of History Publication no. 66 (Washington, D.C., 1967); idem, "Sources for the History of World War II," *World Politics* 13 (April 1961): 435-53.

4. Richard W. Leopold, "The Foreign Relations Series: A Centennial Estimate," *Mississippi Valley Historical Review* 44 (March 1963): 595-612.

5. H. G. Jones, *The Records of a Nation; Their Management, Preservation, and Use* (New York: Atheneum, 1969).

6. See the *Final Report* of the Joint AHA-OAH Ad Hoc Committee to Investigate the Charges against the Franklin D. Roosevelt Library and Related Matters, August 24, 1970, and "A Statement in Rebuttal" by Francis L. Loewenheim, December 12, 1970.

7. See Ernest R. May, "A Case for 'Court Historians,'" Charles Warren Center for Studies in American History, *Perspectives in American History* 3 (1969): 413-32; Herbert Feis, "The Shackled Historian," *Foreign Affairs* (January 1967): 332-43.

8. Arthur M. Schlesinger, Jr., "The Historian and History," *Foreign Affairs* (April 1963): 491-97; Louis Morton, "The Cold War and American Scholarship," in *The Historian and the Diplomat*, ed. Francis L. Loewenheim (New York: Harper & Row, 1967), pp. 123-69.

Problems and Opportunities in Research in the Administration of Federal Policy and Programs Relating to Poverty, pages 153-165

1. D. G. Hogarth, *Accidents of an Antiquary's Life* (London: Macmillan & Co., 1910), p. 2; Sidney Baldwin, *Poverty and Politics: The Rise and Decline of the Farm Security Administration* (Chapel Hill: University of North Carolina Press, 1968).

2. Daniel P. Moynihan, "The Concept of Public Policy in the 1970's" (Address delivered at Hendrix College, Conway, Ark. April 6, 1970.)

3. Austin Ranney, ed., *Political Science and Public Policy* (Chicago: Markham, 1968), pp. 6-7.

4. Henry S. Kariel, *Open Systems: Arenas for Political Action* (Itasca, Ill.: F. E. Peacock, 1969), p. 92.

5. William W. Boyer, *Bureaucracy on Trial: Policy Making by Government Agencies* (Indianapolis, Ind.: Bobbs-Merrill, 1964), p. 18.

6. Simon Ramo, *Cure for Chaos* (New York: David McKay, 1969).

7. Robert Boguslaw, *The New Utopians: A Study of Systems Design and Social Change* (Englewood Cliffs, N.J.: Prentice-Hall, 1965).

8. T. R. Schellenberg, *Modern Archives: Principles and Techniques* (Chicago: University of Chicago Press, 1956), pp. 26, 141.

9. U.S., Advisory Commission on Intergovernmental Relations, *Intergovernmental Relations in the Poverty Program* (Washington, D.C.: Government Printing Office, 1966); U.S., Office of Economic Opportunity, *Catalog of Federal Assistance Programs* (Washington, D.C.: Office of Economic Opportunity, 1967).

10. William R. Petrowski, "Research Anyone? A Look at the Federal Records Centers," *American Archivist* 30 (October 1967), pp. 581-92.

11. G. Q. Flynn, "The New Deal and Local Archives: The Pacific Northwest," *American Archivist* 33 (Jan. 1970), pp. 41-51.

12. Ernst Posner, *American State Archives* (Chicago: University of Chicago Press, 1964).

13. Edwin A. Bock, "Case Studies about Government: Achieving Realism and Significance," mimeographed (1962).

14. Douglas G. Montgomery, "The Federal Delivery System: Impact on the Community; a Case Study of EDA and the West Oakland Health Center," and Murray Seidler, "Manpower Training and the Conquest of Poverty: A Detroit Case Study; (Papers presented at the Sixty-sixth Annual Meeting of the American Political Science Association, Los Angeles, Calif., September 8-12, 1970, Ralph M. Kramer, *Participation of the Poor* (Englewood Cliffs, N.J.: Prentice-Hall, 1969).

15. James L. Sundquist, ed., *On Fighting Poverty: Perspectives from Experience* (New York: Basic Books, 1969).

16. Harry P. Stumpf, "The Legal Profession and Legal Services: Explorations in Local Bar Politics," and Martin A. Levin, "Some Problems in the Evaluation of Policy Impact and the Case of the Criminal Courts" (Papers presented at the Sixty-sixth Annual Meeting of the American Political Science Association, Los Angeles, Calif., September 8-12, 1970).

17. Samuel P. Hays, "Archival Sources for American Political History," *American Archivist* 28 (January 1965), pp. 17-30; *AHA Newsletter* 7 (June 1969), pp. 1-2; Robert F. Berkhofer, Jr., *A Behavioral Approach to Historical Analysis* (New York: Free Press, 1969).

18. Harold D. Lasswell, "Do We Need Social Observatories?" *Saturday Review*, August 5, 1967, pp. 49-52.

Index

Francis, James D., 57
Franklin D. Roosevelt and Foreign Affairs (Nixon), 140
Franklin D. Roosevelt Library, 33, 98, 119, 122, 154
Freedom of Information Act, 75
Freedom of information procedures, 35
Friedrich, Carl J., 29
Fritz, Harry, 148
Fuller, Wayne, 30

Gate, James Lea, 138
Geneen, Harold, 85
General Service Administration, 24, 85, 109-10
Gifford Pinchot, Public and Private Forrester (Pinkett), 5
Gore, Howard, 48
Government agencies, scientist as historian of, 21
  see also Federal agencies
Government historian, *see* Historian
Government history writing, from inside, 7-16
  see also History
Government in Science: The U. S. Geological Survey, 4
Government science
  history of, 17-22
  neglect of primary sources, 21
  scientific vs. historical training in, 20-22
Great Depression, 55, 159, 165
Green, Constance, 139
Greenfield, Kent Roberts, 14, 138
Gremner, Robert, 78
Grodzins, Morton, 157
Guggenheim Foundation, 132
Gulick, Luther, 99, 101

Haas, Frank, 55
Hamilton, Alexander, 44, 136
Hamilton, Francis E., 44
Harper's, 121

Harvard University, 43, 132
Harvard University Press, 140
Hattery, Lowell H., 37-38
Hawaii, University of, 156
Hays, Samuel P., 27, 164
H-bomb debate (1949), 10
Heady, Ferrel, 110
Health, Education, and Welfare Department, U.S., 113, 126, 139, 145
Heinemann report, 121
Henderson, Keith M., 94, 105-14, 124, 168
Henderson, Leon, 59
Herring, Pendleton, 107
Herter, Christian, 43
Hewlett, Richard G., 4, 7-16, 27, 30, 139
Historian
  agency loyalty of, 15-16
  agency support of, 12
  bureaucracy and, 145
  censorship of, 12
  as government employee, 8, 12, 15, 136-37, 141
  government vs. academic, 15
  independence of, 14-15
  as policy maker, 142
  professionalism of, 13
  scientific background of, 20-21
Historian, The, 94
Historical Advisory Committee, 14
History of U.S. Naval Operations, 138
History journals, content of, 9
History writing, from inside, 11-16
Hitler, Adolf, 103
Hoffman, Paul, 88
Hoover Commission, 24, 109-10, 114, 120, 122, 127
Hopkins, Harry, 88
Horsman, Reginald, 148
Hough, Warwick M., 44, 49
House Committee on Appropriations, 17
House Committee on Government Operations, 24, 106
House Select Committee on Government Reorganization, 98

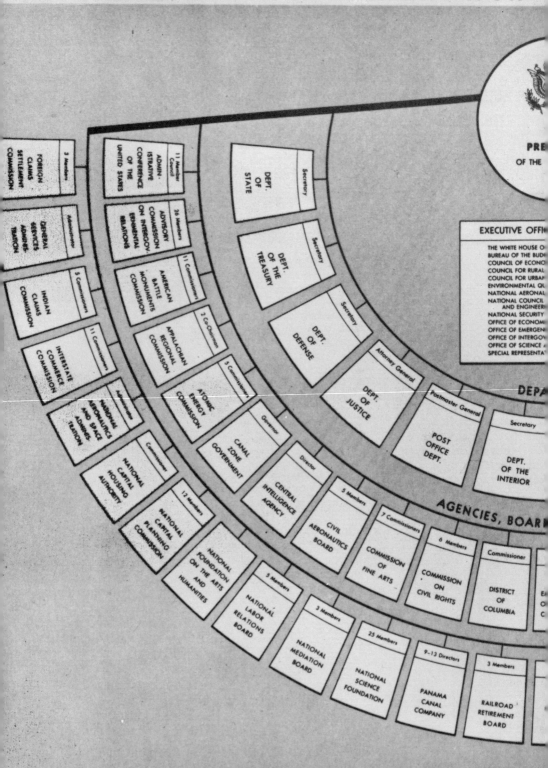

PRE...
OF THE

EXECUTIVE OFFIC...
THE WHITE HOUSE O...
BUREAU OF THE BUD...
COUNCIL OF ECONO...
COUNCIL FOR RURAL...
COUNCIL FOR URBAN...
ENVIRONMENTAL QU...
NATIONAL AERONA...
NATIONAL COUNCIL...
AND ENGINEERI...
NATIONAL SECURITY...
OFFICE OF ECONOMI...
OFFICE OF EMERGEN...
OFFICE OF INTERGOV...
OFFICE OF SCIENCE A...
SPECIAL REPRESENTA...

DEPA...

AGENCIES, BOARD...

DEPT. OF STATE — Secretary

DEPT. OF THE TREASURY — Secretary

DEPT. OF DEFENSE — Secretary

DEPT. OF JUSTICE — Attorney General

POST OFFICE DEPT. — Postmaster General

DEPT. OF THE INTERIOR — Secretary

FOREIGN CLAIMS SETTLEMENT COMMISSION — 3 Members

GENERAL SERVICES ADMINISTRATION — Administrator

INDIAN CLAIMS COMMISSION — 3 Commissioners

INTERSTATE COMMERCE COMMISSION — 11 Commissioners

NATIONAL AERONAUTICS AND SPACE ADMINISTRATION — Administrator

NATIONAL CAPITAL HOUSING AUTHORITY — Commissioner

NATIONAL CAPITAL PLANNING COMMISSION — 12 Members

ADMINISTRATIVE CONFERENCE OF THE UNITED STATES — 11 Member Council

ADVISORY COMMISSION ON INTERGOVERNMENTAL RELATIONS — 26 Members

AMERICAN BATTLE MONUMENTS COMMISSION — 11 Commissioners

APPALACHIAN REGIONAL COMMISSION — 2 Co-Chairmen

ATOMIC ENERGY COMMISSION — 5 Commissioners

CANAL ZONE GOVERNMENT — Governor

CENTRAL INTELLIGENCE AGENCY — Director

CIVIL AERONAUTICS BOARD — 5 Members

COMMISSION OF FINE ARTS — 7 Commissioners

COMMISSION ON CIVIL RIGHTS — 6 Members

DISTRICT OF COLUMBIA — Commissioner

NATIONAL FOUNDATION ON THE ARTS AND HUMANITIES

NATIONAL LABOR RELATIONS BOARD — 5 Members

NATIONAL MEDIATION BOARD — 3 Members

NATIONAL SCIENCE FOUNDATION — 25 Members

PANAMA CANAL COMPANY — 9-13 Directors

RAILROAD RETIREMENT BOARD — 3 Members